Management for Professionals

For further volumes:
http://www.springer.com/series/10101

Taco C.R. van Someren •
Shuhua van Someren-Wang

Innovative China

Innovation Race
Between East and West

 Springer

Taco C.R. van Someren
Shuhua van Someren-Wang
Ynnovate
Hilversum, The Netherlands

ISSN 2192-8096   ISSN 2192-810X (electronic)
ISBN 978-3-642-36236-1   ISBN 978-3-642-36237-8 (eBook)
DOI 10.1007/978-3-642-36237-8
Springer Heidelberg New York Dordrecht London

Library of Congress Control Number: 2013935699

Printed on acid-free paper

Springer is part of Springer Science+Business Media (www.springer.com)

Foreword

In the global race for innovation, the Netherlands and the EU are facing a challenge to keep up with emerging markets like China. As was brilliantly described by Kishore Mahbubani in his book *The New Asian Hemisphere*, we are truly witnessing the rise of Asia.

The global financial and economic crisis has hardly affected Asia over the past few years. Economic growth has been remarkable. Annual rates of 8–10 % have not been uncommon. The result is a growing well-to-do middle class, while tens of millions of Asians have risen out of poverty. Over the past 10 years, two-thirds of worldwide economic growth has come from emerging markets such as China.

Some people are frightened by these developments. Certainly, they have profound implications for people and businesses. Yet I believe that the rise of Asia is first and foremost a tremendous opportunity. As markets worldwide become increasingly interconnected, the whole world—and especially countries with an economy as open as the Netherlands—can greatly benefit from the Asian growth miracle.

Emerging markets, and China in particular, are forcing companies to devise new business strategies and governments to formulate new policies. There are no simple answers to the great challenge of the twenty-first century: creating a sustainable society in partnership with the new global players. But I believe that entrepreneurs and researchers are key in finding the answers. And I fully agree with the authors that sustainability is key to creating future business opportunities around the globe.

It is against this background that I have launched a new economic policy to stimulate innovation and cooperation between businesses, academic and research institutions, and government in nine top sectors of the Dutch economy, such as energy, water, agri-food, and the chemical sector. These are knowledge-intensive sectors that can both strengthen our economy and provide responses to some of the most pressing challenges of our time, from climate change and food security to declining natural resources and clean energy.

This book clearly illustrates how strategic innovation is crucial if Western companies and governments want to secure a leading role in the markets of the future. Yet, as the authors point out, this requires a radical shift in thinking in order to deal effectively with other cultures and develop business concepts that work in the new world markets.

The authors have extensive personal experience with strategic innovation in the private sector, in the government, and in the academic world, both in the West and in China. And they warn that the importance of knowing how to deal with various cultures has not been sufficiently incorporated into today's business models.

I congratulate Professor Taco van Someren and Dr. Shuhua van Someren-Wang on the well-chosen subject and timing of this book. I hope it will contribute to many successful green business initiatives!

The Hague   Maxime Verhagen
The Netherlands   Deputy Prime Minister
                                                  and Minister of Economic Affairs,
                                                      Agriculture and Innovation

Contents

China is becoming the largest economy of the world again. A few centuries ago, when the East met the West, China used to be the Giant Dragon before it turned out to be an ancient dinosaur. Will there be a déjà vu in our days? Or will China become a giant Innovative Nation? Foremost the USA and to a less extent the EU still have their competitive advantage in the field of innovation. But for how long? While the West is busy putting out the fire of crises, they may also be putting out their innovation strength. At the same time, the Chinese government is rolling out innovation policies supported by wide-open money taps and favorable social, business, and legal conditions for innovation. The Chinese enterprises are outgrowing their image of the factory of the world and becoming world players in, for example, renewable energy, telecommunication, high-speed trains, and air- and spacecrafts. The aim of China to be an innovative country by 2020 is not yet taken seriously by the West. In Western eyes, the world still turns on Western norms and values and according to Western principles for international relations and market rules. The Chinese may turn it into a different world. Learning and combining the good market principles from the West with their own heritage and culture, the Chinese may become a giant in innovation using their high-speed top-down and collective long-turn innovation strategy. They may change the game of innovation, but success is not guaranteed. The Chinese aim of being the future nation of innovation is a huge challenge far more difficult than the achievements of the past decades. The Chinese culture was never really pro-innovation until 30 years ago. The Chinese economy is too far integrated into the world economy for the Chinese to develop without the others. There is still a long way for the Chinese to go to turn into an innovative society. The West still has time to use their innovation strength to have a bright future together with China. In our opinion, the field of innovation will be the most important battlefield between China, the USA, and the EU. If the USA and the EU can ride the Chinese innovation wave, there will be an infinitive welfare for us all. The world is now reshuffled and strategic innovation is the necessary answer to deal with it.

T.C.R. van Someren and S. van Someren-Wang, *Innovative China*,
Management for Professionals, DOI 10.1007/978-3-642-36237-8_1,
© Springer-Verlag Berlin Heidelberg 2013

1.1   When East Meets West

1.1.1   The State-of-the-Art Carriage of the British Emperor

A few centuries ago, the Asian Mode of Production (AMP) levied China and its surrounding countries to one of the most prosperous regions of the world. When in the seventeenth century envoy Macartney visited China with the request of the English king to the Chinese emperor Qianlong to open China and to have a dialogue on equal terms, the Chinese refused. Particularly illustrative for this meeting were the refusal of the kowtow by the envoy and the refusal of the gift by Qianlong. The British Emperor sends the most advanced carriage with state-of-the-art suspension as a gift to the Chinese emperor with the hope to create an export market. It was not the technical perfect suspension that took attention of the Chinese emperor but the couch of the coachman. A eunuch explained that the gift could not be accepted because the coachman was sitting higher and with his back turned to the passenger. Nobody can sit higher than the Emperor of China let alone showing his back.

The broader cultural background of denying equal relations was that China regarded itself as the only civilized country in the world. China with 300 million inhabitants and its history could never be equaled by a European country of only eight million people. "It was a dialogue between deaf and the dumb. And Europe had the biggest mouth asking questions and giving themselves answers, the Chinese played the role of the dumb."[1]

Does history really repeat itself? Yes and no. As of the seventeenth century, Western countries took over the lead of Asian economy because all kind of innovations prospered, whereas in China innovations were partly limited to the court of the emperor without practical use or market introduction. Innovations at that time did not fit into the system and trade and manufacturing were not enough to compete with Western innovations.

Meanwhile, Western enterprises have landed in China, but the further expansion is accompanied by trading technology for continued market access. Nowadays, technology gifts are accepted and Western firms indeed expand their business in Chinese market. China is the dreamed export market for many Western firms because of the potential number of buyers. But very often it is still a relation between the deaf and the dumb.

Most Western firms are often blinded by the prospects or even worse the short-term success and ignore longer-term perspectives and aspirations of Chinese government and enterprises. In the time of Macartney, a wave of Sinomania existed, and nowadays China again unlocks a wave of admiration of the speed of development. But also in China the trees do not grow to the sky. Chinese also only cook with water. Therefore, a realistic and below-the-surface view is necessary to

---

[1] Peyrefitte (1991), pp. 47–49; 175–176. Citation is a free translation of Peyrefitte by authors, p. 49

understand the role of any enterprise or nation in the future world co-created by Chinese and other non-Western countries.

1.1.2 World's Challenges: Apocalypse or Phoenix

China has a plan for the Chinese future which may surpass the West, and the West has no answer. China's political and business leaders also have a clear idea about the role and place of China in the future world and its corresponding road map. The opening up by Deng in 1978 was China's Big Bang. Four decades later, in 2011, the leaders of China gave themselves the launch of spacelab Tiangong-1 as a birthday present for the 100-year-old revolution tumbling the 4,000-year-old dynasty system—another clear sign from heaven about Chinese progress and a confirmation of a new era.

The economic interpretation of these signs boils down to the start of a new long-term growth curve. More importantly, the inner dynamics of the new growth curve will be different from the Western-dominated old growth curve. Economic thinking, corporate strategic behavior, management concepts, and business practices belonging to the old growth curve will be replaced by new ones. But will innovation culture change as well or will only some superficial cultural changes characterize the new growth cycle with China in the driving seat?

Although the West has of course observed the rise of China, the recognition of a new growth curve with other than Western (business) practices and roles of business and governments is less clear. Moreover, the majority of business and governmental leaders stick to the traditional way of making corporate strategies and governmental policies, respectively, perfectly belonging to the old growth curve. The West interprets the rise of China as being an extension of the current old growth curve. China should adapt to Western rules, norms and values, and practices. Partly China does indeed take over some useful ideas and integrates them in their institutional development and behaviors, but simultaneously, they will develop their insights, norms and values, and so on. For example, creating a sustainable "green" society combines traditional Chinese values with a joint effort of government and private enterprises to be leader in the new growth curve (see van Someren & van Someren, 2012).

Current Western thinking about both corporate strategy and innovation concepts do not fit to the new growth curve and the role of Chinese players from private and public sector. Classical corporate strategies from private industry boiled down to outsourcing and Chinese market penetration, which most of the time lack long-term strategic insights and renewal of the business models. For most top managers, China is an additional market with a huge potential to contribute to top-line improvement (revenues). But bottom-line contribution (profits) is by far more challenging. Classical strategy concepts and modern innovation concepts are used as framework to which Chinese business partners have to commit. Win–win, knowledge sharing, and open innovation are Western management mantras which the Chinese should adopt as well. The reality is different and the Chinese have other insights and opinions.

The Western innovation function needs to be renewed as well if the Western enterprises want to profit from the upcoming Chinese market. Selling to China and making profit is still difficult for most Western enterprises because they do not really understand Chinese markets and client needs. Already selling existing products and services requires a different approach of every aspect of the value chain from design to marketing and even complete business models. But in the future even more is needed. Chinese enterprises are becoming increasingly competitive in their home market too. Chinese enterprises are not only competitive in low-segment markets, but some are able to translate Chinese customer needs into high-end products and services. They will become formidable competitors for Western companies. Therefore, knowing the Chinese and coping with future Chinese innovative dragons are challenges even more important than selling on the short term.

But Chinese business leaders need also to renew their innovation function when entering world markets and dealing with non-Chinese customers. Only delivering cheap products in large quantities is not the route to future success. Besides branding and appealing designs, it is very relevant to deal with Western human resources management and how to motivate employees and foster creativity. Improving every aspect of the value chain is still a gold mine for most Chinese enterprises. The first step is to improve high quality and service to Western standards. The second step is to improve and renew the innovation function in order to be able to become front-runners. For sure, Chinese business practices like top-down decision making can cause creative input from Western employees and customers unutilized.

Western governments also behave in conformity of our old growth model in which the Western economy is still the centerpiece. The US government spent hundreds of billions of dollars to revive the economy. But where did the money go? Who benefitted? Job creation till 2012 was relatively low and below expectation measured along the governmental money spent. An inward perspective exists leading to an "island economy" like independence of energy resources and bringing back manufacturing jobs. And the EU? Both the failing Lisbon Strategy followed by the Strategy 2020 formulated old innovation mantras in a new jacket. In both plans, China is hardly mentioned. In fact nothing else than an improvement of old policies but no in-depth analysis of the consequences of Chinese rise and its geo-political, geo-economical, and geo-social consequences.

The West is fighting on two fronts. The first are the wars for oil and the second is the Western society taken hostage by the (investment) banks and the linked governmental debt problem. These are all old-growth-curve-born and old-growth-curve-related issues.

The war for oil can economically be doubted due to, first, the huge investments and operational costs and, second, the increasing availability of renewables. It is estimated that the total costs of the war in Iraq and Afghanistan for the USA are $1.3 trillion (accumulated till 2011).[2] Meanwhile, in the same period of time the

---

[2] http://www.costofwar.com.

green energy technology has been developed and is available. With regard to costs they reach grid parity meaning that renewables are becoming competitive with regard to operational costs. Only the failing infrastructure of transport networks needs large investments mounting to 300 billion euro in the EU. The EU invests hundreds of billions of euros in the financial sector to equalize the risks taken by banks, insurance companies, and pension funds in buying debts from low-performing countries like Greece. Moreover, economic senseless investments supported or even initiated by governments have been made in infrastructure in the middle of nowhere and useless expensive but state-of-the-art architectural buildings without a function. Will these buildings in 2,000 years be the tourist attraction for non-Europeans?

In the end, the central bank is not the lender of last resort for saving the banks and their unchanged bonus systems but the European taxpayer. Furthermore, solutions in the EU for the several crises are sought in setting up new European institutional frameworks such as the bank union, the fiscal union, the economic union, and the political union. Even if these measures are thought to be necessary, they are certainly not sufficient. The market system has developed towards a capitalistic system dominated by the financial sector and greed instead of creating industries of the future for renewed prosperity.

Making war, besides the immeasurable loss of life, is peanuts compared to crime fighting the financial crisis. The total size of the annual world economy is approximately $70 trillion (2011). The IMF estimated that the cost till 2009 of cleaning up the financial crisis is at $11.9 trillion or $11.900.000.000.000.[3] These costs include capital injections pumped into banks in order to prevent them from collapse, the cost of soaking up the so-called toxic assets, guarantees over debt and liquidity support from central banks, and amounts to 20 % of the world's total annual economic output. The EU "only" needs 300 billion euro for building a new Pan-European grid structure for distributing renewable energy output but has difficulty to find the money. The US treasury calculates the household losses at approximately $17 trillion between 2007 and 2009. In these estimations, the costs of the debt crisis and Euro crisis after 2009 are not even included. The investments in green energy are very cheap compared to making war and crime fighting against banks, but we cannot find the money.

What is the connection between oil wars, saving banks, and China? The war on oil and financial institutions are signs of the downward phase of the Western growth curve. The rapid rise of China is linked to a new growth curve with focus on creating new industries; conquering markets; assuring (natural) resources; financing their industrial activities by private capitals, banks, and governmental support; and introducing new ways of doing business. Who is better off: the Western society with their financial sector in crisis or the Chinese society with governmental lending? Ten years ago, we would have said the Western market-based financing is better off, but do we still believe in it?

---

[3] http://www.thehill.com (09.08.09) and digitaljournal.com (05.03.10).

Or in other words, the West produced wars and words but no sound grand strategy on how to deal with the greatest change and shift in recent world history. Or in figures: China invests in its country trillions of euros to build up infrastructure and create new industries; at the same time, conditions for innovation are created for more than 700 million entrepreneurs with renewal of the legal, educational, and financial system. But how effective are the investments in Chinese innovation system?

For the Chinese, the Western crises came on time. Due to their exports, they hoped of a quick solution which did not come soon enough yet. The export-oriented labor-, capital-, and resources-intensive growth model with little added value for the Chinese has to be abandoned. This reinforced their thoughts about their growth model and turning to a more innovation-based and domestic market-oriented path. They are also at the point of reforming the financial system. Before the financial crises, a lot of Chinese admired the Western financial system and may want to copy it to China. At this moment, the Chinese do not openly criticize our financial system, but they look with astonished eyes to the Western mess. They can still learn from it, but at the same time, they want to avoid the faults of the Western banking system which can harm growth and development. The Chinese may take advantage of both the governmental control and the private entrepreneurship for their new financial system. The only problem is that they may do not know how without the right innovations in this sector.

But there is one thing more than finance. That is strategic innovation and the ability to renew oneself. In the West, we have turned it around: the financial sector has conquered the top of the pyramid being the primary sector followed by other industries. In the beginning of the growth curve, it was the innovative entrepreneurs and enterprises which needed investment money; now at the end of our growth curve, the taxpayers and companies are the lenders of last resort who have to pay for the financial sector and overspending governments. It is time to turn it around again.

The key of any society is its future earning capacity and competence to renew itself. The institutional internal measures will not increase earning capacity and competence of the EU by one eurocent. The European political reaction was to abandon governmental budget cutting and focus on a growth agenda by governmental spending and investment. But they forgot that a growth agenda needs innovative entrepreneurs, earning capacity, and creative market-based innovations. Creative entrepreneurs should be rewarded for their risk-taking and not finance sector or high bonuses for semigovernmental organizations.

From a defensive and an offensive perspective, future growth in the USA and the EU is coupled with the rise of China. The rise of China is not a revolution but more of a renaissance after the world's economy domination of China till about sixteenth century. But history does not repeat itself as we have seen before. The resurrection can be viewed from at least three alternative views.

In the first interpretation, China is reclaiming its natural position and role in the world as it had in the world the past 5,000 years. The last 300–400 years is only a short intermezzo of different Western countries. The dream of Chinese leaders is to revive the 5,000-year-old notion of a harmonious society and to create a new one for the future. However, this China Number One dream nowadays requires the emulation of the USA, the EU, and several other front-runners.

In the second interpretation, the opening of China puts the Chinese leaders for a historic and tremendous task to create a prosperous and harmonious China in which all citizens can share the benefits of wealth and prosperity. During the past three decades, the Chinese leaders managed to create a middle class of 250–300 million people, but they have more than 1,000 million to go. This is the greatest challenge and worry of future China far away from realizing a renaissance.

The third interpretation reflects the idea that the glorious past of China based on entrepreneurship and trading creating a wealthy class of the happy few is fundamentally different from the current challenge to create an innovative society. Creating prosperity for the whole nation does not only require adoption and diffusion of new technology but also require new leadership styles and the use of people's power to contribute to bottom-up innovative solutions. The context of a new harmonious society has some fundamentally different requirements and characteristics than the long history and recent past of China.

Therefore, whatever interpretation you prefer or combine, the rise of China is only a first step in the attempt to become the new power of the twenty-first century. The USA and the EU still have the opportunity to challenge China and maintain their position as great rivals. But China, the USA, and the EU have to renew their governmental policies and strategies of private and public organizations to prepare for the twenty-first century. In the continuous race for staying ahead and to belong to the top performing nations, due to their different histories and different start positions, they have to create different solutions for the future. Figure 1.1 presents the economic photo of the current situation in China, the USA, and the EU.

The Western growth curves of the past decades have reached their highest point. The growth curves of the USA and EU are reaching the tipping point, and in the coming years, it will be decided whether a new growth curve can be started or a downfall will occur.

All kinds of strong and weak signals indicate the end of the Western current growth curve. Among others some of these indicators are the low growth rate over many years, breakthrough of emerging countries, difficulties in the West with starting up new industries like biotech and renewable energy, extremely long lead times in building new infrastructure, underperforming innovation output, political discussions about distributing wealth instead of creating conditions for generating new wealth, absence of grand political visions, regarding China as a source of cheap labor for outsourcing and additional market instead of a game-changing emergence, empty and ineffective policies about knowledge economy, focus on improving living conditions of several minor pressure groups thereby forgetting about the big challenges of the twenty-first century, difficulty with integrating sustainability issues in current market economy, loss of power in world institutions like IMF, Greece receiving rescue package to be able to save banks and pay salaries and pensions, the Netherlands increases its pension age, the increase and thereafter decrease pension age in France and request for Eurobonds implying that German tax money is used to maintain living standard in other EU member state countries,

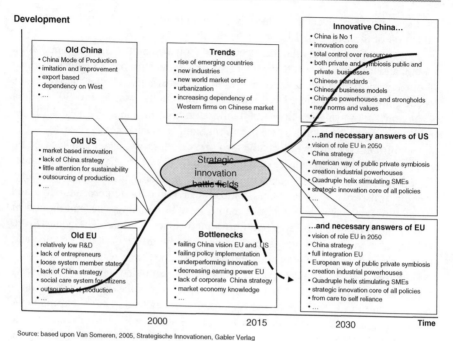

Fig. 1.1 The rise of China reshuffles world economy

lack of competence and governance to avoid bank and currency crisis and worse continued arrogance of banking sector even after crisis and saving actions leading to unchanged behavior instead of creating new foundation, and unimaginable sums of money spent to save banks instead of building the industries of the future.

Are the financial, debt, Euro, and bank crisis the apocalypse of the Western growth curve? Or can the West resurrect as a phoenix from the ashes? Will China wipe away the old world and new world and become the future world's dominator?

Despite these manifold mixes of strong and weak signals, Western governments lack any sense of urgency and business leaders are still blinded by the cheap labor and market prospects. In our opinion, the Western world has to understand the major shifts accompanied by the new growth curve led by China. All the alarm bells in governmental buildings and corporate headquarters should be ringing. But we only hear fancy ring tones of smartphones followed by conversations about old growth curve issues.

The Chinese have the opportunity to become the leading nation of the new world growth curve. But this is not sure at all. The new growth curve will show huge strategic renewal processes of old industries into new industries such as the car industry and the emergence of new industries such as biotech and others. Both strategic innovation trajectories need large sums of capital to invest in experimentation, invention, commercialization, and growth. More relevant for the Chinese are the soft skills and nontechnical innovations such as canalizing bottom-up entrepreneurial activity and organized creativity process without distorting social, institutional, and societal order.

The Western answers on these weak and strong signals are to defend the old growth curve by making war to protect oil supplies, inward focus instead of world view, to stick to old institutions like protecting social rights of a disappearing working class, to shift attention to minor political issues instead of paying attention to big world picture, to primarily improve existing products and services instead of rethinking existing business, and to reward managers and professionals of bureaucratic institutions instead of creative entrepreneurs and bold new policies and strategies.

The only way to survive the emergence of China and other countries is to create a new growth curve. Due to the rise of China and its introduction of new rules in the market economy, it will be insufficient for the USA and the EU to improve their current situation. A new world has to be created in which the behavior of China and others have to be integrated and both government and private sector have to renew themselves. As long as business and political leaders have no vision on China, private organizations disregard the new world order and continue their current business model, public organization are involved in greatest financial scandals, and in Germany the attempt to create a renewable society ("Energiewende") is frustrated by conservative forces, the West will be far away from a new growth curve. Western politicians have been navel-gazing, and private industry limits itself to outsourcing and market development. Instead, new answers are needed by visionary leaders.

From a content view, most books give no answer on the question what the reaction of the West should be and how China should develop. What are the possible strategic answers? It is useless to speculate about future winners or to make scenarios which will be obsolete within a year. Much more relevant is to define the cornerstones of a practical strategy of the future and to be flexible in its content and roll out. This will be the focus in this book. Why did we not ask this question earlier and why was there no proposal in this direction?

The main reason is that the West was busy with itself and convinced that the rising of other world regions could be tackled without greatly adapting the pretended superior Western way of thinking and acting. The past decades since Deng, the Western focus was on several hypes such as the threat of Japan, growth of Asian tiger states, IT, new economy, innovation as the magic stick, oil wars, climate change, and financial crisis. Several of these topics appeared to be a hype such as the dominance of Japan and The New Economy followed by the Internet Bubble and partial innovation topics like creativity sector. Other crises in Middle East and Arabian regions linked to oil and financial crisis consumed large amounts of government spending.

Political and business leaders followed gurus pushing forward hypes like the creative industry as the economic engine of cities and social innovation as the most important nontechnical issue. We still wait on bottom-line results after billions of euros have been spent in fostering these single issue innovations. China did not play a great role in all these hypes except for trade missions of nation states; lower governments and even small cities organized their own dual city ties with Chinese counterparts. For most Western companies China was an excellent outsourcing regions and a future sales market.

Much less attention was paid to China as a competitor or even the possibility of China as the most innovative region in the world. Only two strategies would be sufficient: a low-cost and market entry strategy. This very static approach, which is very common among Western managers due to the dominance of American management literature, will not provide the right answer to our common future. And what about China? China elevated itself to the workshop of the world, raised about 250–300 million Chinese from poverty into middle-class citizens, and is gaining world economic and political presence. The price of the necessary economic development in the past decades is environmental pollution and social inequality.

Furthermore, being the manufacturer of the world within one generation is a tremendous act of economic development but is more or less low-margin business. Here the issue of production factors and value conversion comes into the picture. In the recent history, China has gained a dominance in three of four fundamental production factors: cheap labor (production factor labor), cheap and abundant capital (production factor capital), and fast and flexible decision making combined with accumulation (production factor time). Knowledge is still lagging behind but is improving. Natural resources (coal, oil, gas, renewables, materials, land, water, and air) are the one production factor which will dominate future battles for growth and development, and this is the production factor less developed in China but with high potential for dominant positions from a strategic perspective.

Sustainability is closely linked with all the production factors. Labor is linked with demographics and social issues, natural resources with depletion rate and climate, capital with sustainability criteria, and time with accumulation of knowledge and timing of decisions. Therefore, solving environmental problems and turning these problems into opportunities and creating high-margin industries will be the future bases of economic development, thereby creating stronger social structures. It can be concluded that China also needs strategic innovations to keep the pace of GDP growth and extending prosperity to the rest of their population.

1.1.3 The Dinosaur or the Flying Dragon?

1.1.3.1 The Upside Development of China

The recent era since the opening of China has shown the rise of Red Capitalism. The core of Red Capitalism is the success of Chinese Mode of Production based upon high-volume low-cost exports and investments in infrastructure. Both central and local governments and private entrepreneurs have contributed to GDP growth and a world-class low-cost manufacturing system.

Governmental policies for overall growth and development supported the export-based economy by fostering imitation and improvement. Besides export, the housing and infrastructure sectors are the second pillar of growth and development. But sometimes, policies of central government are countervailed by local interests or individual interest of powerful governmental and business leaders. This internal rivalry led to copycat initiatives resulting in overcapacity in most industries, rapidly rising labor costs, increasing danger of high inflation, ecological detrimental effects, increasing social inequality, and insufficient innovation capabilities.

Combined with future challenges such as aging of population, new social structures, effects of one-child policy, different behavior of younger generation taking much less care of elderly undermining century-old social security of elderly, reform of health-care system, buildup of pension system, capital market, risk management banking, and capturing more profitable parts of value chain, a basis for a new growth curve has to be found.

Moreover, China's world-class manufacturing system consists of many firms earning money with a low profit margin. Rising operational costs threaten the successful business model of high volume, low margins, and export. The next growth curve is Innovative and Green China. In the first instance, Green China implies to shift interest from one-sided economic success to social, ecological, safety, and health issues. Early successes are already present in big players in renewable energy, battery technology, genomics, and so on. But this is only a first step. The next steps are even more important but also more difficult.

Innovative China does not only encompass ecological and social issues but involves creating a new world order in which Chinese norms and values and business rules have a substantial stake. Starting points are China's aim to become the leading world's economy and being independent of Western technology and firms. This shift has been made on a macro-level in all kind of policies and plans, but on meso- and micro-level, economic interest is often dominating decision-making behavior. On a macroscale a national innovation system has to be build up, on the meso-level international expansion and service sector has to be developed, and on the micro-level functional areas like branding and creating new business models have to be implemented.

Since the crisis, in the eyes of the Chinese, the Western model of capitalism has lost its credibility. China's innovation policies are the start of tumbling the Western market system and replacing it by a Chinese market system. Since the financial crisis, the Euro crisis, the bank crisis, and the debt crisis, the Chinese also are strengthened in their moral view on the world that Western norms and values are not necessarily the best and in favor of prosperity of any nation. China will develop its own system developing from Red Capitalism towards Green and Innovative China.[4] This revolutionary road map towards a harmonious society has many dimensions which have to be realized. Moreover, as in any revolution, many dimensions are being renewed simultaneously over a longer time period.

---

[4] See several contributions to these topics: van Someren (1992); van Someren (1997); van Someren & van Someren-Wang (2009a); van Someren & van Someren-Wang (2009b); van Someren & van Someren-Wang (2010); van Someren & van Someren-Wang (2011a); van Someren & van Someren-Wang (2011b).

But the above-mentioned developments are only some impressions of the upside of recent Chinese development. There are downsides as well.

1.1.3.2 The Downside Development of China

In 2011 the Chinese economy showed some serious cracks which indicates that even China has to obey universal economic laws. At least ten serious problems demonstrate that despite rational plans, human irrational behavior disrupts (central) strategic plan making.

First, the bubble in the housing market led to decreasing housing prices and brought serious financial trouble to construction industry, house owners, local governments, and banks.

Second, the number of bankruptcies in the low-margin industries like toys or business cycle-dependent industries like shipbuilding substantially increased. Rising labor costs, reduced demand, and reduced private loans due to financial losses were the cause.

Third, about a quarter or even more of all bank loans are estimated to be bad bank loans which will have to be written off completely. Additionally, too risky loans by local government substantially increase the financial risk. As a consequence, the central government has risen the level of bank reserves which reduced the level of credits to business and private households.

Fourth, the rising labor costs, low-profit-margin businesses, overcapacity in many industries, risky banking loans, economic bubbles in infrastructure and housing, sustainability issues, failing institutional innovation, and a bias towards technology instead of nontechnical innovation represent the big risks for Chinese growth and development.

Fifth, foreign Western companies are questioning their involvement in China and have started considering alternatives like India, Brazil, and other interesting places in the world. In the eyes of Western managers, the unsolved IP rights issues, the preference of Chinese suppliers instead of foreign companies, the unequal treatment between Chinese and Western companies with regard to appliance of laws and regulations, and on average the relatively low profit margins in Chinese market lead to rethink their Chinese presence.

Sixth, Western companies and especially SMEs are increasingly averse of becoming involved in China due to the copy–paste behavior and winner-takes-all mentality of the Chinese counterparts. There are many cases of equality and successful partnerships, but the major feeling and experiences are in the other direction. In this case, learning has a negative influence.

Seventh, the dependency on Western technology and Western export markets is currently very high. Chinese leaders will do everything to reduce this dependency. The increase of homemade innovation and the growth of home markets are necessary.

Eight, the recent focus on economic growth had detrimental effects—social and ecological effects. The social inequality is rising faster than the economic growth and the ecological problems will in the end slow down the spectacular past growth.

Development

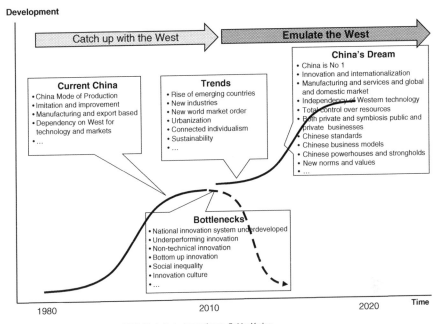

Source: based upon Van Someren, 2005, Strategische Innovationen, Gabler Verlag

Fig. 1.2 China's biggest challenge

Ninth, technology is believed to be the solution for solving the main problems. But the long history of China does not show a long heritage of continuous innovation embedded in its national or industrial culture.

Tenth, human beings are the source of creativity and entrepreneurship. The future question is not how to feed and control them but how to mobilize their knowledge, creativity, and entrepreneurship. New social and organizational structures in both society and enterprises are necessary to create an orderly context for these game-changing issues.

This limited selection of downside issues accompanying the rise of China demonstrates the difficulties and risks to be solved in the future. China will not overrun and wipe away the West, but the West will have to get the best out of themselves to become a countervailing power. Therefore, a balanced view on the rise of China is necessary.

In Fig. 1.2, China's biggest challenge is presented. Top priority of the Chinese leaders is to create prosperity and sustainable wealth for their people. Only then legitimization of government is assured.

In the past decades, the efforts were focused on catching up with the West. Now the time has come to emulate the West. In this respect two big challenges lie ahead of China: firstly becoming an innovative country and secondly creating a sustainable society. Strategic innovation is the answer on both challenges. But this is much more difficult than realizing the upside development of the past decades. Strategic innovation means more than building new business models but requires much more difficult tasks of changing behavior, creating and implementing nontechnical innovations like creating a context and culture of innovation, and allowing bottom-up initiatives in order to mobilize the necessary creativity and buildup of original stock of knowledge. It requires an inversion of their top-down-oriented system. Moreover, both innovation within individual organizations and creating new (Chinese) business models are in their infancy. China is moving towards strategic fields that on first sight are the strengths of Western countries.

1.1.4   The New World Order

The creation of strategic innovation leading to a new growth curve will be accompanied by complete new inner (market) dynamics. These new dynamics shape a new world order. The new world is happening to us, but we are all creating it. Based on this attitude, new trends are external events to us which have to be anticipated, but they can also be created by creative entrepreneurs. Demographics determine societal development due to age structure, ethnic and cultural features, knowledge level, labor supply, future demand for products and services, and its accompanying resource intensity. Asian dominance, respectively, Chinese suprem- acy is likely but not for sure yet, and this will change how the world will tick. European integration especially on a political and economic governance level will be key to create future conditions for the prosperity of European key member states. With the rise of Asian but may be also Arabian, South American, or even African states, Western norms and values will become less prominent than in the past centuries. The same holds for governance structure. The Western governance models based on a separation of managers, shareholders, and other stakeholders differ from private–public symbiotic Asiatic forms and African tribe-relation-based alternatives. Furthermore, sustainability issues will influence and represent a chal- lenge for anyone living on this planet. However, China, the USA, and the EU do have different insights and solutions on how to tackle this problem (van Someren & van Someren-Wang, 2012). In short, a new world is being created.

The increase of the participation of other than Western countries in the world economy requires systematic innovation; otherwise, no position can be conquered, maintained, and enlarged. All these challenges can only be realized when strategic innovations are introduced. Strategic innovations are necessary in every society and private as well as public organization. These challenges will not be the hypes of the future but key areas for future prosperity.

In this context, Innovative China is not a separate or stand-alone topic but is an integral part of all the necessary changes towards China's future. This holistic way of thinking fits with the Asian way of dealing with larger issues. But Westerners will have to get used to this integral approach and abandon their disintegrated way of solving problems. For example, sustainability is not only about emissions and CO_2 but also about dealing with worldwide key challenges related to new world order of doing business. But sustainability is only one top issue; others are China strategy, creating global corporations and implementing institutionalized innovation within public and private organizations.

These key challenges changes top management agenda of political leaders and leaders of private and public organizations. This change of perspective is crucial in finding the right answers (van Someren, 2005).[5] Therefore, Innovative China implies revolutionary changes on many fronts which will dramatically change our world. Innovative China is about roles of government, alternative ways of market organization, roles of networks, individual organizations, and individuals on a global scale. In fact it is about a new world order. The West and China will have different views on this new world order.

1.1.5   The Macro-, Meso-, and Micro-level

From a static view, the emergence of a new world order is a life-changing event such as an event never seen before. But from a dynamic perspective, the new world order is only a step in the world's history. In fact, the new world order is a part of the eternal process of innovation.

In order to understand the future mutual living together between China and the West, we need to understand the way of thinking. In this book we will not go back to a comprehensive overview of Chinese and Western historical foundation of our thinking and acting. We will limit ourselves to strategic thinking as far as relevant and related to business thinking. Western strategic thinking related to our market system is sliced up in three main categories: macro, meso, and micro. These areas are separated not only as a discipline but also in their appliance in organizations; there hardly exists any link between these levels. In case of Innovative China, this has to be changed. The Chinese economic wonder could happen because the Chinese leaders in the last 30 years have initiated fundamental reforms which generate step by step the macro- and meso-conditions for the existence and flourishing of enterprises at the micro-level.

The focus of macroeconomics is on international trade relations, development of nations measured in, e.g., GDP, and currency issues and economic policy for governments and international organizations like IMF. The main macro-indicators in the West show a slow GDP growth and increasing average age in demographic development, population reduction in EU, growing population in the USA due to immigration, a huge debt in the USA and several European member states, and slow economic growth. These macroeconomic indicators are more a result of activities— or absence—than cause of slowing profits and decreasing wealth. No monetary measure can countervail these macro-outcomes; only activities on the meso- and micro-level can keep the West in the race for wealth and prosperity. In China the earned money is partly allocated to several state funds which have to invest in all

---

[5] van Someren (2005).

kind of projects contributing to the realization of national plans. The growth of Chinese GDP is necessary to create the needed wealth to provide the over one billion Chinese citizens who do not yet share in the created revenues. Macroeconomic policy is translated in nationwide plans and projects defined and worked out on the meso- and micro-level.

More important are the changes in the Chinese society which was brought with the macroeconomic reforms. For the first time in history, being a rich businessman is admired instead of despised. Freedom is given for those who dare to try their luck in the business sea. More and more Chinese are educated in sciences instead of Confucianism. More and more Chinese have the chance to study and travel all over the world absorbing the capitalistic values and using it back in China. But the Chinese did not abandon their own value. It is likely that they can combine the best from both sides. If so, they may be able to create an innovation wonder.

Mesoeconomics is linked with issues like mergers, cartels, industry analysis, and policies. In Western countries mesoeconomics gets relatively little attention. The main focus is on maintaining fair competition within the system of market economy. Mergers and acquisitions are controlled by cartel organizations to protect consumers from too dominant suppliers. But active involvement of governments in creating new (sub)industries always touches the boundaries of the market system. In the USA, it is strongly believed that market-based innovations will eventually lead to new industries. In France, the government has in many instances a more direct involvement in individual companies and emergence of industries than in Germany. The European Commission has only supportive programs which are however dwarfed if compared to the budgets available by the Chinese government. Moreover, the Chinese government is directly and indirectly involved in industries by state-owned enterprises (SOEs) besides the privately owned enterprises (POEs). Moreover, the Chinese government initiates forced mergers within an industry to create powerhouses and stimulate the growth and development of industries.

Business strategy is linked with the micro-level representing the strategies of individual firms. Business strategies are mainly formulated on a micro-level (from the perspective of a singular organization trying to survive in a changing world). Innovation is in first instance also formulated on an individual organization level, but also cooperation between organizations, i.e., meso-level, is used to develop innovations. Sometimes individual entrepreneurs or firms are able to create a new industry (micro- and meso-level overlap). The focus of Western business strategies is from micro- to macro-level and much less the other way round. Moreover, the relevance has the inverted relevance meaning that the micro-level is supposed to be more important than the meso- and macro-level.

Chinese strategies more or less are characterized by the opposite order. Till now the focus of Chinese strategies is dominated by macroeconomic strategies of which five-year plans are still the iconic example. But also Chinese increasing penetration in relevant natural resource markets are an illustration of Chinese macro-power politics. On a meso-level, the development of a certain industry is more important than the fate of individual firms belonging to these industries, except for the selected and privileged organizations. On the micro-level, classical strategic development in the Western sense is more or less in its infancy in China. The Chinese strategies are mostly competition tactics from The Art of War. There are Chinese enterprises which tried to use Western-developed strategic methods, but they do more harm than good when the Chinese character is missing. They still have to find out their own strategy with Chinese character. For example, Chinese takeovers and new market penetration and developments are not as successful yet as their macro-policies. For example, the entrance of the automotive sector by Landwind in Europe failed due to misjudgment of the role and relevance of car safety criteria in Europe. But Chinese business strategies of an individual firm are much more linked with the meso- and macro-level than in the West. For example, in the renewable energy market, Chinese government forced the most important wind mill manufacturers to merge in order to reduce overcapacity and to create world-class players needed for realizing macroeconomic goals of going West macro-policy. For both the West and China, the greening of industry requires the involvement of all three levels, and this is the reason that the West and China can learn from each other. Because of the nature of sustainability, all three levels are relevant.

As a result, future strategies will have a completely different content and scope than existing traditional business strategies. Long-term success does not depend on how to deal with technology such as the cloud but how to deal strategically with China and the bottom-line performance in time. The strategic innovation theory (SIT, van Someren, 1991, 2005) blurs the distinction between the micro-, meso-, and macro-levels. Western-style approaches include the American way (including the UK) of focusing on individual entrepreneurship and shareholder value compared to European (continental Europe) with a more dirigistic governance of innovation and stakeholder approach (Rhineland model). However, differences in the interpretation of the Rhineland model between countries like France and Germany exist. France has a more centralized and top-down governance than the German innovation system. The financial crisis was the trigger to revive this discussion again because the shareholder approach connected with its short-term orientation and bonus system in relation to governmental spending and lending was regarded to be the central cause of the crisis. Additionally, discussions about the macroeconomic financial system, the depreciation of the renminbi (RMB), the survival of the dollar as worldwide leading currency, and the viability of the Euro cover the real foundation of prosperity.

The real foundation of growth and prosperity is the ability the convert production factors into value by means of introducing strategic innovations. It took China more than 30 years to build up a strong economy with high future earning potential. Instead of giving in on the demands of the USA to depreciate the RMB, the government of China issued on early March 2011 the policy to set first steps to let the RMB become the world's leading currency. Chinese firms exporting should do business in RMB instead of the dollar—or simply stated: work hard, do something new, and earn money and as a sound bite: the earning capacity.

The Chinese are able to conquer the world markets because they earned money by working hard. But meanwhile a Chinese way is being developed of which the current features are a symbiosis between firms and government with the aim to achieve nationwide goals and at the same time private businesses. Future strategic innovations applied by firms and policies will contain a mix of these three levels. It is necessary to understand these different approaches which all will determine the future of business world. As the coming chapters will reveal, on all levels, different approaches and choices with regard to context and strategic innovations are applied in China and the West.

1.1.6 Create, Combine, and Cash

In the coming decade it will be decided in which direction this new world order will be developed. At the moment alternative directions of the path to the future are still possible. The scale, scope, and pace of this change should worry every other world player because when adequate reaction and action is taking too long, other societies will be dominated instead of a peaceful living together as the harmonious society is striving for. But within the emerging new world, everyone has to conquer its place again. However, every country, region, and organization will generate its own strategic innovation fitting to its history, experiences, context, and ambitions. This holds for both the West as well as China. The reason is that in the past, our society has constantly been renewed. In Fig. 1.3 this way of thinking is schematically presented.

China, the USA, and the EU have only three options to deal with each other in the future: to cooperate, to compete, or to coexist. It is about the ability to create and combine generating something new to cash. Based on the history, the context, the starting positions, and the future needs, it is inevitable that the decisive future battlefield will be strategic innovation.

1.1.7 Infinitive Innovation

The whole history of societal development and along the development of the (market) economy is a process of emulation. Emulation comprises the will of individuals, organizations, and nations to be the best and surpass the other by means of any kind of small or big technical and nontechnical innovations. In fact the development of mankind is a history of eternal or infinitive innovation. The symbol ∞ represents the process of eternal innovation as presented in Fig. 1.4.

In our book the ∞ symbol embodies several notions reflecting our core issues. First, the ∞ symbol means the totality of the universe full of paradoxes represented by the yin–yang design (Chap. 1). Second, the ∞ symbol in the West means eternity or infinity representing the never-ending race between humans, organizations, regions, countries, and other organizational forms of humans and its institutions. The West and China as the yin–yang of the world economy and the influence of Chinese heritage, thoughts, culture and institutions on innovation (Chap. 2). Third, the ∞ symbol is a lying number 8 which is the number of fortune in China and represents forever prosperity (Chap. 3). Fourth, the symbol ∞ also

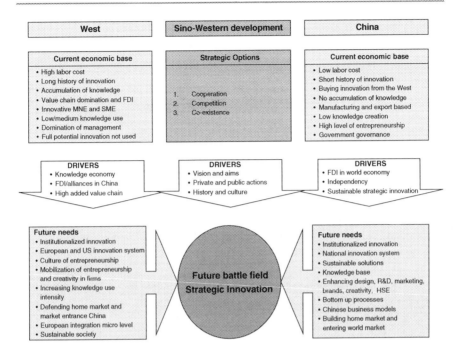

Fig. 1.3 Sino-Western future perspective

Fig. 1.4 Infinitive or eternal
innovation

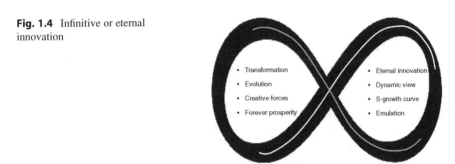

means transformation, evolution, and creative force. It represents the dynamic view
in which the role of time is essential (Chap. 4). Fifth, the symbol is made of the
combination of S-shaped growth curves. Two successive S-shaped growth curves
reflect the old and new (Chap. 5). Sixth, in our terminology, all the dynamic
changes taken together are called emulation (Chap. 6). These interpretations all
fit to the concept of strategic innovation and each chapter of this book will refer to
one of these meanings.

At the moment the West is at the end of its growth curve, and China is
experiencing a period of acceleration. With the use of the ∞, this situation is
schematically represented in Fig. 1.5.

Fig. 1.5 Crossroad between
China and the West

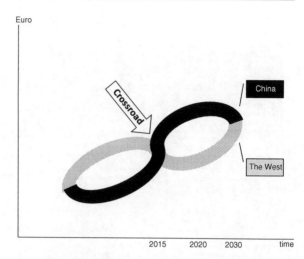

China and the West are on a crossroad. Strategic innovations are the only means to become the winner of the future. But winning and having competitive advantages are only temporarily.

In this view it is necessary to derivate a theory of innovation which comprises technical and nontechnical innovations taken together called strategic innovations. Innovative entrepreneurs are the driving force of innovation.

1.1.8   Setup of This Book

The key message of this book is as follows: new conceptual thinking about the fields of strategy and innovation is necessary to support private and public organizations preparing themselves for the twenty-first century. The rise of China leads to a new growth curve accompanied by a complete new (market) dynamic of growth and development. The world economy will be transformed by new economic rules introduced through strategic innovations. The West needs strategic innovations to countervail China's aim to build up an innovative economy to overcome the restrictions of labor-, capital-, and resources-intensive growth model. This growth model resulted in too little added value and too many problems like polluted cities and vulnerable copycat businesses with pig cycle syndrome. The ongoing crisis is another drive for the Chinese to find the new strategic direction. China wants to outgrow their image as the factory of the world. If China continues to have the right leadership and goes on renewing the Chinese economic system, they may overcome the non-innovative culture for thousands of years. This may lead to a new world order.

The new world order will not be completely Chinese but a combination of Western and non-Western rules, a convergence of Western and Red Capitalism, or a new set of (market) rules. It depends to which extent the West can recover and be a countervailing power to the rise of China. However, the West lacks an adequate strategic response on this biggest challenge of the last centuries. If there is not a strategic answer, then the Western world will indeed lag behind. China is already successfully trying to generate a green economy to keep up the need of growth and to give answers on the question how to achieve a sustainable society. This process is not a rhetoric phrase or a hype but fits in its history and cultural roots. The issue of sustainability in China, the USA, and the EU has been elaborated in another book Green China (van Someren & van Someren-Wang, 2012).

The foundations of the recent economic success are being used to transform China in an Innovative and a Green China. The strength of the Chinese culture like the power of hierarchy and collectiveness is being used strategically. The holistic long-term pragmatic approach helps the Chinese to see the national economy as a system which needs the whole-package approach. A strong symbiosis between Chinese government and Chinese firms forms the basis of a new sustainable growth curve. These new economic power houses may dominate domestic Chinese markets and stimulate the forming of national champions in most of the industries and at least in the defined strategic industries. These new Chinese firms in, for example, the green sector, may conquer the world markets like the labor intensive Chinese export industry do now.

At the same time, Chinese entrepreneurs enjoy the most favorable conditions for business in Chinese history. Respect and protection for individual property is growing. Chinese people are from nature hardworkers and risk-takers. All over the world, from "peanut Chinese" in the Netherlands to "railway Chinese" in the USA, many Chinese started their business from nothing under desperate circumstances but worked hard to become successful businessmen. Financial support from family and friends make it possible for them to start business very quickly. Chinese people seem to be born entrepreneurs. The interaction with the world brings market economy value into China. The overseas Chinese entrepreneurs rash back. Millions of domestic Chinese entrepreneurs are awakened. These Chinese are also forming the power of the Chinese economy.

But a balanced view on the perceived success of several industries is necessary. For the Chinese case, there is always another side of the story. The strength of the Chinese can be their weakness too. For example, too strong hierarchy can kill the bottom-up innovation which contributes to the success of Western economy. Both the advantage and the disadvantage of the Chinese way are presented in this book. China still has a long way to go. The only way is to continue to strategically renew itself again and again.

The current answer of the West on Innovative China is insufficient. The sign of missing the ride of the new growth wave is already showing in, for example, the green energy sector with the invasion of Chinese solar panels in Europe. The main strategy of Western companies is to be present in Chinese markets mostly by trading off technology against (promised) market share. The core argument is that presence in the largest future market is necessary in order to survive. It is a self-destructing strategy because the future dependency of revenues, profits, R&D, knowledge, and human resources will become dangerously dependent on China due to the size of operations scale of local earnings. It will be shown that several Western multinational enterprises from various industries are increasingly dependent on revenues from Chinese markets. To outrun the fast imitators in China, they need to innovate strategically both in technical and nontechnical aspects of the business.

Without alternative strategies the Western economy will lose the vitality to sustain our welfare society. Not only Western individual corporate organizations but also policy makers in the USA and EU and its member states need to study the new Innovative China, to take the Chinese megatrends into account, and to create necessary new strategies.

Strategic innovations help the policy makers to find the right policy and the organizations to formulate the right business model. Most ideally, the public and the private sector join forces in the strategic innovation process to create a symbiotic growth strategy. The strategic innovation theory presented in this book can be used to reach the symbiosis. In our opinion, strategic innovations can be stimulated from the macro- through meso- to micro-level. The relevance of innovation, sustainable development, and rise of China can be coped with connected mega issues with a coordinated approach from all levels. But apart from the linkages with the macro- and meso-level, Western private and public enterprises have to formulate a China strategy and more importantly to build the abilities to renew these strategies according to the changing Chinese business conditions.

This book gives insight into these necessary strategic innovations to build up a countervailing power in which all can win. Ideas of the strategic innovation directions for the USA, the EU, and Chinese governments are discussed. Methods for enterprise strategic innovation are presented. Cases are analyzed to show the strategic innovation theory in practice. In this book, except China, we leave aside other BRICS countries or even the TIMZ countries of Turkey, Indonesia, Mexico, and South Korea, because the different culture and historical backgrounds also should be taken into account for strategic innovations. A central shift will occur from Western thinking and acting towards Asiatic thinking and acting. It is expected that China will be leading; we therefore concentrate on China and leave aside other Asiatic countries which can differ from each other as much as Western countries. Hence, a few thoughts about the Chinese culture and its influences on strategic innovations are illustrated.

1.1.9 Overview of This Book

Both Western corporate strategy and innovation thinking need to be renewed due to the changing context belonging to the new long growth curve. The core message leads to the following overview presented in Fig. 1.6 of content and connection between the chapters.

The main line of thoughts which connects the chapters is as follows: Chap. 1 makes clear that a new long growth cycle is appearing characterized by the rise of China and sustainability as core challenge. New growth cycles are accompanied by, e.g., new modes of technology, organizational forms, and governance structures, leading to a new world order. New growth curves alongside with emerging new

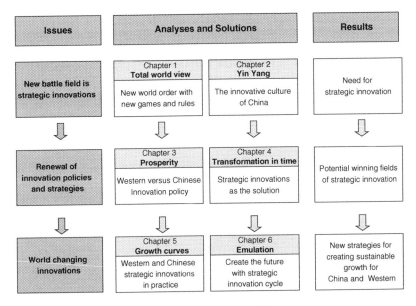

Issues	Analyses and Solutions		Results

Fig. 1.6 Overview of content of chapters and their connection

dominant countries are accompanied by new world views or even norms and values of these new power nations. Hence, Chap. 2 elaborates on the nature of the innovative culture of China. In the historical context of China, the role of government has been pivotal. Therefore, governmental policies are at the center of Chap. 3. But it will be concluded that policies are senseless and useless without innovative entrepreneurial activity and strategic innovations within private and public organizations. Consequently, the world of strategic innovations and particularly the Chinese context are discussed in Chap. 4. It is shown that strategic innovations within individual organizations are a prerequisite for developing the growth curve. But new business practices like involvement of governments and new measures of success will accompany the new growth curve. This background is necessary to understand the practical cases in Chap. 5 which reveals the different approaches and solutions of enterprises in the West and China. Chapter 6 integrates all the previous results and concludes that each organization within its own context has to create its own tailor-made solution.

Chapter 1 presents the total world view highlighting the necessity to be aware of a new world order. But the new world does not happen; it is shaped by our own decisions, and that is why strategic innovation is the instrument of governments and private businesses to create the new world. This chapter made clear that a new world is being shaped in which new battlefields based on strategic innovation will dominate the process of emulation between China, the USA, and the EU. China, the USA, and the EU are on a crossroad. In the following chapters, the issue of strategic innovation will be tackled from different perspectives.

Chapter 2 focuses on the basic philosophical and cultural pillars of Chinese society and other Chinese cultural aspects. In Chap. 2 some relevant Chinese historical and cultural issues influencing the innovative competence are elaborated. These insights help to understand the difficulties and opportunities of a possible future Innovative China. Some elements of culture and behavior will foster innovation and other elements will slow down or even prevent innovation. A balanced view on both sides of the Chinese paradoxes is discussed.

Chapter 3 takes up the meaning of prosperity which is often used by governments as their legitimacy for their role in society. Chapter 3 deals about the main innovation policies in China, the USA, and the EU. It will become clear that the Chinese ambitions on paper are huge. The policies such as the five-year plan aim at creating an innovative country by 2020. In most policies the focus is on technology. Some of the aims directly attack the current Western position. For example, China aims to become independent of Western technology by 2020. Furthermore, in China's plans for the future, several strategic sectors are selected which are the drivers of innovation.

But the focus on technology disregards the crucial and in our opinion decisive aspect of, for example, bottom-up initiatives. In the USA the role of government is relatively low compared to China and also compared with the EU or most of its member states. Nevertheless, an innovation policy exists, but the main hope of the USA is on market-based innovations. But future challenges such as sustainability and the rise of China require a different governmental role than in the past. With regard to the EU, the policies of both the European Commission and most member states were till now not very successful. Many of the ambitions such as to become the most innovative region of the world have not been achieved.

The American way is market-based innovation despite government. In the EU, it is government alongside with private business but with no idea how, what, and when. The Chinese way is business alongside and/or together with government. Hence, innovation policies but also governmental institutions with regard to innovation and the rise of China require renewal. Therefore, in the West, the main contribution should come from private sector, whereas in China, the government takes the leader's role, but also private organizations are in the lead.

The US policy is an extension of market-based innovation, the EU moves into the direction of top-down central planning, and China tries to involve individuals and individual organizations. As a result, all policies on all levels are being tried out. Policies alone cannot solve these issues of innovation and prosperity needs input from innovative entrepreneurial action to create something new. The creation of something new can be done dependent on policies, irrespective of policies, or despite policies. In fact Chap. 3 is the top-down approach of governments, and Chap. 4 represents the bottom-up approach of innovative entrepreneurial activity by individuals, enterprises, and all kind of alliances.

Chapter 3 is about the power of governmental institutions with their policies and Chap. 4 about the power of people with their creativity and conceptual solutions to foster innovation. Therefore, a conceptual approach towards innovation is necessary to deal with the different perspectives on innovation, creation of new industries, and market development. This is the link to Chap. 4 which focuses on the theory of corporate strategy and innovation.

Chapter 4 puts the notion of strategic innovation related to time at the core of the world development. In Chap. 4 it is made clear that current theories of corporate strategy and innovation are not able to deal with the issue of the coming changing world order. The rise of China accompanied by the issue of sustainability requires a new approach. The value creation process is being changed with regard to the role of time, the increased scope from micro to meso respectively macro-level and the necessary dynamic view on business development.

The strategic innovation theory offers a new perspective which enables to create the public and private organizations of the future. The strategic innovation theory opposes popular hypes and vested opinions such as myopic advocacy of technology, open innovation, sharing knowledge, and cooperation and networks as the solution for the future. Alternatives views are being presented which fit to the new world order. Chinese firms steadily expand their activities beyond manufacturing throughout all activities in the value chain. R&D and brands are being developed.

In this respect, in China Total Innovation Management (TIM) has been developed to increase the innovation output. However, TIM is insufficient to deal with the issues of sustainability and market-driven innovation in non-Chinese markets. Innovative entrepreneurs are able to make unique new combinations of production factors leading to new products, services, organizational forms, and business models. Innovation is about change and new things, but the history of innovation also offers a constant which is the common determinant of renewal. The determinants of any innovation are economies of scale, economies of scope, and economies of time. This constant or modus operandi of strategic innovation is called Triple E which explains the value conversion. Triple E offers the basic law of our dynamic view on innovation. All these elements—innovative entrepreneurship, production factors, technical, nontechnical innovation, emulation, Triple E, innovation context, value conversion—are brought together in a coherent theory.

To be able to describe, understand, and predict future corporate behavior of participants in the new growth curve, it is necessary to introduce new notions and strategic concepts. Based on the strategic innovation theory, Chap. 4 introduces new notions fitting to the new world order and growth wave like dynamic value conversion instead of short-term profit, membrane innovations instead of open innovations, and symbiosis between private and public organizations instead of separation and industrial governance instead of corporate governance.

Chapter 5 relates to search and creation of strategic innovations symbolized by new growth curves. The strategic innovation theory is applied in Chap. 5. Several business cases from Western and Chinese organizations from various industries are being discussed and evaluated. These cases reveal the strengths and weaknesses of American, European, and Chinese organizations. They also show the different influence of cultural- and institutional-based business development of individual organizations. One of the most striking differences is the bottom-up versus the top-down approach for fostering innovations. Another is the different approaches to the symbiosis between private business and government.

Furthermore, insight is given in the increasing dependency of Western firms on Chinese markets. For many Western companies, the new situation emerges that the share of Chinese revenues of total world revenues is becoming dominant. Combined with the knowledge that China wants to become independent of Western technology by 2020, a dangerous cocktail is brewed together. By the comparison, it becomes clear that the battle for strategic innovation requires to deal with many aspects which are partly depending on conditions, context, content, and creativity.

Chapter 6 focuses on the integration of all discussed issues forming the process of emulation—emulation as eternal or infinitive innovation. In Chap. 6, based on the innovation policies and market-based innovation, ten battlefields of strategic innovation are identified which will decide the emulation race between China, the USA, and the EU. With the help of the Global Strategic Innovation Index (GSII), the standing of China, the USA, and the EU can be compared. For all involved, a huge potential for untapped improvement and progress is existent. But there exists no readymade solution for anyone; instead tailor-made solutions have to be created. This holds for both private and public organizations.

References

Peyrefitte, A. (1991). *China en het Westen. Kroniek van een historische ontmoeting.* Kampen: Kok Agora.

van Someren, T. C. R. (1991, June). *Innovatie, Emulatie en Tijd. De rol van de organisatorische vernieuwingen in het economische proces* (Tinbergen Institute Research Series, No. 9) (diss.). Rotterdam: Tinbergen Institute.

van Someren, T. C. R. (1992, March). *Reference framework for Environmental Performance Indicators, Environmental Performance Indicators, European Green Table,* Oslo, Norway

van Someren, T. C. R. (1997, November). *Greening Economies in Transition. Some practical aspects based on a case study in Eastern Europe.* In 6th International Conference of the Greening of Industry Network, Santa Barbara, USA.

van Someren, T. C. R. (2005). *Strategische Innovationen. So machen Sie Ihr Unternehmen einzigartig.* Wiesbaden: Gabler.

van Someren, T. C. R., & van Someren-Wang, S. (2009a, September). *Nederland moet zich spiegelen aan China* (p. 6), Financieele Dagblad.

van Someren, T. C. R., & van Someren-Wang, S. (2009b, December). *Groene Strategie nodig* (p. 9), Financieele Dagblad.

van Someren, T. C. R., & van Someren-Wang, S. (2010, January). *Een spook van Chinese makelij waart door Europa* (p. 7), Financieele Dagblad.

van Someren, T. C. R., & van Someren-Wang, S. (2011a). Building new business models for sustainable growth and development (B. Kh. Krasnopolsky, Trans.). In *Spatial economics* (No. 3, Vol. 27, pp. 40–55) (ISSN 1815-9834). Russia, Khabarovsk.

van Someren, T. C. R., & van Someren-Wang, S. (2011b, December). *Kans na harde landing* (p. 7), Financieele Dagblad.

van Someren, T. C. R., & van Someren-Wang, S. (2012). *Green China.* Heidelberg: Springer.

Chinese Culture, Strategy, and Innovation

2

Despite the amazing innovations like paper, printing, gunpowder and compass in Chinese history, ancient China was not innovative. The agricultural centered dynasties were ruled according to Confucian ideology and bureaucracy, dynasty after dynasty until China was shocked awake by gunpowder powered cannons. The underdog role forced Chinese to think about the down side of the Chinese culture for innovation. The locked country and society as a stable unity enforced by strict hierarchy, the education emphasizing reproducing the same five Classics, the discrimination towards merchants all contribute to lack of innovation in ancient China. Pragmatic leaders like Deng Xiaoping found a way for Chinese to become rich quickly. The conditions for innovation in China was greatly improved. Combining with long term strategic thinking, China is outgrowing imitation towards strategic innovations. One needs to know the basic Chinese philosophy to understand where China came from and is heading to. Confucianism and the Chinese strategies should be looked at from both sides of their paradoxes. This can help China to overcome its shortcomings. It can also help the West to ride with the Chinese innovation wave.

2.1 History of Innovation in China

Why is there no Steve Jobs in China? Proud Chinese, those pro-China Westerners, and even the China-threat predicators are all impressed by the Chinese inventions in history. From cast iron to chain suspension bridge, from wheel barrow to silk textile, from gunpowder to porcelain, from paper to printing, and from compass to sailboat, many Chinese inventions are still part of our daily life. But China does not have a history showing innovative mind-set. On the contrary, during long periods in Chinese history, Chinese have been ruled, trained, and forced not to be different than what the layers of rulers, the teachers, and the parents wanted.

Intellectually, the Chinese are smart enough to be innovative. When they have the space to be creative, they can be very surprising in turning knowledge into value. The strategic insides and programmatic way of looking for solutions have

T.C.R. van Someren and S. van Someren-Wang, *Innovative China*,
Management for Professionals, DOI 10.1007/978-3-642-36237-8_2,
© Springer-Verlag Berlin Heidelberg 2013

generated Chinese entrepreneurs all over the world. Even today, this heritage has its influence on innovation and the way Chinese people deal with innovation.

Therefore, it is necessary to get some insight into some main cultural foundations and their relation to strategic and innovative behavior.

2.1.1 The Center of the World Turning Around Itself

A simple description of Chinese ancient history is that China was almost the same a hundred years ago as two thousand years ago. Dynasties came and went all considering itself as the center of the world. The same form of hierarchy was used dynasties after dynasties. The power of the Chinese culture was so strong that even the foreign rulers like the Mongolians and the Manchus were assimilated using the Chinese state system and language to rule.

China did have impressive inventions which changed the world. For example, in China Eastern Han period Cai Lun invented papermaking technology. Papermaking was spread to the Middle East when China's Tang Dynasty and the Islamic Army fought a war in the year 751. The Chinese lost the war and those captured were transferred to the Middle East and brought the papermaking technology with them. A few hundred years later, it reached Europe. Then came the Renaissance in Europe. Among other innovations, such as compass and paper, these have accelerated the progress of Western civilization.

Chinese also invented printing before 220 AD. Printing with the movable type was developed by Bi Sheng around 1045 in China. The printing press developed by Johannes Gutenberg in the fifteenth century is a more efficient printing process for Western languages. It is often regarded as the most important invention of the second millennium. The same invention "printing" led to different results for the West and China. While printing triggered social leapfrogs in Western countries by stimulating critical and creative reading and writing; printing only generated more Chinese reading only the Five Classics and tried to live up to those ancient social standards. Printing stimulated innovation in the West but restricted the freedom of renewal in China.

The Chinese invented the compass already in the Song Dynasty around 1040. Zheng He started in 1405 his first of seven voyages to different regions in Asia, Arabia and some say America by using star navigation technique. But it is the Westerner who found the new continent America and sailed all over the world to create their golden age using the compass.

Gunpowder was discovered in the ninth century by a Chinese alchemist searching for medicine for immortality. The Chinese did not come further than making amazing-looking fireworks to drive away the evil ghosts. But they were surprised by the killing capacities of fire guns when the Chinese gates were forced open many centuries later. Why did the brilliant inventions not take China to an innovative modern society? Because the Chinese treated innovation as a black box or even did not notion the black box at all. Figure 2.1 shows the difference between white and black box.

For example, in the case of China, the relevance of nontechnical innovation is a white box element for future success instead of the focused view on technology.

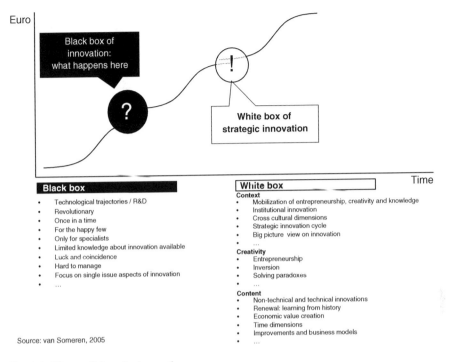

Source: van Someren, 2005

Fig. 2.1 The conditions for innovation

If we look at the theories about innovation, innovation does not only come from a lucky hit in a smart head. There are certain conditions which stimulate the smart heads turning to the right direction. China has its unique philosophic concept like Confucianism, national tradition, social custom, languages, fairy tales, religious belief, literatures, and mode of thinking. That implies that the Chinese conditions for innovation are totally different.

Based on strategic innovation theory showed in Fig. 2.1 and the Chinese historical cultural background, a few examples of the bad conditions for innovation in China can be listed (Table 2.1).

For thousands of years China was a self-centered locked system. It was not always closed because it held open many trade relations with different countries. It was locked in certain ideas about societal progress and prosperity. The Chinese character for China—"Zhongguo"—literately means "the country in the center of the world." The Chinese early civilization gave ancient Chinese a superior feeling that all the others were barbarian. The few interactions with the outside world were mostly one-way traffic. The most flourishing time in the Chinese history were those periods when China was interactive with the outside world. For example, during the period of Tang Dynasty from 618 to 907, China was an international trade center attracting people from all over the world. The Chinese society allowed the dynamic mix of deferent layers of the hierarchy. Many inventions were made in the field of medicine, engineering, and the sciences. Welfare also brought welfare disease like

Table 2.1 Why ancient China was not innovative?

Conditions for innovation	What's wrong in ancient China?
Receptive system	Rigid and non-accessible country and society
Creativity	Unity
Demand for renewal	Top-down
Competition	Too organized hierarchy
Environment	Self-centered
Entrepreneurship	Anti-merchandise
Human capital	Wrong education and selection criteria
...	...

diabetes. In the Tang period, diagnosing diabetes by testing sugar levels in the urine was developed. Treatment for diabetes using thyroid glands of sheep and pigs were successfully carried out. These thyroid extracts were not used until 1890 in the West. An engineer named Yi-Xing invented the world's first clockwork known as the famous astronomical clock. The first wine server was invented around that time. It was carved out of iron and placed on a lacquered-wooden tortoise frame. This mechanical device consists of a hydraulic pump that draws wine out of a metal-headed faucet.

The creativity of the Chinese has being repressed since Qin Shi Huang united the various warring kingdoms and created the first Chinese empire in 221 BC. The Legalist practice of absolute power of the emperor, complete subjugation of the peripheral states to the central government, total uniformity of thought, and ruthless enforcement of law is the character of the short regime of Qin Shi Huang. To enforce the mental unity, books from the "Hundred Schools of Thought" were burned and scholars were buried alive. Soon after Qin Shi Huang had been overturned and Han Dynasty had been founded, Confucianism—which emphasizes correctness of the family-centered social relationships and the hieratical rituals—became the dominant code of conduct in China until now. Confucians, applying the family metaphor to the community and the country, illustrated the emperor as the Son of Heaven, the king as ruler–father, and the magistrate as the "father–mother official." Confucianism was deeply entrenched in the Chinese bureaucracy. The court and the government were separated. But the emperor as the Son of Heaven had the absolute power over his ministers. The capabilities of the emperor directly had influence of the capabilities of his ministers. The possibilities for renewing also largely relied on the insights of the emperor and the space he gave to his subjects to be creative. Unfortunately, there were too many weak emperors and leaders in the Chinese history.

Confucianism was dominant for thousands of years forming unity of mind-set to serve the hierarchy. The family-centered social structure, the agriculture-based economy, and the educational network are the key elements of Chinese culture from Confucius on. Confucian ideas were also firmly rooted in the legal system as ritual became increasingly important in governing behavior, defining social relationships, and adjudicating civil disputes. The other two important ancient Chinese philosophies, Buddhism and Taoism, teach conflict reconciliation. This is attributed to the Chinese culture of looking for similarity, unity, compatibility, and tolerance.

Confucian philosophy advocates harmony between different value systems. Harmony, cooperation, and convergence of different thinking should be the ultimate goal. In this way, other cultures were always smoothly assimilated into the Chinese mainstream culture. Confucian students integrated Buddhist and Taoism into Neo-Confucianism in the Ming Dynasty, which became a new unified way of thinking until today. On the other hand, new ideas which could endanger the hierarchy were punished severely; even the whole extensive family of the "innovator" could get killed. Bureaucratic unity was developed and enforced by dynasties after Confucius. Comprehensive bureaucratic systems enabled the emperors of China to directly control vast territories. The Chinese history looks like alternating periods of political unity and disunity, with China occasionally being dominated by others. But the bureaucratic unity was so strong that the same bureaucratic system was used over and over again. Only the degree of pressure in the system was different. It was mostly enlightened in the beginning regime of a dynasty or an emperor. Carried by successive waves of immigration and expansion, cultural and political influences from many parts of the world did not change China but were in turn assimilated. Even in modern China, many Western companies and Western people are so overwhelmed in China that they tried to be more Chinese than the Chinese themselves.

Because of the absolute power of the hierarchy, the demand for renewal in China came mostly from top-down. In 747, during Tang Dynasty an emperor complained about the heat in the summer. He had a cool hall built in the imperial palace. This cool hall had a device known as Tang-Yulin, which had water-powered fan wheels that functioned like air conditioning and also had rising jet streams of mountain water. This is the first air conditioner in the world. The gunpowder was invented by an alchemist trying to please the emperor by finding the long-life medicine. When he found out that the exploding flash made the emperor laugh, the amusement use of gunpowder was enriched. Another Chinese alchemist invented porcelain while researching for the long-life medicine. It was a dust-repelling and waterproof cream that works like vanish for clothes, for weapons, for silk materials, and for polishing bronze mirrors. When heated the powder turned into shiny thin coating. It was used widely later on status given houseware called China. The top-down demand can easily create new markets like renewable energy. But it can also waste resources to generate prestige-driven flops. Even today, Chinese central and local governments sometimes still invest in ghost high-tech campus and not-connected-to-grid green energy parks.

Chinese people are competitive. But free competition was not appreciated. For the sake of harmonious hierarchy, competition is mostly organized, under the surface and between groups. From childhood on, Chinese are told that it is normal that the mother should give in to the father and the younger sibling should give in to the older sibling. In return the weak will be taken care of. This mind-set created many passive followers. But this attitude also generated many Chinese women and younger siblings who were forced to be very creative to get what they wanted. To improve the family capability, explicit and implicit family (hierarchy) rules need to be developed to make sure the best came out of the competition. For example, the fifth Qing Emperor Yongzheng made clear rules how he should be followed. Hoping to avoid repetition of the succession crisis and making sure that his fourth son Hongli, a favorite of the grandfather and himself, get the throne, Yongzheng entrusted a number of important ritual tasks to him and included him in important court discussions of military strategy while Hongli was still a princess. He wrote down the name of Princess Hongli as the successor and placed in a sealed box secured behind the tablet over the throne in the Palace of Heavenly Purity. The name in the box was to be revealed to other members of the imperial family in the presence of all senior ministers only upon the death of the emperor. When Yongzheng died suddenly in 1735, the will was taken out and read out before the entire Qing Court, and Princess Hongli became the famous Qianlong emperor. The Qianlong emperor proved to be a very capable emperor and his early years saw the continuation of an era of prosperity in China.

Chinese had the wrong way of education for innovation. As a result of the dominant position of Confucian who was favored by the rulers, the Confucian Classics was the core curriculum for all levels of education since Wudi of the Han Dynasty until the fall of the last dynasty. In 124 BC a kind of imperial university was set up only studying the approved Five Classics, which had been determined by scholarly conferences and research groups under imperial auspices for several decades. According to Confucians, governmental officials are the "father and mother" governing over common people. They also should enjoy the status, rights, and privileges accordingly. Becoming officials is the ultimate goal of a common Chinese who wants to reach the highest level of the social hierarchy. This is still the case even now. Officials were appointed through the dual mechanism of selection and recommendation. Talents from different backgrounds were selected by Confucian examinations administered by the state. Those came into power often recommended their students and study friends to get a good position. Those with a Confucian education staffed the bureaucracy.

Entrepreneurship was discouraged in most of Chinese history. Businessmen used to struggle at the bottom of the society. Even since the Zhou Dynasty (1045–256 BC), Chinese professional classes were divided into four major groups: Shi, scholars and/or warriors; Nong, farmers; Gong, artisans or craftsmen; and Shang, merchants or businessman. This grouping represented a kind of hierarchical order. This historical sentiment leaves even its traces in modern Chinese society. In the late 1980s, the majors for business like economics and finance were looked down by those who were studying sciences (Fig. 2.2).

Shi is always at the top of the Chinese society. The Chinese character for Shi looks like a weapon. Earlier on in the Chinese history, the Shi were renowned mostly for their battle skills. As philosophical thinking flourished in China, the rulers shifted their requirements for Shi from physical to intellectual qualities. Because of the high status of Shi, study and martial arts were always very important in China. After the state exam system was established, etiquettes for clothing, special to show the level of the exam a scholar has passed, was developed. More

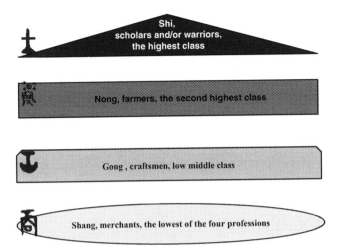

Fig. 2.2 The hierarchy of ancient Chinese professions

and more value was attached to become a Shi. The Chinese farmers were the foundation of Chinese society. The Nong were appreciated by the rulers for their stability, skills in cultivating the land, and its essential in the economy. Many soldiers turned into farmers in peaceful times. The land owners were often family members of Shi (war heroes or famous scholars) and were highly respected.

Because the demand, which usually came from the court or the higher-class officials and farmers, was very traditional and stable, innovation was not always appreciated. The Chinese craftsmen were necessary because of their skills to provide weapons or tools. The skills went from father to son, emphasizing the precision of reproduction than creating something new. This is partly comparable with the medieval guild system in Europe.

Merchants had the lowest status in ancient China. The Chinese character for merchant Shang shows a round and slippery man. In Chinese old literatures and dramas, businessman had the image of being greedy, cunning, and cooked, which was the opposite of what Confucius called a moral man should be. These were typically traders, sellers, bankers, and money changers who engaged in monetary exchanges of goods and services. Members of the Shang class were generally mistrusted by the public. They were also clearly suppressed and discriminated by the rulers. In Qin Dynasty, merchants were not allowed to wear silk clothing no matter how rich they were. In Han Dynasty, when the state exam system was established, businessman, their family, and their offsprings were not allowed to participate in the exams, which was the only way to improve the social status in China. Even in the much enlightened Tang Dynasty, businessmen could not enter civil service, while foreigners could. The low status lasted until the late Song Dynasty. In Yuan Dynasty under the Mongolian rulers, merchants were temporarily promoted to the second layer of the social hierarchy. But the majorities of Han (Chinese) people did not change their mind.

The low status of the businessman was the result of the ruling class trying to rule by household and governmental tax. Unlike farmers, merchants moved around which made it difficult to trace either their household or their property at that time. They could not easily be called in for labor forces and military services. The businessmen were also threats for governmental restrictions on the circulation of materials (such as salt, iron) in ancient China. The rulers were also afraid that the wealth could enable merchants to finance rebels. There was always an unspoken rule for the rich to hide their wealth in China. The science and technology which could bring more wealth was not attractive enough than knowing philosophical classics which could bring higher status.

2.1.2 The Shock of the Sleepy Dragon

Until 1820, there was not a big gap between the income of the Chinese and the others. Considering itself a mighty dragon, China acted like a sleepy frog in a warm bath, while the heat was built up in the West with the fire of Industrial Revolution.

The Industrial Revolution started around 1750 in the UK. Not only the technological innovation, like the iron-making techniques and the increased use of refined coal, but also the social and economic innovation formed the force for the Industrial Revolution. Great Britain provided the legal and cultural foundations that enabled entrepreneurs to pioneer. Trade expansion was enabled by the introduction of canals, improved roads, and railways. The transition from an agricultural-based economy to machine-based manufacturing shifted the mayor population from the countryside into the towns and cities.

The Industrial Revolution was seen as a major development in human history. In the long emulation process, at the end huge changes happened in manufacturing, mining, transportation, and technology from that time on. Geological, social, economic, and cultural conditions were fundamentally reshaped. It changed almost every aspect of our daily life. Most important is the growth of welfare. In the two centuries following 1800, the world's average per capita income increased over tenfold, while the world's population increased over sixfold.

Started in the UK, the Industrial Revolution subsequently spread throughout Western Europe, North America, and Japan during the nineteenth century. The rest of the world followed in different tempo.

But China did not wake up on time. The English came and won the first Opium War (1839–1842) forcing the signing of the first unequal treaty the Treaty of Nanking (29 August 1842) in the Chinese history. China paid the British an indemnity, ceded the territory of Hong Kong, and agreed to establish a "fair and reasonable" tariff. Five ports including Canton and Shanghai were forced open to free trade. After that, China is called the Asian Sick Man loosing war after war. During the nineteenth and early twentieth centuries, more unequal treaties were forced upon China by foreign imperialist powers, like Great Britain, France, Germany, the USA, Russia, and Japan. China was forced to concede many of its territorial and sovereignty rights. The dragon was cut into pieces. China became the underdog.

2.1.3 The Copycat Who Caught the Mouse?

Since the reform and opening-up policy initiated by Deng Xiaoping in 1978, China has developed itself into a labor-, capital-, and resources-intensive socialistic market economy with severe competition, private property rights, and rich entrepreneurial spirit.

Napoleon Bonaparte said when China was an underdog in 1803: "China is like a sleeping giant. And when she awakes, she shall astonish the world." China is now becoming one of the largest economies in the world again. From toys to shoes, from handcrafts to arts, from mobile phones to iPads, and from bikes to cars, made in China is a routine rather than exception.

China is also trying to outgrow its image as the factory of the world. Chinese are put into space and sent to the deepest sea bottom. Thousands of kilometer high-speed railways, the most modern airports, and highway networks have been built. The automotive market flourished driving the foreign carmakers to green figures and greener cars. ICT companies such as Huawei, ZTE, Weibo, and Tudou compete head-on with their international likes. Eco-cities are rising one after another. Alternative energy is no longer a propaganda but a booming business. Innovation is occurring in China in both the business-to-consumer (B2C) and business-to-business (B2B) sectors.

Holding on to the critics towards Chinese imitation behavior, breakthroughs are generally unrecognized by the broader global public. At the same time, Chinese companies increasingly outdated their reputation for being imitative not innovative. Product innovations in China are tested in domestic market and so escape the notice of the foreign competitors until it is too late. For example, advances by local companies in domestically oriented consumer electronics and white goods built the foundation for them to compete aggressively abroad. The home market was flooded by Chinese entrepreneurs from all over the world. There is almost no place for outsiders in upcoming new market like instant messaging and online gaming.

How can a country like China follow such divergent development paths in different times? The answer can be found in governmental policies and institutional reforms to create and support the Chinese individual entrepreneurship. Figure 2.3 showed our understanding of the change in Chinese innovation conditions in the last 30 years.

The visionary leadership, the path to develop Chinese business, the attempts to institutionalize innovative organization, and the building up of the governance system all formed a solid condition for fundamental change. The seeds of entrepreneurship inside the Chinese people are their diligence and strategic insights. Once they get to the right soil for business, the results are obvious.

There is a Chinese saying: "If you want to catch the dragon, you have to catch the head." The most important for China is the right leadership since Deng

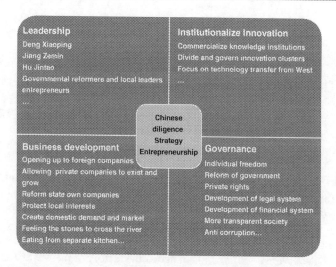

Fig. 2.3 Developed conditions for Chinese economic wonder since 1978

Xiaoping. Deng Xiaoping used his famous pragmatic speech: "white cat or black cat, the cat which can catch the mouse is a good cat" to end the theoretical discussion about socialism.

For him and the successive Chinese leaders, giving the Chinese people welfare is the most important bottom line for Chinese socialism. The Chinese successes in economic reform mostly come from the top-down initiatives. To catch up with the rest of the world, China opened up to the international trade and investment with attractive policies. Deng Xiaoping allowed the establishment of economic special zones where experiments of policies, financial instruments, and tolerance for local and private freedom and properties were tried out. Many foreign companies and overseas Chinese were recruited and stimulated to invest in those economic zones with favorable conditions like 5-years-tax-free and one-stop service.

By allowing the local governments and private persons to keep part of the benefit they generated, bottom-up initiatives were stimulated. To organize the new situations, the Chinese used their famous "feeling the stone to cross the river" method. A series of reforms were carried out to deal with the institutional, legal, and financial challenges. Table 2.2 shows a few examples of the reforms the Chinese carried out in the way of crossing the capitalistic river. The result is the development of a Chinese society with on the one hand dynamic capitalistic economy and on the other hand which is still very Chinese: hierarchical, traditional, and holistic.

At the same time, respect for being rich grows. In 1992, when Deng Xiaoping visited the south of China after the economic setback followed by 1989 Tai An Men incident, he praised the Chinese entrepreneurs in his "South Touring Talk." "Being rich is glorious" is from then on the new ideal for young Chinese. Wealth is also showed off by driving the most expensive cars, wearing famous brands and calling with expensive phones. When we had dinner in a Chinese restaurant in 1996, it was

Table 2.2 A few examples of Chinese reform since 1978

Time	Reform	Result
1978	The "Four Modernizations" reform program	Light industry grew, legitimating of township and village enterprises(TVEs), de-collectivize agriculture
1978	Opening up to foreign trade and investment	Attract foreign investment, explore international market
1988	Legalizing Entrepreneurs' status	Private sector coexists and develops, until 100 million private companies now
1993	Establishment of a Socialist Market Economic Structure	Being rich is glorious
1995	Reform of state own enterprises	Large state enterprises more independency; the smaller ones privatized
1998	Reform of knowledge institutions	The Knowledge Innovation Program
1998	Financial reform	More than $16 billion in state-owned venture capital funds
2001	Joined WTO	Support international business development

amazing how many Chinese businessmen were calling each other with the newest mobile phone while they were seated at different tables in the same room. Chinese entrepreneurs are doing very well all over the world now. The private sector now accounts for around 65 % of GDP and 70 % of tax revenues. They contributed 60 % of China's total output and export volume and employed 75 % of the workforce. China surpassed Japan in trademark patent filings in 2009.

The changes in education are another important aspect for the Chinese economic wonder. The reopening of the universities after the high education stop during the Cultural Revolution in the 1980s generated a new generation knowledge hungry talents. Those students farmed in poor countryside knew how important science, technology, and welfare are. New curriculum emphasizing science and technology was developed. The State Education Commission (SEC) issued the "Reform Plan of Teaching Contents and Curriculum of Higher Education Facing the 21st Century" in 1994. Two hundred and eleven large projects and nearly a thousand subprojects to improve teaching and curriculum in higher education institutions were carried out.

At the same time, talents went outside China to seek knowledge and opportunities. First they were sent with governmental money, then came the wave of student gold rush going abroad financed with family saving and scholarships. Some stayed abroad and made their fortune. In 1998, Chinese Americans, including Chinese who came to the USA as students, account for less than 1 % of the US population at the time. But they provide 17 % of all Silicon Valley firm owners and 10 % of the professional workforce in the valley. According to the 2010 US Census, Chinese American had one of *"the highest year-round, full-time median earnings having one of the highest median incomes among any ethnic minority in United States."*

There is also a powerful group of Chinese-born investment bankers carrying out influence on investment strategies by the major American investment banks—Goldman

Sachs, Morgan Stanley, and Citigroup. Some of whom were paid $10 million a year. Some overseas' Chinese invested in China and hit the jackpot. For example, Andre Yan and Jung Huang of Softbank Asia Infrastructure invested $40 million in an online gaming company in Shanghai called Shanda in 2003. In January 2005, they sold their stake for $500 million. Overseas' Chinese are called "sea turtles" now in China because they chose to return to where they were born carrying new values, new knowledge, and sometimes "gold bags" with them. They are more and more valued for their knowledge than for their money as China is getting rich quickly. Some even get governmental financial support if they chose to start business back in China. The golden glow on their head is also disappearing, while Chinese universities are becoming world famous institutions.

As the result of tradition for thousands of years, the best students were also recruited by the Chinese government. Because of the vacancy created by absence of high education in the 1970s, the new scholars populated the civil service and became the drive behind the reform in China. Some of them became part of the new leadership in China. Every few years, there is a new wave of governmental recruitment to attract new and younger scholar talents. For example, in the early 2000, scholars were recruited to enrich the local and central governments. Some of the study mates of the coauthor were suddenly transformed from professors into mayors. There is an exam system for the selection of civil servants at all levels. Nowadays, if one wants to get promotion in Chinese governmental organizations, one needs at least a master's degree from a famous university. The favorable kind is called "wu zhi mei shao nu" in Chinese, referring to "no party," "scholar," "educated in the USA," "ethnic minority," and "woman." That is why there are so many capable Chinese technocratic civil servants who have Dr. titles.

In the last 30 years, Chinese higher education experiences transformations through expansion of enrollment, decentralization, diversification, and merging universities. University enrollment exploded from under three million in 1995 to over 18 million students enrolled in 2007 resulting in devaluation of Chinese high education. Since 1999, the number of undergraduate and graduate students has grown at nearly 30 % per year. Chinese high education now moves to establish world-class universities, privatization, and internationalization.

Turning science and technology into economic power is the new focus of Chinese high education. In 1998, the Ministry of Education initiated Project 985 in order to strengthen existing research and to catalyze new areas for research. Education and knowledge institutes were reformed and transformed into internationally recognized institutes. Young, talented scientists who were educated abroad were attracted to return to China and those in China were kept by financially attractive policies for research and high-tech business supported by central and local governmental funding. Since 1999, funding for universities are more and more linked with academic results. Faculty members are contracted according to their academic and commercial achievements. Some universities even require faculty members to publish three articles in international journals each year or run profitable projects. Under this pressure, a few chose for academic fraud. Some

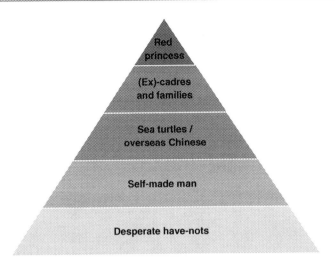

Fig. 2.4 The positions of Chinese entrepreneurs

bright heads are forced to become entrepreneurs. At the same time, many renewals are generated by the high educations.

China is not perfect yet. If one has a good look at the Chinese economy, the gap between the haves and the have-nots is becoming larger and larger. Conditions for business are still not equal for everyone. The people with good background are still having the favorable position to do business better than others. It will not change soon.

An illustration of the positions of the Chinese entrepreneurs can be like Fig. 2.4. The red princess are from the highest Chinese communist elite families. They mostly enjoyed very good education attending elite elementary schools and world famous universities. Some also took their chances and became rich when the economic reform was carried out. Because of their background, doing business was easier for them, resources were easier to get, and even the clients which were not always a state-owned company were eager to pay.

The opposite group of the red princess are those who do not have anything to lose. The first group Have-nots is the farmer. In the 1980s, many farmers grasped the chance of the agriculture reform and started from nothing their small business. Some became collectives and later on grew into big companies. The second group have-nots is the jobless. There were a lot of jobless who could not get jobs mostly because of their background. There were also millions who lost their jobs during the reform of the state-owned companies. A new group of well-educated unemployed are being formed too, while high education enrollment exploding and studying abroad becomes easier. These jobless Chinese cannot fall back to a social security system. They are too ashamed to burden on their family. The only way is to start their own business and try their luck. From selling things at street corners too making apps in their small rooms, some are doing very good. The story of Steve Jobs is an inspiration for millions of Chinese also dreaming to become rich from the "garage." They are forming the grass roots of Chinese innovations. Because they usually do not have big financial resources, smart ways of doing business are tried out. Many business innovations were generated in this way.

China is getting rich, but the Chinese are still Chinese. To do business with them, to innovate together with them, or to try to surpass them, one needs to understand their cultural background. Because 1,000-year-old stable family-oriented Confucian culture is still deeply rooted inside the Chinese value, attentions should be paid to its influence on the Chinese organizations and their way of innovation.

2.2   Chinese Culture and Innovation

2.2.1   Confucianism and Chinese (Not)-Innovative Organization

Confucianism is actually the Chinese code of conducts followed by billions of Chinese. It is the most durable ethical and social edifices in Chinese history. It shaped Chinese thought and character. Confucius was concerned with the existential problems of man. He tried to deal with these problems pragmatic by showing rules for the practical matters of daily and personal relationships. The essence of his philosophy is relationships, which formed the fundament to his social order: ruler and subject, father and son, husband and wife, older brother and younger brother, and older friend and younger friend (Confucius, 1998).

The most important is everyone should know his position in the hierarchy and acts according to the rituals (Li). One of the famous Confucius quotes is: *"Let the ruler be a ruler, the subject a subject, the father a father, the son a son* (Confucius, 1998)." The ultimate goal is to order all human relationships resulting in an ideal social structure and harmony. Table 2.3 gives some other examples and their influence on innovation.

This relevance of Confucianism for a Chinese organization was very often underestimated. To understand how a Chinese organization functions (or should function), we need to look at the relationships between rulers and ruled, within the family, and between friends (see Fig. 2.5).

This illustration demonstrates how an ancient Chinese government looked like. In ancient China, the emperor had the nature power as the "Son of Heaven," but that also requires him to act like one. Confucius said: *"To govern is to correct. If you set an example by being correct, who would dare to remain incorrect?"* He should be an example, have wisdom and knowledge, and rule with humanity. His subjects should in return to be loyal to him and to do their best to serve the ruler according the rituals. Confucius said: *"In serving one's lord, one should approach one's duties with reverence (respect) and consider one's pay as of secondary importance."*

To our understanding, the relationship between ruler and ruled in ancient China can be applied in modern Chinese organization.

First of all, leadership is the most important thing for a Chinese organization. But the Chinese leadership is not the same as Western leadership. To govern the relationships there should be attitudes like benevolence in rulers and loyalty in

Table 2.3 A few examples of Confucian thoughts and the advantages and disadvantages for innovation

Advantages	Challenges
Knowing what you know and knowing what you don't know	Self reflection without improvement
Discover new from study of old	Imitation without innovation
Hear much, observe more and remember. Study in greater depth to know more. Pick and follow those that are good	Learning without entrepreneurship
In harmony with heaven and earth	Fatalism without renewing
Know at both extremes and exhaust all possibilities	Contradiction without consolidation
From one corner to think about the other three	Multiplan without focus
Rituals (Li): proper system of norms and propriety	Limitation without exception
Loyalty (Zhong): sense of obligations of the ruled to the ruler	Followers without input
Hieratical relationships improve resources efficiency	Top-down without bottom-up

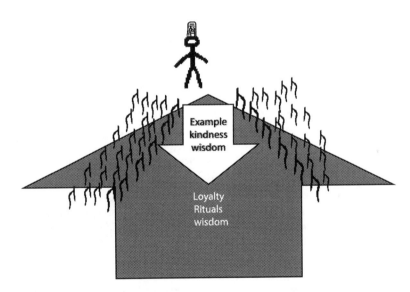

Fig. 2.5 The relationship between ruler and ruled in ancient China

subjects. A leader ruling by fear will not win loyalty. A leader avoiding responsibility will not be respected. A leader showing weakness will not be followed. We always advise Western companies to put someone with natural charisma on the top of their Chinese organization. Unfortunately, many failed to do so (van Someren & Van Someren-Wang, 2012).

Second, the hierarchy of the organization should be clear so that everyone knows his/her place. We once asked a group managers of a very innovative Dutch company to draw their organization charts for both the Dutch headquarter and their Chinese daughter. Because they have a matrix structure, no one could draw the right relationship between the units and project groups. If even the headquarter managers do not know it, how should the Chinese know? That is why their innovative way of developing projects was not carried out in China. The Chinese were pushed and pushed by different units and project groups, but they only could choose to do the thing they know, which is to listen to their own boss in China. A lot of frustration for both sides was generated by this misunderstanding.

To have the complete picture, we also need to know the relationship within a Chinese family. According to Confucius, family is the base of the society. All layers of the society should be governed like a family is being run. The ruler should be like the father in a family and the ruled like a son. Confucius said: "...*Fathers cover up for their sons, and sons cover up for their fathers. Straightness is to be found in such behavior.*" The father should rule with love and the son in return should serve the father with filial piety. For many Chinese organization, the good character, for example, filial piety, of an employee is much important than the other qualities. Remembering what Confucius said: "...*Being good as a son and obedient as a young man is, perhaps, the root of a man's character.*" Questions in a job interview, like "Where do your parents live?," are not for small talk; they are meant to find out how the candidate treats his/her parents. The Chinese family relationship is illustrated in Fig. 2.6.

The father and mother are not equal. In Fig. 2.6, you can see that the Chinese character for man is the one who stands up and works hard in the field for his family. The Chinese character for woman is much gentle and half kneeling to the man and trying to hold a foundation for the whole family at the background. So righteous behavior is expected from the husband and loyalty and support are expected from the wife. The siblings are not equal either. There should be gentility in the oldest brother and humility and respect in the younger and humane consideration in elders and deference in juniors. If we translate this family relationship to a Chinese organization, one can say that in a good functioning Chinese organization, there is always a strong "father" (leader), a kind "mother" (the good cop, not necessarily a woman), "elder brothers" (seniors in age and/or competence), and "younger brothers" (mostly from the same group background as the elder brothers). If one wants to make the "younger brothers" to do their best to innovate, the "parents" should point out the directions and the "elder brothers" should support them.

The friend–friend relationship is the only equal relationship in China as shown in Fig. 2.7.

It is very important to have friends in the Chinese business. The Chinese character for friendship looks like two people with equal power supporting each other. They stand on a basis of a very big mouth which represents good communication. We used the overlapping of groups of friends to show the Chinese network. A shortcut to enter the network is being the friend of a friend. Confucius emphasizes the importance of trust between friends: "*Make it your guiding*

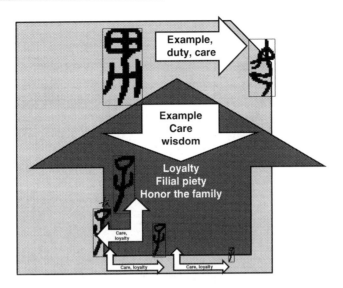

Fig. 2.6 Chinese family relationship

Fig. 2.7 Chinese friendship

principle to do your best for others and to be trustworthy in what you say. Do not accept as friend anyone who is not as good as you. When you make a mistake do not be afraid of mending your ways." The Chinese business used to base on the trust, loyalty, and support between friends. But friendship was sometimes misused. Like Confucius warned: *"He stands to benefit who makes friends with three kinds of people. Equally he stands to lose who makes friends with three other kinds of people. To make friends with the straight, the trustworthy in word and the well informed is to benefit. To make friends with the ingratiating (flattering in order to gain favor) in action, the pleasant in appearance and the plausible (possible) in speech is to lose."* One needs to be very careful to say that Guanxi (relationship in Chinese) can be built by inviting people to diners or giving presents. These gestures are meant to show one's good will to build a relationship. Real friendship one can call Guanxi needs years to build. *"A gentleman makes friends through being cultivated, but looks to friends for support in benevolence (goodwill)."* One first needs to develop and prove to be a moral man, than becomes a friend. Bribery is also not the way to do business in China.

2.2.1.1 Chinese Mentality

For many Chinese culture fans, Chinese civilization is brilliant because it had "another way" of doing science. It is true that Chinese innovators are pragmatic. They do not always try to find the roots of the truth while believing in coexistence of multiple truths. But one also needs to see the downside of this cultural background. What we are trying to do is not to give a complete definition of Chinese innovation mentality but to show how to look at both sides of the mentality attitudes. For the Chinese who want to outgrow their culture restrictions and for those who want to understand Chinese to cooperate with them, knowing that there is always another side of the story is a beginning towards an innovative future of China.

In Table 2.4 a few common Chinese proverbs are linked to Chinese innovation behavior.

Some examples of Chinese behavior can be seen in daily practice. For example, the gambling behavior of some entrepreneurs is no exception. Contrary to Japanese quality management, sometimes pragmatic half solutions are preferred above finding the ground cause of failures. Similar is the easy pragmatic solution of becoming rich by reverse engineering instead of transforming basic research into cash cows.

2.3   Chinese Strategy and the Art of Innovation

2.3.1   From Sun Tzu's The Art of War to the Chinese Art of Innovation

Sun Tzu is the godfather of Chinese strategy. Every Chinese businessman knows some of his famous quotes from his famous The Art of War. His way of thinking was widely carried out by successful Asian companies. If we want to understand the way Chinese deal with the future and innovate, we should pay attention to their strategic way of thinking. The strategic thinking of Sun Tzu can be summarized like in Fig. 2.8 (Sun Tzu, 2002).

According to our understanding, there are five foundations for a good Chinese strategy.

Typical for Chinese, the most important is visionary and strong leadership. The leaders should have the whole picture of their own organization and their surroundings and counterparts. Sun Tzu said:*"It is said that if you know your enemies and know yourself, you will not be imperiled in a hundred battles"*; if we apply this to innovation, it is about turning the "black box" into the "white box" (van Someren, 2005).

The leader also needs to judge for the right timing and the right position to take. Sun Tzu found time and timing very important: *"He who knows when he can fight and when he cannot will be victorious."*; *"When torrential water tosses boulders, it*

Table 2.4 From a few examples of Chinese proverbs to see the Chinese innovation mentality

Chinese proverbs	Chinese innovation mentality
A fast foot is first to climb	Fast vs. over speeding
The ship will reach the end of the bridge in due course	Pragmatism vs. half solutions
If you don't enter the tiger's den, how will you get the tiger's cub?	Risk taking vs. gambling
It's better to rely on yourself than on the help of others	Self reliance vs. self centered
There is no person that has 1,000 good days in a row and no flower that stays red for 100 days	Failure acceptance vs. lack of failure reflection
When entering a village, follow its customs	Adaptation vs. imitation of competitors
Three unskilled cobblers are superior to one Zhuge liang	Group effort vs. individual ingenuity
Thirty years on the east side of the river, thirty years on the west side of the river	Innovation cycles vs. negative spiral
A mountain cannot turn, but a road can	Reverse engineering vs. circumventing basic innovation
Three feet of ice is not the result of one cold day	Long term vs. flexibility
The starving can't choose their meals	Asset based innovation vs. lack of ambition
One cannot get fish and bear's paw at the same time	Focus vs. missing chances
. . .	. . .

Fig. 2.8 Chinese innovation strategy based on The Art of War

is because of its momentum. When the strike of a hawk breaks the body of its prey, it is because of timing."; "The quality of decision is like the well-timed swoop of a falcon which enables it to strike and destroy its victim."; "Speed is the essence of war."

A good leader should make sure that his command is clear and implemented to all layers of the organization correctly. A good clear hierarchy is a necessity. *"Management of many is the same as management of few. It is a matter of organization."* Sun Tzu emphasized: *"If words of command are not clear and distinct, if orders are not thoroughly understood, the general is to blame. But if his orders are clear, and the soldiers nevertheless disobey, then it is the fault of their officers."*

The harmony within the Chinese organization is crucial. Almost the same as what Confucius may say, Sun Tzu mentioned father and son like relationship between ruler and rules: *"Treat your men as you would your own beloved sons. And they will follow you into the deepest valley."* His way of motivation is not only the reward but also the other soft skills: *"A leader leads by example not by force.";* *"Bestow rewards without respect to customary practice; publish orders without respect to precedent. Thus you may employ the entire army as you would one man.";* *"The art of giving orders is not to try to rectify the minor blunders and not to be swayed by petty doubts.";* *"A skilled commander seeks victory from the situation and does not demand it of his subordinates.";* *"Engage people with what they expect; it is what they are able to discern and confirms their projections. It settles them into predictable patterns of response, occupying their minds while you wait for the extraordinary moment — that which they cannot anticipate.";* *"If our soldiers are not overburdened with money, it is not because they have a distaste for riches; if their lives are not unduly long, it is not because they are disinclined to longevity."* He even warned the danger of using rewards unwisely: *"Too frequent rewards indicate that the general is at the end of his resources; too frequent punishments that he is in acute distress."*

To have all the aspects right for a victory, one needs to know that there is always the other side of the coin in China. Sun Tzu gave a few examples of the paradoxes one should consider for a winning strategy. These paradoxes are part of Chinese philosophy and are still being applied to carry out Chinese innovation (Fig. 2.9).

For example, a company can still win a competition even when it is relatively weak. Sun Tzu showed how: *"It is the rule in war, if ten times the enemy's strength, surround them; if five times, attack them; if double, be able to divide them; if equal, engage them; if fewer, be able to evade them; if weaker, be able to avoid them."* Many Chinese companies avoid the confrontation abroad and only focus their product innovation for Chinese, knowing that they have more chance at home comparing to their strong foreign counterparts. Some did go abroad but focusing on niche when they are weak. When Haier first tried the American market with their small size refrigerators only for hotels, they were very smart to avoid the main competitor in household white goods. But the contrary also happens. Because of cutthroat competition in Chinese market, export and overseas market development has a higher rate of return than same activity in home market.

From Western perspective, a very interesting one is the damage—profit paradox. In Chinese eyes, not all profits are beneficial for the future prosperity of an enterprise. Gaining short-term profits can harm future long-term profitability when relations have been disturbed acquiring a quick buck. It is better to create value on a long term and invest in durable relations instead of focusing on short-term results. This "playing" with the factor time is extremely important in China. A dynamic interpretation of the profit criterion characterizes Chinese enterprises. It fits into the dynamic value conversion principle as will be explained in Chap. 4.

Yin	Yang
Counterpart	Self
Visitor	Local
Few	Many
Weak	Strong
Offense	Defense
Charge	Retreat
Victory	Failure
Strange	Mainstream
Fake	True
Brave	Afraid
Labor	Leisure
Calm	Move
Curvature	Straight
Damage	Profit
Death	Life

Fig. 2.9 A few examples of Sun Tzu's paradoxes of innovation according to The Art of War

Sun Tzu gave many examples of how to use paradoxes: *"The ultimate in disposing one's troops is to be without ascertainable shape; Be extremely subtle, even to the point of formlessness. Be extremely mysterious, even to the point of soundlessness."*; *"when we are able to attack, we must seem unable; when using our forces, we must appear inactive; when we are near, we must make the enemy believe we are far away; when far away, we must make him believe we are near."*

Sun Tzu even allowed entrepreneurship: *"If fighting is sure to result in victory, then you must fight, even though the ruler forbid it; if fighting will not result in victory, then you must not fight even at the ruler's bidding."*

All the strategy should serve one goal: to win the war. This should also be kept in mind by the leaders calling for innovation: *"What is essential in war is victory, not prolonged operations."* This attitude and market behavior should frighten Western business managers not the copy–paste behavior.

2.3.2 A Few Stories of the Chinese Innovation Tactics

2.3.2.1 Borrowing of Arrows with Straw Boats

Zhuge Liang, who lived in the third century, is a famous strategist in Chinese history. His stories were told in *Romance of the Three Kingdoms* (Luo, 1976 [c. 1330]), one of the four best sellers in the Chinese history which has been turned into dramas, films, and TV series again and again. Almost every Chinese knows his stories of winning from his enemy using wisdom in place of forces. Since Chinese are brought up with the idea that one needs to learn from great men's wisdom, Zhuge Liang's wisdom was widely told and used in the daily life.

Zhuge Liang was once assigned the task of making 100,000 arrows in 10 days, or he would face execution for failure in duties under military law. Zhuge Liang prepared 20 large boats, each manned by a few soldiers and filled with human-like figures made of straw and hay. At dawn, when there was a great fog, Zhuge Liang deployed the boats, and they sailed towards Cao Cao's camp across the river. He ordered the troops to beat war drums loudly and shout orders to imitate the noise of an attack. Upon hearing the noise, Cao Cao's troops rushed out to engage the enemy, but they were unsure of the enemy's strength, because their vision was obscured by the fog. They fired volleys of arrows towards the sound of the drums and the arrows became stuck in the straw figures. The boats with more than 100,000 arrows returned to camp when the fog cleared.

The development of many of Chinese strategic sectors knows phases that the arrows were borrowed. Unfortunately, Chinese also know how to turn borrowed arrows into icebreaker. They studied the "old" (borrowed arrows) and improve it to generate their "new" like Confucius told them to do. From green energy to aircraft industry, traces of borrowed arrows were everywhere in their infant time. Once they mature, the borrowed arrows turned into flying rackets which may destroy those who do not want to ride along.

The development of the Chinese high-speed train gives a good illustration of how it happens. Policies to develop high-speed train system were developed in the 1990s by the Chinese central government. A grand future with network of thousands of kilometers of high-speed railway was pictured and planned. China initiated high-speed trains by first importing and building under technology transfer agreements. The market signal was quickly picked up by advanced train-makers. Foreign train-makers including Siemens, Bombardier, and Kawasaki Heavy Industries, limited by the slow development at home, were blinded by the possibilities in China.

They all underestimated the Chinese technology improvement capability and aimed at the Chinese straw boat by signing the technology transfer agreements. Chinese localized first the easy part, the low-tech components. Meanwhile, most of the China Railway High-speed (CRH) train components are manufactured by local Chinese suppliers. Comparing, combining, and eliminating the faults of the different technologies, the Chinese engineers successfully redesigned internal train components and built indigenous trains that can reach operational speeds of up to 380 km/h (240 mph). Foreign train-makers are left to sell only certain high-tech components in place of train sets and signal systems they aimed at the huge China's high-speed train market. Reports differ over the extent to which Chinese engineers absorbed or expropriated foreign technology in building indigenous train sets and signal systems. The fact is that China currently holds close to 1,000 local and international patents for high-speed rail technology which have partly been acquired from their former cooperation partners like Siemens (www.news.sina.com.cn, 2012).

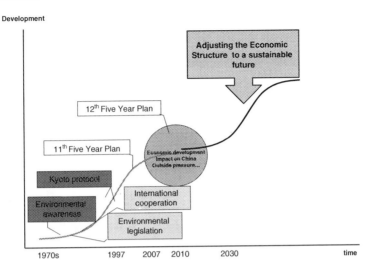

Fig. 2.10 China's policies and actions on climate change

2.3.2.2 Praying for the Eastern Wind

Another story of Zhuge Liang is about his wisdom of timing. Before the major winning against Cao Cao, preparations for the fire attack on Cao Cao's fleet had been made; the general in charge Zhou Yu suddenly realized that the eastern wind, which was required to enhance the fire attack, was not blowing to their advantage. Zhuge Liang studied the weather and anticipated that the east wind will come in a few days. He pretended to pray for the eastern wind. Days later, the eastern wind started blowing making the fire attack one of the most famous winning of a weaker army over a strong one in the Chinese history (Luo, 1976 [c. 1330]).

The same tactic is also seen in the development of Chinese climate change policies and actions as illustrated in Fig. 2.10.

In the development of the Chinese policies and actions against climate change, Chinese environmentalists have worked their way up towards a sustainable economy patiently. Early as 1972, before the opening-up policy and economic growth, Chinese representatives were sent on the path of environment diplomacy to attend the First United Nations Conference on the Human Environment held in Sweden. They brought back the massage that environmental issues were becoming social and economic issues which attract attention of the international community. To have a voice in the international community, China had to pay attention to the environmental issues. In the next year the Environmental Protection Leadership Group was established.

In the following 10 years, Chinese scholars and policy makers absorbed the knowledge of foreign colleagues and struggled the ignorance to environmental concerns in China. Young talents were educated in universities like Beijing Normal University which has one of the earliest environmental institutes in China. When they graduated, under the pressure of pointing-fingers of the international community, the need for these talents was urgent. The talents, mostly students of the same mentor like Professor Wang Huadong (also professor of the coauthor) who is one of the founding fathers of Chinese environmental sciences, soon populated high-level governmental organizations and knowledge institutions. They become the drive behind the Chinese environmental policy. Because they came from the same nest, they sometimes back up each other's policies from different governmental organizations. In 1983, the Chinese government announced that environmental protection would become a state policy.

The Chinese knew that they knew little about environmental protection. The international community wanted to get China on board. International cooperation was stimulated from both sides. Studying, combining, and localizing different environmental legislation from the EU and several member states, the USA, and Japan, comprehensive environmental legislation was built up. Although it is not always enforced because economic interest was higher ranked in the agenda. In 1998, China went through a disastrous year of serious flooding. The consequences of neglecting the environment were pointed out by the environmentalist educated in the 1980s and getting into decision-making position in the 1990s. Then the Chinese government upgraded the leading group to a ministry-level agency, which later became the State Environmental Protection Administration after a series of environmental disasters.

It is again promoted to Ministry of Environment in 2010 when China decided to turn into a green economy. Some smart leaders in Chinese environmental protection sector also used the media strategically. For example, the Vice-Minister of Ministry of Environment, Pan Yue, has been one of the most vocal high-level officials in the Chinese government critical of the old development model. He warned that "the Chinese miracle will end soon" if sustainable issues were not addressed urgently again and again in Chinese and even foreign medias.

China was ready for a new growth model. Gradually, sustainable development was integrated into Chinese economic plans like the 11th and the 12th Five-Year Plans. Supporting sector policies and financial instruments were built around it. Demand for environmental technologies and solutions was created by tightening up the law enforcement. The only thing missing is the "east wind."

The 2009 Copenhagen Climate Change Conference was the "east wind" for the Chinese. Let us have a look at

"China's Position on the Copenhagen Climate Change Conference"

IMPLEMENTATION OF THE BALI ROADMAP

China's Position on the Copenhagen Climate Change Conference

May 20, 2009

I. PRINCIPLES
---
1. The UNFCCC and its Kyoto Protocol as the Basis and the Mandate of the Bali Roadmap as the Focus. . . .
---
2. The Principle of Common but Differentiated Responsibilities. Developed countries shall take responsibility for their historical cumulative emissions and current high per capita emissions to change their unsustainable way of life and to substantially reduce their emissions and, at the same

(continued)

time, to provide financial support and transfer technology to developing countries. Developing countries will, in pursuing economic development and poverty eradication, take proactive measures to adapt to and mitigate climate change.

3. The Principle of Sustainable Development. *Sustainable development is both the means and the end of effectively addressing climate change. Within the overall framework of sustainable development, economic development, poverty eradication and climate protection should be considered in a holistic and integrated manner so as to reach a win-win solution and to ensure developing countries to secure their right to development.*

4. Mitigation, Adaption, Technology Transfer and Financial Support on the Same Footing and as Equal Priorities. *Mitigation and adaption are integral components of combating climate change and should be given equal treatment. Compared with mitigation that is an arduous task over a longer time horizon, the need for adaption is more real and urgent to developing countries. Financing and technology are indispensible means to achieve mitigation and adaptation. The fulfillment of commitments by developed countries to provide financing, technology transfer and capacity building support to developing countries is a condition sine qua non for developing countries to effectively mitigate and adapt to climate change.*

Source: National Development and Reform Commission (NDRC)

Until then, China was always the underdog trying to organize the developing countries to avoid the pointing-fingers. For the first time China made concrete commitment to reduce CO_2. A set of plans with detailed actions towards quantified targets was published. China has turned the pointing-fingers from the international community into their "east wind" to develop a sustainable economy (Van Someren & Van Someren-Wang, 2009 december).

2.3.2.3 Empty Fort Strategy

This is one of the risky tactics Zhuge Liang used. During the first Northern Expedition, Zhuge Liang found his army in peril of being attacked by the enemy. His main force was deployed elsewhere; only a small group of soldiers were left in the city. Zhuge Liang had to do something to save his city from being crashed. Zhuge Liang ordered all the city gates to be opened and instructed soldiers disguised as civilians. A few old men were ordered to sweep the roads while he sat on the viewing platform above the gates with two boys flanking him. He put on a calm and composed image by playing relaxing music on his Guqin. When the enemy arrived, the general was surprised by the scene before him and ordered a retreat after suspecting that there was an ambush inside the city (Luo, 1976 [c. 1330]).

Under the influence of 2008 financial crisis and the ongoing Euro crisis, some Chinese companies are suffering problems like dried-up orders, lack of cash flow, and heavy loans. But many of them are invisible for the outside world except the few caught the media attention with panicking owners who tried to escape or kill themselves. Empty Fort Strategy is used mostly by those who are desperate. Instead of showing panic, they choose to deceive the outside world to win time to recover.

One of our clients used it with great success. The factory is a young company set up in 2008. They make high-tech components for windmills. Almost all the employees enjoyed high education with specified knowledge which were hard to recruit when the business was booming. The company managed to get the best people by offering options for share if the company goes public in the Chinese stock market. The company made millions in the first 2 years supplying unique products no competitors could. Soon came the imitators in the market. The managing board decided that new products and market have to be developed to surpass the others. Thanks to their high-quality employees, they started testing a series of innovative products. At the same time, millions were invested in developing other business like investment in building wind energy plants. When the overheating happened in the wind energy business in the summer of 2010, the company faced severe cash flow problem because the clients were not paying them on time. With several new products in the pipeline and a wind energy plant waiting to be connected to the grid, the managing board expected that the company could survive if they could hold on long enough. A kind of Empty Fort theater was carried out. All the board members were sent out to get new investors riding BMW 7 Series or Audi A8 which they borrowed from their friends. Potential investors were taken to diners in an exclusive restaurant which the company made a deal of open account paid once a month. They could not pay the salaries. So they send the less needed employees to collective trainings which they do not need to pay in advance. With a few million RMB, new investment came and they hold on. Half year later, many of their Chinese competitors were wiped out of the market.

The world is now facing serious problem with the US economy recovering too slowly and the EU threatened by struggling monetary union. China faces serious problems too. Some analysts say that China is manipulating its growth figures and bad loan burdens. We do not know if China is carrying out an Empty Fort Strategy. What we can see is instead of panicking, the Chinese are rolling out policy packages to secure the economic growth. For example, China's banks are expected to issue trillions of RMB of new loans each quarter in 2012. China's banks used to operate within tight limits. The central bank used to impose a ceiling on the interest rates they may pay to depositors and a floor under the rates they may charge borrowers. The loan policy of the state-owned banks was directly generated from the economic agenda's with favorable conditions for certain sectors. At the same time, more freedom is given to the Chinese banks. It said that banks could offer depositors an interest rate 10 % above the benchmark and borrowers a rate 20 % below it. The cut in lending rates could allow banks to revive credit. The rise in the deposit ceiling could attract depositors. The Chinese government is carrying out a reform of the financial system. Empty Fort or not, China is trying to pass the storm with peace. It may work out better than the panicking news from Europe we hear every day now.

2.3.2.4 Create Something from Nothing
This is the story of Shi Yuzhu. Shi Yuzhu is one of first Chinese high-tech entrepreneurs with a legendary story of ups and downs typical for many pioneering Chinese self-made entrepreneurs. Entrepreneurship accompanied with sometimes overheated head with gambling behaviors makes them grow or fall. Some managed to be born from ashes again and again. With China growing into a market economy, new generation of Chinese entrepreneurs are learning from Shi Yuzhu-like lessons. They may overcome the same fault. If not they can learn that there is always hope for a true entrepreneur. Not only the favorable policies but also these entrepreneurs

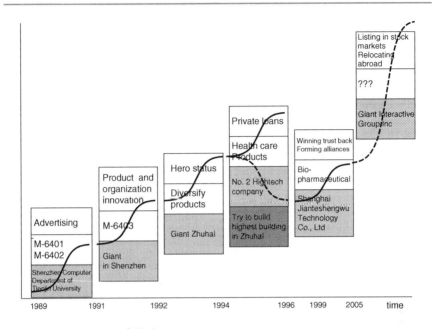

Source: based on news about Shi Yuzhu

Fig. 2.11 The history of Shi Yuzhu's giant

will bring China to an innovative market economy. Figure 2.11 shows the development in time (www.news.sina.com.cn, 2012).

Shi Yuzhu is from the first-generation well-educated Chinese after the culture revolution. He graduated from the Department of Mathematics of Zhejiang University at the age of 22 in 1984. As an excellent talent who was hardly needed after years of pause of the high education during the Cultural Revolution, he was assigned to the Anhui Province Bureau of Statistics and became a civil servant, which is a dream job for millions of Chinese students, even today. He gave up the dream job to study further in the Graduate School of Shenzhen University. Shenzhen is the lab for Chinese reform. Entrepreneurship was booming under the less strict governmental control. The border of Hong Kong and Macao attracted thousands of Hong Kongnese and other overseas Chinese to start business. Under this business optimism, in 1989, Shi Yuzhu jumped into the business sea as the Chinese may say. Using his software knowledge, he developed a Chinese desktop word processing systems named M-6401. With only 4,000 RMB, he leased the business license of the Shenzhen Computer Department of Tianjin University, which only had a business license without even a computer. At that time, import of computer was restricted. The price of a computer in Shenzhen was at least 8,500 RMB. Shi negotiated with a computer supplier offering 1,000 RMB more for one computer if he could pay 2 weeks later. He arranged at that time a very bold advertisement with collateral payments in the Chinese magazine "Computer World" with a total budget of 17,550 RMB (at that time less than $1,800) which he did not have. Thirteen days after the advertisement appeared, the sales exceeded $100,000. Shi paid off outstanding loans and used all the money left to invest in advertising. Four months later, the M-6401 sales exceeded one million. This was the story of the first growth curve of Shi Yuzhu's business, which did not only come from technical innovation as M-6401 but mostly is driven by the innovative way of sales and marketing. In 1991, Shi founded his own company named Giant (JuRen) in Shenzhen.

In 1992, the headquarters of Giant was moved from Shenzhen to neighboring Zhuhai. M-6403 achieved a profit of 35 million RMB. In 1993, Giant launched the M-6405, a Chinese laptop computer enabling Chinese handwriting. The annual sales of only handwriting Chinese computer and software reached 360 million RMB. Giant became the second largest private high-tech enterprise in China. Shi Yuzhu also got hero status. Shi Yuzhu was honored the Rewards of Intellectuals in Zhuhai and was elected one of the top 10 reformers in China. National leaders like Deng Xiaoping and Jiang Zemin praised his effort in public.

At the same time market for Chinese computers was changing. The restriction of import of computers was loosened. Shi Yuzhu anticipated the change and started to broaden the scope of Giant. Real estate and healthcare products should bring new impulse to the company. The dream of a nice headquarters was heavily encouraged by the local government. The design of the headquarters grew from a 16-floor building into a 70-floor building which would become China's tallest building at that time. The required funds exceed one billion RMB which Giant did not have yet. Private loans were easily raised by Shi Yuzhu because of his big name. The business of healthcare products was also growing. In 1995, Giant launched 12 kinds of healthcare products using a billion RMB in advertising. Shi Yuzhu was ranked by Forbes as the Mainland China's No. 8 richest man. In 1996, the Giant headquarter building faced a major setback because of the unexpected high cost of the foundation. Cash flow became a problem. Shi Yuzhu decided to tape the healthy healthcare diversion to save the financial emergency of the building of Giant's headquarters. The healthcare division suffered from financial blooding and excessive mismanagement, coupled with the rapid boom–bust. In early 1997, the Giant building is not completed on schedule. Media reported that Giant faced financial crisis and was at the edge of bankruptcy. Shi Yuzhu settled with the loans owners with his Giant building as guarantee and promised to pay back every penny he borrowed. Giant was not forced to file for bankruptcy.

Starting from nothing again, Shi Yuzhu registered a biopharmaceutical company Shanghai Jianteshengwu Technology Co., Ltd. in 1999 to produce healthcare products. He teamed up with the original friends of entrepreneurs in Shanghai, Jiangsu, and Zhejiang to do the business of "melatonin." Shi said: "the people's money, I have to repay." and set a timetable repay the debts at the end of 2000. In 2001, after he cleared his credit, Shi Yuzhu applied for registration of a new Giant company seeking listing in Shanghai Stock Exchange. It was realized on 15 November 2005. On 26 July 2006, Shi Yuzhu and the other 18 company executives officially registered "Giant Network Technology Limited" in the Cayman Islands. On 11 June 2007, "Giant Network Technology Limited" changed its name to Giant

Interactive Group Inc. On 1 November 2007, Shi Yuzhu Giant Interactive Group Inc.'s successfully launched its stock at the New York Stock Exchange, generating more than $4.2 billion market value. It is the largest private enterprises listed in the foreign stock market. In China, Shi Yuzhu is estimated worth more than 50 billion RMB. He is still the marketing genius with news about him bidding excessive amount of money for commercials time on CCTV. His imperium reached out from healthcare products, biological technology, health wine to investment banking, online games, education, and consulting. The story of Shi Yuzhu has not ended yet. We do not know if he has to be a phoenix again.

2.3.2.5 Make the Host and the Guest Exchange Roles

China is realizing the dream of being a great nation on aerospace technology. China has always played the modest guest admitting that its aerospace technology was far less advanced than that of the USA and the EU. Afraid of being copied, the advanced countries have always refused to see the possibilities for cooperation. At the same time China is developing itself into the owner of advanced aerospace technology which is also widely transplanted to civil usage generating impulses for economic transition.

The push on aerospace technology development has put enormous pressure on study fields like physics, chemistry, mechanics, earth science, and materials, hence generating advances in these fields quickly in recent years in China. The way from lab to market is very short because most of the involved research institutes and companies have direct link to "military" industry or even have their own subcompanies. According to Xinhua News, 80 % of the developed space technology is used in other sectors like ICT, new material, renewable energy, medicine, and agriculture; nearly 2,000 space technology achievements have been ported to various departments of the national economy. For example, China Aerospace Information Co., Ltd. developed and launched the "Golden Tax Project," the "Golden Shield Project," and the "Golden Card Project." The "Golden Tax Project" used advanced cryptographic techniques for the country to solve the major issues to curb tax evasion and fraud crimes. The "Golden Shield Project" is the national ICT system for law and order. The "Golden Card Project" generated the earliest IC card products for the Chinese market. It is playing an important role in the field of intelligent transportation; 70 % of the nation's highway network is using the intelligent transport system. More than 1,000 kinds of new materials are developed by the Chinese aerospace industry. The Chinese photovoltaic industry is turning to use key technologies from the development of Chinese space solar cell technology being more and more independent of the foreign development. New medicines are developed and tested in the space since Shenzhou I is launched in 1991. Seeds were mutated in the space and developed quickly for the market. The giant 90 kg pumpkins you see in the normal Chinese farms came from the 10 g pumpkinseeds that traveled the space in 2001. In the future, we will see more and more of Chinese aerospace technology in the normal life (www.news.sina.com.cn, 2012).

With the weakening financial position of the USA and the EU, less and less will be available to be invested into aerospace technology. China is turning from the guest into the host at the aerospace feast table. Those who did not believe in Chinese innovation strength have to be careful with their conclusion that China only can copy. It may be the case in the beginning of the development. But China has the tradition of long-term pragmatic thinking; once the Chinese find the right direction to go and commit to it, the power of the Chinese collectively can be astonishing.

China came from a 1,000-year-old culture which emphasizes reproducing the master thinking and following orders according to the hierarchy. The freedom to innovate and the turning focus of education have worked out well for the Chinese who used their long-term pragmatic strategic thinking. China, especially in the eyes of Westerners, is full of paradoxes and will continue to be so in the future. It is important for the Chinese to find the right balance to continue their road of innovation. The West will be growing with Chinese innovations too if there is more attention to the Chinese culture and the right way to deal with the Chinese paradoxes.

References

Confucius. (1998). *The analects of Confucius: A philosophical translation* (R. T. Ames & H. Rosemont, Trans.). New York: Ballantine.

Sun Tzu. (2002). *The art of war*. Boston: Shambala.

Luo, G. (1976) [c. 1330]. *Romance of the three kingdoms* (M. Roberts, Trans.) New York: Pantheon Books.

van Someren, T. C. R. (2005). *Strategische Innovationen. So machen Sie Ihr Unternehmen einzigartig*. Wiesbaden: Gabler.

van Someren, T. C. R., & van Someren-Wang, S. (2009, December). Klimaattop? Welnee, er wordt een markt verdeeld (p. 29). *Trouw*.

van Someren, T. C. R., & van Someren-Wang, S. (2012). *Green China. Sustainable Growth in East and West*. Heidelberg: Springer.

http://www.news.sina.com.cn (2012)

Innovation Policies in China, the USA, and the EU

3

Governmental policies in China, the USA, and the EU have different roles, scope, and impact. In the USA market-based innovation is by far more important than governmental innovation policy. In the EU, market-based innovation is also the main driver of renewal, but on a European level, innovation policies gain momentum. However, the role and scope of innovation policy differs between member states and interfere with Pan-European initiatives. For China central planning and policies are the core of economic growth and development. But the five-year central planning cycle changed into a five-year strategic growth agenda supported by numerous issue-based policies. China is developing according to a 4I-scheme consisting of imitation, improvement, innovation, and internationalization. The biggest challenge for China is the move from being a copycat country to an innovative country by 2020. Moreover, becoming independent of Western technology is one of the main goals. Triggered by world issues like sustainability, the West is searching for "Chinese" like grand innovation policy plans, whereas China is searching for individual firms innovation policies. For both sides, China and the West, the paths of policy making are new, and it depends on the speed of learning and its acceptance in society who will win the policy race. In this respect, the pivotal policies to become leading edge technology country are decided by nontechnical issues. The world game changing policies focus on nontechnical aspects. Therefore, the crossroad of innovation policies is also deciding about the outcome of the strategic innovation battle.

3.1 No Wind No Waves

The role and involvement of government differs per geographical region. But the common task is to take care of general interest of the country or region. With regard to innovation, the government issues policies which are trying to ensure future prosperity. A few characteristics of these policies in China, the USA, and the EU are presented in Fig. 3.1.

T.C.R. van Someren and S. van Someren-Wang, *Innovative China*,
Management for Professionals, DOI 10.1007/978-3-642-36237-8_3,
© Springer-Verlag Berlin Heidelberg 2013

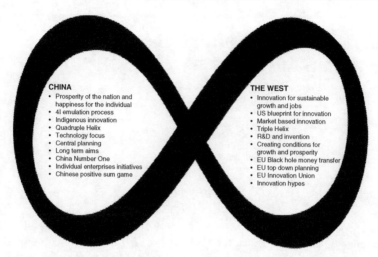

Fig. 3.1 Policies for prosperity

The approaches, aims, and time frames differ among China, the USA, and the EU. The central thought is that without wind, there will be no waves, but whether and how governments should be wind maker differs. In this chapter, the main subject is the pivotal role of innovation policies in China, the USA, and the EU in realizing an innovative society.

3.2   Gales of Creative Destruction

Governments and policy makers think they rule the waves. Sometimes they do, but regularly they are overruled by strategic innovations being the gales of creative destruction. Being aware of this phenomenon, policy makers try to create these gales and shift the innovation frontier. But where and when do these gales and waves occur? They are identifiable on world scale, the level of the nation, region, and even cities. The strategic innovations are also to be seen in any period of time. To make it simple, we will start to illustrate the strategic innovations from the macro-level and then descending to the meso-level followed by the micro-level. This chapter makes clear that innovation policies of China, the USA, and the EU are converging and in the end cover identical issues. But successful policies are rare, and imitating each other's successes is not the solution due to differences in context. Strategic innovations often happen without policies. Therefore, successful innovation requires in-depth knowledge of the innovation process and its context.

The next sections will investigate to what extent the gales cause waves throughout the economy and what the policies of China, the USA, and the EU are.

3.2.1   Macro-waves

One common and accepted way of showing the relevance of innovation is the format of successive waves of innovation. The history and future of worldwide

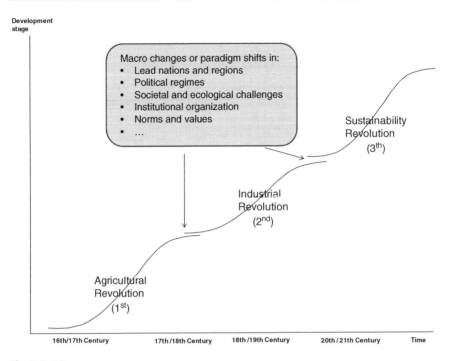

Fig. 3.2 Macro-waves

societal development are congruent with the waves of innovation. However, there are many different ways to make a categorization of waves. Historians but also current policy makers favor the macroscopic classification of revolutions. According to the historians, since the Middle Ages in the development of the (market) economy, two revolutions have taken place, and we stand on the eve of a third (see Fig. 3.2).

The first revolution is the Agricultural Revolution in which several new techniques leading to higher productivity were introduced. The second revolution is the Industrial Revolution which started around nineteenth century in the UK. Of course, the steam engine and iron were the most eye-catching new techniques characterizing the second revolution. In this scheme, sustainable development is regarded to be the Third Revolution.

This is a birds' eye view of historians covering decades or even centuries. But this macro-view is a Eurocentric view on world history, neglecting the economic scale of Asian economy before the rise of the West. If sustainability is the next industrial revolution, we are witnessing its beginning. In that respect, it is insightful to understand the change processes on macro-level which are influencing the buildup of the new gales and waves.

From a macro-perspective, the industrial revolution consists of several long waves. The big macro-waves are an accumulation over time of strategic innovations addressing new issues and challenges accompanied by the rise of new nations. The sustainability macro-wave takes off, and the rise of China is not a coincidence (van Someren & Someren-Wang, 2012).

Only policy makers and top managers with strategic foresight did see the connection between sustainability as the next industrial driver of prosperity and the rise of China. However, the large majority missed the strong and weak signals on the meso- and micro-level and focused on China as a low-cost country. Although these developments sometimes look as revolutions, big dramatic changes in a very short period of time, they are not. The reason is that the causes of these changes have been active for many years, sometimes decades. But only a few spent attention to these weak signals of upcoming change. Most of us ignore them being occupied with daily business. When we discover them, the momentum and accumulation of new societal development are huge, and it cannot be stopped anymore. To discover these developments, we have to dig deeper in underlying processes of change and innovation on the meso- and micro-level.

3.2.2   Meso-waves

On meso-level, a classification very often used by innovation experts are the eras in which new technologies and new materials emerged and followed by organizational forms. Figure 3.3 demonstrates the radical changes in the industrial sectors and the emergence of new firms and (sub)industries together with their technical and nontechnical innovations.

The meso-level covers industry-wide issues such as mergers and acquisitions, new industrial standards and shifts in ways of doing business, or dominant technology and organizational forms. Sometimes new entrants or incumbent firms introduce a strategic innovation, thereby shaking existing industries. For the future, the megatrend of clean energy and sustainable mobility are the big challenges. Linked to renewable energy, a big issue is energy storage such as batteries. Chinese BYD is currently worldwide the biggest battery manufacturer, and they jumped in the market of electrical cars. Chinese business models will accompany the shift to the new era of sustainability and the greening of industry with China as leading countries in runner-up Asia.

With regard to innovation, on the meso-level, some features of innovation in different cultural settings become clear. The rise of China and some other countries leads to a mix of interpretations of innovation. In Table 3.1, a few characteristics demonstrate the different context of innovation in the USA, the EU, and China.

From all different criteria, innovation has a different meaning and content in the EU, the USA, and China. Maybe the most relevant is the driving force of having a dream. Everybody knows about the American Dream of getting rich by setting up your own business. Chinese have similar dreams, and besides getting rich, they want to possess the biggest company in their industry. At the moment of writing, there is no collective European Dream except for the political elite creating a unified Europe and several individual entrepreneurs.

Therefore, it is no surprise that both the American and Chinese economies are full of creative entrepreneurs trying to realize their dreams and achieving bottom-line

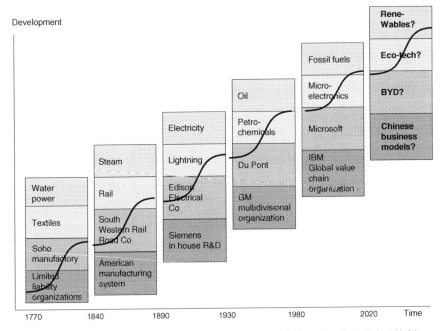

Source: based upon Van Someren, 1991, Innovatie, Emulatie en Tijd, 2005, Strategische Innovationen, Gabler Verlag, table 2.1

Fig. 3.3 Meso-waves

results. Finding practical solution is key in the USA and China, as shown by the American "fix-it" mentality and the Chinese pragmatism in creating solutions.

Another aspect is the regulations and characteristics of the economy. An example is the ownership of firms which has an influence on innovation output.

In Table 3.2, the rise of private companies compared to state-owned companies in China is illustrated. The conclusion is that state-owned firms are not an outmoded model. On the contrary, public owned will remain very relevant in China because they are the instruments and vehicles of the political leaders for realizing central planning aims. It demonstrates the pragmatism to allow both forms of ownership in different situations.

3.2.3   Microwaves

When we zoom in even more, a third microscopic succession of waves can be constructed. As an example, we take the topic of sustainability as presented in Fig. 3.4.

Each of the waves in Fig. 3.4 was for the individual company a big step, but only the accumulated effect contributes to the changing of industry. But sometimes strategic innovations initiated by individual entrepreneurs or single enterprises like the introduction of the solar panel can cause the desired gales of creative

Table 3.1 Some features of the innovation context in the EU, China, and the USA

	EU Manager based	China Entrepreneurial based	USA Technology based
Innovation	Company-based governance Technology orientation Incremental innovations	Government-based governance and FDI based High-tech orientation Imitation and improvements dominate	Company-based supported by institutions Technology and market orientation New business model creation Revolutionary innovations
Organization	Wide dispersed knowledge Cooperation and sharing knowledge is often but not always leading principle	Institutions still dominate Cooperation best between internal networks Sharing knowledge only with internal network members	Firms lead Concentratred centers of excellence with tight cooperation with private business Cooperation and sharing alone if profitable
Entrepreneurship	Managerial entrepreneurship Large knowledge base not transferred in products, processes and services Leaders focus on short-term as well as quick results	Creative entrepreneurship Leaders see relevance of innovation for long-term survival and long-term aims of China Bottom-line results relevant	Innovative entrepreneurship Individualistic approach dominate Although innovation performance is good; leaders focus on short-term results Bottom-line results dominate
Culture	European dream is absent Manager culture Risk avoidance orientation Analytic Conceptual Trust	Chinese Dream Family business High risk takers/gamblers Pragmatic Innovation Distrust	American Dream Entrepreneurs are heroes High risk-takers Practical solutions that work Fixing and doing it Legally ensured trust
Time	Short term Accumulated knowledge	Long and short term Learning and accumulation	Short term and flexible Accumualted knowledge andrenewing stock of knowledge

destruction with a profound impact on the meso- and macro-level (van Someren, 1991, 2005)

In the remainder of this chapter, we focus on what role policy makers in China, the USA, and the EU played in these macro-, meso-, and micro-developments. Table 3.3 gives a helicopter view on some of the current policies.

Table 3.4 shows different focus and approaches towards establishing a kind of innovation system. The aims, key dimensions, key actors, programs, and obstacles

Table 3.2 Ownership of firms in China

Employment	1998 (in millions)	2009 (in millions)
State-owned entities	90.58	64.20
Limited liability companies/companies limited by shares	8.94	33.89
Private companies or self-employed	32.32	97.89

Source: Information Office of the State Council of the People's Republic of China. September 2010, Beijing

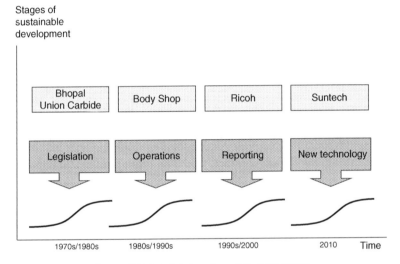

Source: based upon Van Someren, 2005, Strategische Innovationen, Gabler Verlag, table 2.1

Fig. 3.4 Microwaves

to overcome show similarities and differences between the EU, the USA, and China. A more detailed view is necessary to understand the real world and meaning behind on first sight apparently similar policy statements.

3.3 China's Innovation Policies: Temple of Innovation Heaven

China is in the transformation phase from world's manufacturer to a high-value innovation-based economy. This "Innovation Revolution" puts China but also the West for big challenges and a lot of opportunities. But it must be kept in mind that even Western societies like the European Union and its individual nation states have many difficulties over many decades to realize such an innovative economy. Moreover, for both many Western individual firms and policy makers, innovation is

Table 3.3 Overview current innovation policies

	China	USA	EU
Ambitions	Independency of West by 2020 Technological powerhouse by 2020 Global technology leader 2050	US-based innovation	Innovative Union 2020
Strategy	From improvement to innovation	Reviving market-based innovation	Fostering innovation
Finance	Investment in top sectors	Primarily private sector	Private sector, member states, and EU
Key dimensions	Top-down	Bottom-up value creation	Bottom-up and uncoordinated top-down knowledge creation
Key actors	Symbiosis private and public	Triple Helix	Uncoordinated policies in member states
Programs	Key sectors	Innovation strategy and blueprint for America	EU innovation and members states
Main obstacles	Bottom-up	Long-term investments	Investment in social security Managerial instead of entrepreneurial spirit

Table 3.4 Some relevant Chinese innovation policies

Policies	Aim
Science and technology reform	Improving cooperation between research and actors in economy
Torch Program	Stimulating spin-off enterprises from the R&D institutes
Regional Innovation	Stimulating entrepreneuralism and transfer of Western knowledge
White paper "Peaceful Development"	Strategic adjustment of growth mode and becoming (technologically) independent of the West
Economic and Social Development Plan	Enhance capacity for independent innovation, building innovation-oriented country and promoting original innovation; strengthening role of enterprises
National Medium- and Long-Term Program for Science and Technology Development (2006–2020) (MLP)	China as a world power in science and technology field by the middle of the twenty-first century; creating indigenous innovations
11th Five-Year Plan	Harmonious development and endogenous innovation
12th Five-Year Plan	Inclusive growth and indigenous innovation

still a black box, and many innovation opportunities are being missed. And future business in China will take place in this transformation towards an innovation society.

Many businessmen from the West and the East always got dollar signs in their eyes when thinking of the size of the Chinese market. But earning the quick buck does not exist because developments in the past decades went very fast, the conditions are changing almost constantly, and competition is fierce. In the next years, this will not change, and the challenges will even be greater because of the coming Innovation Revolution.

There are short-term and long-term developments which transform the Chinese society and economy. On the short term, the market conditions are determined by demand and supply side, and the conditions set by government change on a daily basis. Central and local governments frequently submit new institutional rules ranging from tax laws to environmental regulation. On the supply side, Chinese private and state firms changed, and Western firms entered markets. Basic industries developed relatively quickly and new industries have been born. On the demand side within a period of 20 years, demand has been created for household products, housing, telecommunication, and cars. Additionally, Chinese consumers change their preferences very quickly. All these developments taken together created a dynamic society.

The long-term development is dependent on both external and internal developments. External developments include issues like world economy, climate change, natural resources supply, political tensions, and upcoming new markets. Internal developments include central and local governmental policies, market structures in industry, consumer demand, and education. The following sections show the attempts of China's policy makers how they tried to cope with these developments and prepare China for the future.

3.4   The Chinese Innovation System from 1950 to Present

The 11th and 12th Five-Year Plans are not the first time innovation that has been addressed as an important policy issue for China's future. In the 1950s the technological policy was based on imitation from the Soviet Union and the affiliated Eastern European countries (Xu & Wang, 2000). It was called "Learning from the Soviet Union." After 1950 the policy changed and own adaptations were pushed. In this system thinking the notion "Learning Movement" was the leading principle and put thinking freely and creatively at the center. It enabled people to be more creative and less conventional resulting into more participation of workers. However, in this period from 1950 till 1970s, a highly centralized plan system existed, and plans belonged to an administrative department or government. In the late 1970s, besides the open-door policy and reform of the economic system, also a new foundation for innovation has been proposed. Till the 1970s, R&D in China was concentrated in institutes and foremost initiated by government programs or new missions. This means that firms played no role in R&D or technological innovation. Firms did not have the decision power or the necessary resources to act. Chinese government saw the need for another reform as a result of the increasing globalization of their economy and the aim to emulate the West. In Table 3.4, some of the most relevant Chinese innovation policies are summed up.

The short discussion of these policies reveals the struggle and various attempts of China to get control of innovation.

3.4.1   The Search for R&D and Inventions

The science and technology (S&T) reform aimed at a better cooperation of research and the actors in the evolving market economy. Different organizational relations have been built. Till that time, the demand side (the production side) and the supply side (the science and technology institutions) were highly separated. Or in market economy words, R&D and innovation were almost completely separated from the firms. Governmental institutions were responsible for innovative activities. Consequently, a fruitful exchange of knowledge to create new products, processes, or services was disabled. As a consequence, development of a special category of machines was absent because the system could only generate general purpose machines (Gu & Lundvall, 2006).

In 1985, the aim of the decision of the Central Committee of the Communist Party of China was to tear down the wall between both sides. In fact, policy makers hoped to create a market for science and technology. However, institutional players showed another reaction. Instead of forming a market, the science and technology suppliers organized a vertical integration. On the one hand, the demand for the services was too low, and on the other hand, the demand side was not able to adopt the technologies offered.

A new reform followed to stimulate the merger of R&D institutes into enterprises. One year later, 1988, the Torch Program was initiated with the aim to stimulate spin-off enterprises from the R&D institutes. These new technology enterprises (NTE) transformed technical knowledge into commercial activities. In the beginning of the 1990s, the next policy reform followed transforming individual R&D institutes into production entities. In this way science and technology suppliers transformed into producers (Gu & Lundvall, 2006). As a result more applied research projects had been carried out sometimes, leading to spin-offs from research institutes and universities. Nowadays, well-known companies like Stone, Legend (Chinese Academy of Sciences), and Founder (Beijing University) are examples of this development.

The other reforms of the 1980s and 1990s boil down to decentralization and privatization. Bureaucratic decentralization was another notion for a series of measures such as increasing the autonomy of firms in decision making on production planning, investment and acquisition of technology, marketing, pricing and personnel, and with more autonomy to local governments in financial, budgetary, and administrative issues.

After the mid-1990s, several institutional and organizational reforms were implemented. Besides introducing more transparent rules, also taxation and banking were reformed. This period also showed the changing governance structures in state-owned enterprises (SEO). The SEOs were corporatized. The road to privatization included less restrictions for township and village enterprises (TVEs) in the early 1980s followed by allowances for private initiatives in the mid-1990s. The TVEs were sometimes a mix between governmental participation and investment by private investors.

These institutional reforms now enabled the government to exploit economies of time because capital could now be accumulated. Whereas about 20 years ago, the state owned dominated the output, in 2003 the three types of ownership—state owned, FDI, and other domestic—equally split the output (Gu & Lundvall, 2006). Of the category other domestic, especially the TVEs, contributed to the fast growth. Connected with this fast growth was also the creation of "Special Economic Zones."

In the late 1990s, the Chinese government tried to improve the ability to have an indigenous technological capability of industry. The 1997 National Conference on Technological Innovation further stimulated the intensification of R&D within firms (Cong Cao, 2004). Soon after the conference, the Chinese visible hand appeared and selected a few SOEs—Baoshan Iron and Steel, Changhong, Jiangnan Shipbuilding, and Northern China Pharmaceuticals—to experiment with technological innovation. Two years later, on the 1999 National Conference on Technological Innovation, the government pushed the level higher and required that high-tech enterprises spend at least 5 % of their annual sales on R&D.

Despite the successes of, e.g., the spin-offs and other policy measures, the overall picture looks a little bit different. In 2000 about 71 % of Chinese enterprises did not have an independent R&D unit. Even the Chairman of Legend (now Lenovo), Mr. Liu Chuanzhi, once said that Legend has only played a role as mover for foreign companies. Legend's profit margin was between 3 and 4 %. Value chain functions like design and setting standards belonged to the dominant Western players. This holds not only for Legend. In general Chinese high-tech export was largely based on processing and assembling with supplied materials from abroad for export.

About 90 % of China's high-tech exports in 2002 were based on foreign supplies (Xu & Wang, 2000). But at the same time we know that assembly was the first step in China's emulation process to acquire additional manufacturing technologies. Additionally, the relatively low labor costs enabled China to start with low-tech assembly lines and to improve them to a higher level. These low labor costs attracted Western FDI into China.

In 2000, for example, 92.5 % of computer systems and 96.4 % of mobile communications equipment were exported by foreign-invested enterprises. In 2002, wholly owned foreign enterprises (WOFEs) contributed 55.4 % of China's high-tech exports, while state-owned enterprises (SOEs) have seen its portion declining year over year (Xu & Wang, 2000). In 2004 Vice-Minister of Commerce Ma Xiuhong says China Daily, 12.09.04: "Despite robust economic growth and some gains of the government-backed go-global drive, the international competitiveness of China's industries is still at a relatively low level...Generally speaking, Chinese companies are weak in fending off international competition due to the lack of technological innovation, own brands and sale networks... Chinese companies are generally poor in management and operating efficiency, which hampers the overall improvement of industrial competitiveness." China Daily reports that "For example, China only owns 60 per cent, 50 per cent and 15.8 per cent of the core technologies that are needed to manufacture color television sets, cell phones and DVDs respectively...What makes things worse is that the enormous number of small and medium-sized enterprises (SMEs) are less competitive. Many of them operate with outdated technology and are fragile in the face of fiercer overseas competition." Others come to the same conclusion.

In a report by the Jiu San Society in 2005, it is stated that "The Chinese enterprises' spending on technological innovation for imported equipment accounts for only 0.7 per cent of that of Japan and South Korea... China has invested very little in research and development of its enterprises, with the annual spending per capita equal to 1.2 per cent and 1.1 per cent of the amount in the United States and Japan, respectively... In large and medium-sized enterprises, the ratio of R&D spending to sales revenue was 0.83 per cent in 2002, compared with 2.5 per cent to 4 per cent in major developed countries. In 2001, only 25 per cent of China's large- and medium-sized enterprises have set up their own research and development centers" (Asia Pulse, 10.03.06).

Chinese firms have spent on average a very low portion on R&D. Large- and medium-sized enterprises have spent on average 0.5–0.8 % of their sales on R&D. According to a survey, firms within high-tech parks spent an average 1.9 % of their sales on R&D, far below the 5 % standard by the Chinese definition of a high-tech firm, as noted above, while those outside the parks merely 0.63 %.

Besides the financial investments, also some cultural factors come into play. Chinese entrepreneurs, especially the new generation, lack patience. They want to earn money quickly. Importing Western technology is then the easy way. Between 1991 and 2002, a very limited amount of the spending on technology imports was used to obtain a technology license, while 95 % went on hardware (Xu & Wang, 2000). Additionally, enterprises also lack interest in engaging domestic institutions. Although the 1980 reform increased the enthusiasm of researchers, Chinese firms did not substantially buy from the Chinese institutions. In fact, the cooperation between institutions and firms was on a very low level.

The imitation and improvement scheme led to a relatively low level of original patents for Chinese firms. Based on small improvements, Chinese firms have only patented minor technical improvements. Since the 1990s, out of the more than 273,000 invention patent applications, only 47,452 (or 17.4 %) were from Chinese firms, which were granted 5,876. In contrast, foreign entities possessed 63.2 % of total invention patents from China (Xu & Wang, 2000).

A research study gives some examples (Xu & Wang, 2000): "China's pharmaceutical industry is built on modeling generic or off-patent drugs from abroad; of the more than 1,000 core patents on color TVs, none belong to China; 92 % of the 426 third-generation (3G) mobile communications invention patent applications filed in China were from abroad, while China's Huawei Technologies ranked eighth with 23 applications, about a quarter of Samsung's; in the petrochemicals industry, patent applications from MNCs accounted for 90 % of the total; and in the aerospace industry, there are 30 times more invention patents filed by foreign firms than by domestic ones. Of the invention patents received by China's Patent Administration between 1987 and 2002 in the areas of optical technology, photography and information storage, 75 %, 81 % and 89 % were from foreigners."

But there are some firms which increasingly do invest in original research—about 10 % of sales revenue—such as Great Dragon, Datang, Zhongxing, and Huawei. However, also these companies followed the emulation scheme by first adopting foreign technologies before starting to create their own products. They now employ a higher rate of scientists and engineers with high education.

Not only the big companies try to invest in R&D, but also the smaller ones show recently signs of investing in R&D. Of the more than 10 million medium- and small-sized firms, 150,000 allocate more than 5 % of sales to technological development (Cong Cao, 2004). In addition to all developments, Western multinational companies are adding value chain activities to their existing operations. More and more R&D facilities are being opened, and alliances with universities and institutes have been agreed upon.

3.4.2 Regional Innovation

An organizational phenomenon which should be mentioned is the clusters of creative entrepreneurial activity in Special Economic Zones. These clusters are called Regional Innovation Systems (RIS). Like Silicon Valley in the USA, China has started with three clusters of economic zones located in China Pearl River Delta, Yangtze River Delta, and Bo Hai Rim. However, Silicon Valley emerged without interference of the state, and the opposite is the case with China's clusters. Central and local governments have stimulated and supported all three regions. Furthermore, part of the FDI to China has been invested in these regions, giving the cluster an extra swing by transfer of knowledge and management capabilities. All these factors together caused an internal dynamic of each of these clusters. These Special Economic Zones were at the core of the opening up of China and represent an organizational innovation with great impact on the development of Chinese economy.

The most innovative regions are the well-known regions of Pearl River Delta (Guangzhou–Shenzhen–Hong Kong region), Yangtze River Delta (Shanghai–Jiangsu–Zhejiang region), and Bo Hai Rim (Beijing–Tianjin–Hebei region). The immediate consequence of the previous promotion of these regions is the huge regional differences in innovation capabilities and output. To close this gap and also to increase the opportunity to participate in the prosperity thereby reducing social inequality, the Chinese central government launched policies to promote cooperation between eastern and western regions. It is a follow-up of "the Great Western Exploration" which stimulated traditional industries to start activities in northeast and central parts of China. The challenge is to keep up or even close the gap with the mentioned regions which is not easy due to their early start, their momentum, and their multiplier effect. This clustering in China is not new. On the contrary, decades ago with the aim to increase learning and competition followed by industrial zones and Special Economic Zones to attract foreign companies and nowadays new enterprise zones to foster innovation.

Despite all the efforts of the Chinese government to foster innovation, around 2005, they had to conclude that foreign companies were dominating the innovation field. Western firms gained more advantage of the opening up of China than original Chinese firms. In the eyes of the Chinese government, this trend had to be reversed. Several policies were issued to transform China into a more innovative country. Some relevant policies will be discussed below.

3.4.3   Being Independent of the West

The White Paper "Peaceful Development" of 2005 states China's long-term aims.[1] For Western readers, the literal text might be rather vague, but when reading between the lines, the relevance for the West can be distilled. It also shows the deep impact of historical events which were felt as a humiliation, and now for the Chinese, the time has come to set things right. The White Paper refers to China's history and culture and concludes that China always has followed the road of peaceful development. In the future, the same road will be followed and trying to:

• Achieve a peaceful international environment to develop itself and promote world peace through its own development
• Achieve development by relying on itself, together with reform and innovation, while persisting in the policy of opening up
• Conform to the trend of economic globalization and strive to achieve mutually beneficial common development with other countries
• Stick to peace, development, and cooperation and, with all other countries, devote itself to building a harmonious world marked by sustained peace and common prosperity

With regard to its future role in the world, again the past is being referred to as a learning moment for the Chinese. The White Paper reminds of the 100-odd years following the Opium War in 1840. During this period, China has "…suffered humiliation and insult from big powers. And thus, ever since the advent of modern times, it has become the assiduously sought goal of the Chinese people to eliminate war, maintain peace, and build a country of independence and prosperity and a comfortable and happy life for the people."

The White Paper continues with the statement, among others, that "new modes for growth" have to be created. This new mode refers to the main problem of its development till now. China is facing the contradiction between its underdeveloped economy and its people's over increasing material and cultural demands and the

---

[1] The full text of the white paper has been printed in China Daily, 23.12.05 under the title "China pursues peaceful development." Some of the excerpts are cited here.

contradiction between economic and social development and the relatively strong pressure of the population, the natural resources, and the environment.

The White Paper concludes that China has to rely on its own strength, reform, and innovation. China seeks multilateral economic and trade relations and regional economic cooperation. China's demand for capital-, technology-, and knowledge-intensive products keeps increasing, offering great opportunities for foreign products, technologies, and services as the market has now evolved into an internationally acknowledged big market.

The White Paper "Peaceful Development" is a forebode of the 11th and 12th Five-Year Plans. The main message however is that China should become less dependent on Western technology and develop its own technology basis without getting at war with the West. The West is still needed to learn and copy from, and at the same time a Chinese innovation system should be build up. As soon as this Chinese system works, the West will not be needed anymore, and the peaceful development will be realized in its full glory. Two plans are central to this aim: the Economic and Social Plan and the National Medium- and Long-Term Program for Science and Technology Development (2006–2020) (MLP). These will be shortly discussed below.

3.5 China's Future Innovation System

In China's Economic and Social Development Plan, it is announced that the capacity for independent innovation will be enhanced and an innovation-oriented country will be build.[2] As a core policy, it is necessary to promote original innovation, integrated innovation, and improvement of imported technologies through digestion and absorption.

The Economic and Social Development Plan mentions how foreign firms, technology, and know-how will be used to realize the policies and to implement an open, win–win strategy to improve the quality and level of China's opening to the outside world.

In order to realize these economic and social plans, the core element is innovation. For this reason, another plan focusing on technology has been issued. This plan is the National Medium- and Long-Term Program for Science and Technology Development (2006–2020) (MLP) issued in February 2006. In the MLP, the Chinese government reveals its innovation guidelines (Gov.cn; 09.02.06).

The MLP is a comprehensive long-term development plan, and in Table 3.5, an overview of some main elements is presented.

As Table 3.6 reveals, the ambitions are sky-high which requires a lot of effort to realize the plan. At the same time, Western policy makers and corporate leaders should carefully consider what the consequences and impact of these Chinese ambitions are.

---

[2] Fourth Session of the Tenth National People's Congress, March 5, 2006.

Table 3.5 MLP highlights

MLP blueprint highlights
China as technological powerhouse by 2020 and global technology leader by 2050
Increase R&D investment from 1.3 % in 2006 to 2.5 % of GDP by 2020
Contribution of technology to economic growth more than 60 %
Lower dependency on imported foreign technology from 60 % to no more than 30 %
Lower dependency on foreign companies
Selection of 11 key sectors for technological development, 27 breakthrough technologies, 4 basic research areas, 16 megaprojects
Fostering Chinese IP and brands (brand economy)
Chinese patents belong among world top 5
Chinese scientific papers belong to most cited ones and rank among world top 5

Table 3.6 Policy on indigenous innovation and its governmental institutions

PRC governmental institution	Main role in indigenous innovation policy
The State Council on Leading Group on Science, Technology and Education	Members are representatives of ministries (e.g., MOST, MOF, NDRC, MIIT, Ministry of Commerce, Chinese Academy of Science) Formulation, discussion, and approval of science and technology (S&T) policies Coordination of departments and agencies
Ministry of Science and Technology (MOST)	Leading reform of indigenous innovation, science, and technology
National Development and Reform Commission (NDRC)	Formulating long-term economic development policy
Ministry of Industry and Information Technology (MIIT)	Implementation of industrial policies
Ministry of Finance (MOF)	Formulates governmental procurement procedures and criteria

The priorities to support the aims of China in its socioeconomic area are the development of energy, water resources, and environmental protection. For the goals to strengthen the industrial base, the areas of innovation in information technology (IT), new materials, and advanced manufacturing technology are selected. In the aim to reduce the detrimental effects of diseases and to improve health standards, biotechnology has been put forward.

China's former President Hu elaborated on these new guidelines and said China will embark on a new path of innovation with Chinese characteristics. The core is (1) to adhere to innovation, (2) seek leapfrog development in key areas, (3) make breakthroughs in key technologies and common technologies to meet urgent requirements in realizing sustained and coordinated economic and social development, and (4) make arrangements for frontier technologies and basic research with a long-term perspective, and raising innovation capability should be given prominence to and the nation's competitiveness should be enhanced broadly (People's Daily Online, 09.01.06).

Furthermore, "The government would play a leading role in the scientific and technological innovation, while the basic role of market will be given a full play in the allocation of scientific and technological resources," he said. "Companies would play a principal part in the innovation, while research institutes and universities across the country would assume a key and leading role in the innovation," he said. China will introduce more overseas talented people and attract overseas Chinese graduates back to start businesses in China, Hu said. China should not only inherit and develop traditional culture but also absorb the advantages of the cultures of other countries, said Hu. Chinese research institutes and universities are encouraged to build joint laboratories and research centers with overseas research organs. China will support enterprises to increase export of high-tech products and establish research and development (R&D) bases overseas, said Hu. International enterprises are also encouraged to set up R&D organizations in China, Hu added.

3.6   Indigenous Innovation (*Zizhu Chuangxin*)

"The Guiding Principles of Program for Mid-to-Long Term Scientific and Technological Development (2006–2020) (MLP)" has two main strategies: sectoral development of chosen industries and enhancing the innovation capabilities referred to as indigenous innovation. The purpose of indigenous innovation is to stimulate domestic development of technical innovations. Indigenous innovation is a logical consequence of the aim to be independent of Western technology. Indigenous innovation also inverts low added value high-waste manufacturing in sustainable high added value nonmanufacturing activities.

It should turn China from the world-class manufacturer into the world's leading technology center. The sky-high ambitions of Chinese central government are chrystal clear. But how should it be achieved? Examples of instruments issued by Ministry of Science and Technology, National Development and Reform Commission and the Ministry of Finance are "Methods for Determining the National 'Indigenous Innovation' Products (Trial)", tax incentives, financial support, technological investment, and governmental procurement.

This was followed in November 2009 by "2009 Explanatory Report Regarding the National 'Indigenous Innovation' Products" putting forward six high-tech industries as products of "indigenous innovation", namely, computers, telecommunication installations, modern office equipment, software, new energy, and energy-saving products. These sectors get preferential treatment in process of governmental procurement. On 15 November 2009, the release of the public draft issued by MOST, the NDRC, and MOF called "Circular on Carrying Out the Work on Accreditation of National Indigenous Innovation Products" became known as Circular 618. This Circular 618 led to a discussion within the worldwide business community because it was feared by Western companies that they would be excluded from participating in procurements bids. After a few amendments, the greatest fear was taken away.

But how do all these plans fit together? Even for Chinese, it is sometimes like seeing the wood for the trees. In the recent years, innovation policies have gained relevance, and many governmental institutions are involved in formulating and coordinating the formulated plans and aims. There are two levels of coordination. The first is governance of the involved organizations, and the second is the Five-Year Plan ensuring top-level priority and availability of capital and other resources.

In Table 3.6, the main involved governmental institutions and the main role in indigenous innovation are mentioned.

In this simplified presentation, it becomes clear that on the one hand the governance structure of the indigenous innovation policy is complex and sometimes accompanied by contradictory interest. On the other hand, indigenous innovation is in the hands of the top leaders of China. Furthermore, it is organized by involving not only the technology institutions itself but also the ministries allocating the budgets and support for hard and soft infrastructure.

On the highest level, the five-year plans try to integrate some relevant notions of earlier issued policies and to sketch a grand design for the country. Therefore, some notions discussed before will come back, but in the five-year plans, they are now levied to national aims supported by central government budgets.

3.7   Five-Year Plans

The five-year plan is the center core of the Chinese planning mechanism. However, this does not mean that the content and appliance did not change over time. On the contrary, in the beginning, the five-year plans were static production planning schemes focused on output, whereas the current five-year plans are now strategic plans for the future and less fixed targets.

In the 11th and 12th Five-Year Plans, both innovation and sustainable development were and are at the center of future policies, making China better. This is already remarkable because it was the first time that consecutive five-year plans address the same single subjects in the spotlights. It demonstrates either big challenges, big problems, or both. It is indeed both as we will see. To understand the future China, we have to know where the innovation programs are coming from and where they are heading to. Not only the 12th Five-Year Plan addresses innovation as a core theme; China's 10th Five-Year Plan from 2001 to 2005 and 11th Five-Year Plan from 2006 to 2010 mentioned technological innovation as a central issue (see also Motohashi and Yun (2005)). In the beginning of the new millennium, the government took several other measures such as allowing R&D expenditures to be counted as costs and implementing a technology standard- and patent-focused strategy in enterprise innovation endeavors, and government purchases of made in China software will be stimulated. Another important measure is the industrial power. With regard to the topic of innovation, Table 3.7 reveals the importance of innovation and sustainability in both plans.

Table 3.8 demonstrates that the issue of innovation is addressed in both plans under different names. It indicates the time needed to get acceptable results which

Table 3.7 A comparison between the 11th and 12th Five-Year Plans

Triple P dimension	11th Five-Year plan	12th Five-Year Plan
Economical	GDP growth rate 7.5 % From unitary to regional differencesgrowth mode Harmonious development Endogenous innovation Circular economy Foster technical innovation Support 11 sectors	GDP growth rate 7 % From growth mode to long-term prosperity Globalization Inclusive growth Indigenous innovation From export to domestic consumption Develop service industry Nine key industries Support of seven emerging industries
Ecological	Reduction of energy use per unit of GDP Reduction water consumption Reduction of major discharge pollutants	More mandatory green targets and green development indicators for keeping officials accountable Energy saving, promote renewables
Social	Educational programs Start with social security and pension plans Fostering middle-class development	Close urban–rural divide Close income gap and reduce inequality From Eastern to Western regional development Well-being/happiness of Chinese people

go beyond a five-year time period. Although the terminology is different, "endogenous" and "indigenous" innovation, the purpose remains the same. Moreover, the aim of fostering technical innovation on technology has been maintained in the 12th Five-Year Plan. During a meeting of the Central Political Bureau on 29 May 2012, about the deepening the reform of the science and technology management system, the core aims of the 12th Five-Year Plan with regard to innovation have been reconfirmed. During the meeting, it has been concluded that China should rely on the power of technology, and the buildup of an independent innovation system is regarded to be crucial.

Based on the official readings of the meeting (Xinhua Press Bureau, 29.05.12), many of the popular innovation vocabulary and notions have been addressed and used such as strengthen collaborative innovation, strengthen coordination, optimizing the layout of the structure, classification reform to promote scientific research institutes, and strengthen the open sharing of scientific and technological resources, the establishment of basic research, applied research, technological innovation, achievements coordination the development of mechanisms to improve the overall effectiveness of the national innovation system. For a more extended interpretation and evaluation of the five-year plans, we refer to Green China (van Someren & Someren-Wang, 2012). But more important are the concrete actions and implementation plans behind the impressive notions.

Table 3.8 The 4I emulation process of China

Phase Issues	Imitation *Manufacturing*	Improvement *Made in China*	Innovation *Knowledge economy*	Internationalization *Designed in China*
Period	1950–1980	1970–2010	2000–2020	1990–2020
Knowledge	Copying Learn Diffusion	Export needs Adoption Western Know How Trading Technology for Market entrance by West	Technical innovatons Developing new industries Independency of West	Self-sufficient and learning Start in small launch markets
Organization	State companies Collective organizational forms HR-Transfer Five-year plans	R&D in state institutions Cooperation with Western firms Mingling Western with Chinese principles Five-year plans	Dominant market power Chinese innovation Five-year plans and private initiatives	Initiatedby central government Multi-country strategy Foreign R&D Securing resources
Time dimension	Short term History/ Tradition	Short term and flexibility Rapid accumulation and diffusion of manufacturing	Timing/long term Accumulation	Competitive home market Long term
Economic engine	Production Economies of size	Chinese Mode of Production Economies of scale Low profit margin Governmental support and private financing China as monopsony	Strategic innovations Value circle Economies of scope Governmental support andprivate financing	Chinese Mode of Innovation Export and domestic consumption Chinese firms and brands Economies of scale, scope, and time
People	Lethargy followed by pioneer mentality	Participation Entrepreneurship Central and local government The Chinese Dream	Innovative entrepreneurship Development of SME	China as world power Global political and economic leadership
Business model	Production orientation Low cost manufacturing	Export Quality improvement Logistics Product and process innovations Enhancing involvement in other linear value chainsegments	Circle value chain End user orientation R&D, design, branding, and marketing Triple P business Chinese home market	Global powerhouses Total control value circle Chinese standards FDI and global M&A
Main ways of Innovation	Innovation almost absent	Cost reduction Low quality/high volume segment	Added value Radical innovations	Triple P value Strategic innovations

(continued)

Table 3.8 (continued)

Phase Issues	Imitation *Manufacturing*	Improvement *Made in China*	Innovation *Knowledge* *economy*	Internationalization *Designed in China*
		Product and process improvement	Technology orientation	
Barriers	Insufficient infrastructure andmanagement Value creation absent	Insufficient experience with managerment inquality, logistics, M&A, innovation Insufficient products and services Insufficient organization Copy cat behavior leads to overcapacity Unsustainable growth	Technical Chinese standards Development of Chinese business models Leading Chinese firms Freedom of creativity Empowerment/ bottom-up	Worldwide protection of interests Penetration in foreign worldmarkets Balancing Triple P

The realization of the bold goals of China depends on the practical results and how to apply and implement these notions of innovation mentioned in all the above policies and plans. For this purpose, we review the development of innovation in China named as the 4I emulation process.

3.8 The 4I Emulation Process

The 4I emulation refers to the successive but sometimes also parallel development stages of imitation, improvement, innovation, and internationalization. The most developments within different industries fit into this scheme. However, one should keep in mind that the underlying process is a continuous process of smaller and bigger innovations.

Long before Deng gave the signal to allow more market mechanisms, the evolution of the Chinese economy had already taken place. Many Western firms were already present in China for many years. For example, Philips has a history of over 60 years in China. The big leap forward however was the restricted opening up of the markets by Deng. Since then, multinationals and small- and medium-sized companies from almost every industry flooded China's coastal regions. The Chinese government established Special Economic Zones giving entrepreneurs to develop business. On the one hand, this bonanza was partly chaotic, but on the other hand, government clearly governed this process.

In many boardrooms of Western multinational firms, the opening up led to overenthusiastic reaction. Several investments in car manufacturing went wrong like for Peugeot and GM in the mid-1990s. In fact, the development of a Chinese manufacturing system in certain industries like automobiles was not a spontaneous action. It has been and still is being directed by central and local government. Out of the over 100 car manufacturers in China, a few were selected to being promoted by government. These more or less privileged firms should become the dominant car manufacturers of China in the future.

Furthermore, private entrepreneurs were allowed to develop their business without much interference of government. Many family businesses took their chance and prospered. But also firms partly owned by state and private entrepreneurs were present. At the same time, state companies are being transformed. On top of this, many of these different organizations have relations with Western firms. This process of change seems to look quite chaotic, but in fact, a certain pattern exists. This pattern is shown in Table 3.8.

Several elements in the emulation process of any country intermingle with each other. At the core is the transformation from a society based on copying from others to a society taking the initiative themselves. More or less, it develops along the phases of imitation, improvement, and innovation.[3] A fourth element which changes its face in each of these stages is the international orientation and activities.

This scheme of 4I development is not only applicable in the Chinese context but in many cases. Human behavior is based on copying. Babies copy their parents, students copy their tutors, and young managers copy their senior managers before deciding to find their own way.

3.8.1 Phase 1: Imitation

Da Fen, located west of Shenzhen, houses one of the four biggest art imitation factory regions of China with five to six thousand artists (NRC Handelsblad, 09.10.05). In Da Fen, Mona Lisa, van Gogh, and other famous artists are being copied for a worldwide market. Internet enables them to download paintings and to imitate them. Da Fen started in the mid-1990s, and in the beginning, the earnings of each Sunflower painting from van Gogh were about 20 €. Due to heavy imitation by other Chinese artists firms, each copy of painting nowadays sells for only 2–3 €. The founder of Da Fen, Huang Jiang, taught painting in Hong Kong. Now 70 % of his competitors were his former students. In 1997, his sales totaled 10 million RMB (about 1 million €), and nowadays it is only one-fifth of this amount. Competition is cutthroat because of the abundant supply of partly low-quality artists. This example from a niche market represents current Chinese economy very well.

China has always been a very entrepreneurial society. However, the degree of freedom, the direction to act at free will, and the institutional setting differed throughout history. Long-term planning by the Communist Party—the five-year plans—presented the aims and direction of China. Before and directly after the

---

[3] A 3I scheme for technological innovation has been suggested by Chen and Xu (2000) (Innovation strategy for building indigenous technological innovation capability in China, *Journal of Zhejiang University SCIENCE*, 2000, Vol. 1, No. 2, pp. 229–232) and earlier work of Xu et al. (1997). However, emulation fits better to the relevant aspects to be tackled to institutionalize innovation within firms and nations (van Someren, 1991).

opening of the markets at the end of the 1970s, imitation of Western technology dominated the learning process of Chinese firms. The creation of joint ventures and other cooperation forms between Chinese and Western firms and regions throughout the world were the foundation for an increased transfer of technology. It enabled Chinese firms to learn and adopt Western technologies and management principles.

Due to the low labor costs, Western firms increasingly followed outsourcing and offshoring strategies to lower manufacturing costs. Chinese government closely governed the development of industries by setting rules and restrictions for the involvement of Western companies. The danger was to be overruled by the power of multinationals. In the Western perspective, firms invented and adopted a new value chain management model.

One of the new Western business models boils down to the role of value chain manager instead of managing the whole value chain. To put it simply, only design, R&D, marketing, and distribution are maintained as the core competences of the Western firms. Manufacturing is in the eyes of Western managers not anymore a function which creates added value. In the view of the Chinese, the manufacturing function enabled to play an essential role in the world economy and putting China on the map. It strengthened the local economy, and China became the manufacturer and supplier of the world.

The manufacturing capabilities enabled the Chinese firms to increase the export volume substantially. Industries like textile, shoes, toys, white goods, electronics, and machine tools were based on the exploitation of economies of scale and low labor costs. Firms like Galanz manufactured 90 % of all magnetrons worldwide for foreign clients. Initially Galanz only assembled magnetrons without having their own brand. Only US retail giant Wal-Mart buys Chinese goods to a total of almost $27 billion a year. The imitation phase made China the factory of the world, and their earning capacity filled the cash register of firms and holder of the largest foreign currencies.

However, for the Chinese, it was only a first step. Based on their cultural dimension of long-term planning, this first step would be the basis to decrease the dependency of the West and to develop Chinese firms dominating the Chinese market. Being a manufacturer is not enough to play a role in the world economy. The ultimate ambitions of most Chinese entrepreneurs and the central government are to be the best and to be number one. First, it was necessary to become member of the World Trade Organization (WTO). When this step would have been mastered, the official policy in different sectors is to learn from the West and to slowly but decisively take over the lead. For example, in the car manufacturing industry, the old policy was that in 2010, 50 % of the cars sold in Chinese markets should come from 100 % Chinese firms. This is the perspective of the Western firms tied up in joint ventures or other alliances. Therefore, these steps attack the Western business model of being the value chain manager.

3.8.2 Phase 2: Improvement

Producing low-cost goods with less quality is only good for a start. Improvements in, for example, product quality, production management, and logistics, would be necessary to continue the market development. These incremental innovations would enable to manufacture better products for the Western companies and products under own label made in China. Trends in markets and customer demand got a greater influence on the manufacturing capacity. Short-term flexibility together with long-term development plans characterized the developments within enterprises. Chinese entrepreneurs have always been extremely flexible, and they can react very fast on new demands or developments.

But still cooperation with Western firms is necessary to get access to knowledge and technology. However, the nature of the cooperation and involvement of Western companies is changing. From a Western perspective at a first glance, it looks not bad. Some Western companies are now allowed to have fully owned subsidiaries, the so-called wholly owned foreign enterprises (WOFE). Other Western companies try to get a majority holding instead of 50 % joint ventures.

However, some Western companies have made the experience that despite agreements to jointly operate activities, suddenly firms were founded with exact the same products or services. In these cases, joint ventures were used by Chinese to gain knowledge in order to be able to create their own firm. Here, economies of scope were being introduced by expanding the business model from copying to improving. This game is still being played. As said before, copying is a natural human behavior. But another aspect of culture is relevant here.

In the eyes of Western people, knowledge belongs to an individual person or an individual organization. In the Western society, we even have a system of laws to protect this specific knowledge. We created property rights. The Chinese society has a complete different attitude towards knowledge exists. In their eyes, knowledge does not belong to an individual person or institution. Knowledge belongs to everybody. It is like fruit on a tree: it is free, and everybody can take it. It depends on who is first and makes money out of it.

Making a perfect imitation is first a recognition and respect for the product to be imitated, and secondly, the imitator must have excellent skills and competences which makes him or her a very respectable person. Therefore, copying is not something criminal but a deed of high respect for both parties involved. In the European medieval society, the guilds and, in nowadays, German handcrafts sector, the principle of copying and delivering your masterpiece was used as the ultimate exam.

In fact, Western companies do it, but they give it other names. Competitor analyses and benchmarking are the Western notions of copying and learning from the other. Furthermore, being able to imitate also indicates the timing to enter the phase of improvement. The accumulated knowledge, experiences, and capital give many Chinese firms the opportunity to increase their market share on the Chinese home markets and to intensify exports. At the same time, since about 2002 in almost every industry in China, a national price war is going on.

Despite growing markets and spending volumes of consumers, price is a major weapon in Chinese market. Why does this paradox situation exist? Because Chinese firms who started with imitating Western firms are being copied themselves by Chinese fast follower firms. Fast follower strategy is possible because many products are being homogenized or standardized and commoditization is the result. In the consumer electronics market and PCs, this can be seen clearly. Chinese copycat firms increase supply faster and on a higher level than demand can follow. In a flooded market with identical offerings, price wars are the logical result. These fast followers are able to bring out products within months or weeks at 40–50 % lower prices.

This cutthroat competition also affects Western firms active in China. A survey of the Chinese Economic Quarterly indicates that American firms do earn money and make profits, but compared to other markets, these profit levels in China are rather low. According to these statistics, the earnings for US companies in the period between 1999 and 2003 rose from $1.9 billion to $4.4 billion (and $8.2 billion when license fees are included). Earnings in Australia totaled $7.1 billion and $8.9 billion in Taiwan and Korea (Business Week 21.02.05). Of course, the growth potential of China for American firms has not ended yet, but it shows how difficult it is to earn money in China.

The phase of improvement is however for China for some industries extremely important. In the transport sector, the Chinese were able to copy and improve technologies from different suppliers coming from Japan, Germany, and France. It enabled the Chinese to establish their own fast train subindustry. This industry is now supplying China, but also export to the United States has started.

The same happened in the solar panel industry. Technologies from other countries were used to form their own low-cost and subsidized solar energy industry. For example, within 10 years, Yingli grew from scratch to one of the biggest worldwide manufacturers. Paradoxically, one of their biggest export markets is Germany where the German taxpayer supports renewable energy. So, Yingli earns money from the German taxpayer, thereby increasing scale and scope of markets enabling a fast growth and intensifying competition with German manufacturers.

For the short term, living from German tax payers money is an excellent business model, but there are many risks for the long term. Solar technology is developing very fast, and new technologies can undermine existing businesses. Yingli has to decide whether to follow fast copy strategy again or to invest in innovation. Also in other industries, these improvement strategies have been followed and lead to success such as in the mobile phone and automotive sector.

Therefore, the Chinese imitation and improvement strategies only have a very short-term effect. There are three strategies to tackle this problem: first, increase the level of foreign direct investment; second, increase domestic consumption; and third, increase the level of innovation. Globalizing business and innovation are connected issues to be tackled simultaneously. Moreover, mergers and acquisitions of Western firms will accompany the globalization strategy. The new mantra will be "align or buy and invest" instead of "imitate and overtake."

The business model of being a low-cost manufacturer is shifting to a business model of integrating the value chain in the home market. Manufacturing has the lowest profit margins, whereas brands and distribution offer higher margins. For this purpose, many Chinese cooperation partners try to get access to other additional sources of their Western business partners. For example, in the car industry, Western companies set up assembly lines. Then they had to expand other manufacturing functions like the high-technology-intensive transfer paint shop. But the quality of the coating is also dependent on the specific welding techniques of the metal. In negotiations, getting access to the welding technology is a condition to increase involvement in the Chinese market. Western firms see themselves forced to give in.

In other market sectors, Chinese firms create their own standards, thereby excluding former Western business partners. Illustrative is the mobile phone market first dominated by companies like Nokia. Now a Chinese technical standard is coming up which makes it very difficult for Western companies to play a part in the game. The size of Chinese home market allows such own standard.

At the same time, in some industries such as steel, automobiles, and oil, the central government selects Chinese companies to increase/improve their performance and extent their involvement in home markets or even world markets. The organizational vehicle for this improvement is setting up alliances with both governments as well as firms in the West. Cooperation treaties between cities and regions in Europe and Chinese cities, provinces, and central government are being established. These treaties give the Chinese access to additional sources and opportunities to establish a bridgehead in Europe. For example, Hamburg has the largest community of Chinese firms in Germany.

Many of these Chinese firms are buying small- and medium-sized family-owned firms with sophisticated technical knowledge but without own financial resources to expand and to compete in a global economy. Besides patents and knowledge, European subsidiaries of Chinese firms also allow them to deliver quicker delivery and after-sales service.

Moreover, multinational firms are setting up R&D laboratories in and outside China together with Chinese companies and institutions. Joint R&D is for Western companies the key to stay alive in the Chinese market. If company A does not want to join because of being afraid to give away the core competences, companies B, C, D, etc. will take over the vacancy. These tactics of the last decades make the Western companies think. Criticism has come up after the announcement of Airbus to set up a production facility in China as a part of the biggest single deal of Airbus to sell 150 A320 airplanes to China (FAZ, 15.02.06, Spiegel-online.de, 14.02.06). Airbus competes with its rival Boeing for market share in China. And the Chinese airplane market is the fastest-growing market in the aircraft industry. Boeing has together with China Aviation Industry Corporation a R&D facility in Xian. Observers are afraid of losing airplane business in the long term. For this reason, it is tried to get the majority position for Airbus in the joint venture. Others say that a transfer technology only of the relatively old A320 will not harm the position of Airbus. And why should Airbus not try to earn money as long as it can. Both arguments are however shortsighted.

Even from a minority position, the Chinese are masters in getting the knowledge and increase their influence over time. The joint venture is not only managed by the managers, but also several governmental institutions influence decision making from behind the curtain. In fact, local governments have the power to make or break the joint venture. And earning money as long as possible irrespective of strategic maneuvering by Chinese parties is a very short-term view on markets. This leads definitely to losing in the end.

Western managers underestimate this Chinese capability to get what they want. It shows how difficult it is to judge the long-term consequences of these kinds of moves. But the emulation process shows that what starts from a relatively safe start position can become a big threat. Chinese tactics to attract both competing companies in different fields—Boeing in R&D and Airbus with assembly— accumulate the knowledge of China in the airplane industry. It already happened in the car industry.

The basic market economy mechanism of rivaling companies trying to get additional market share at a single buyer leads to favorable outcomes for the buyer. Especially in these markets where governments, large state firms, or selected joint venture partners are more or less the single buyer, China smartly positions itself in what economists call a monopsony situation. These situations are rare in the market economy, but China knows how to increase their bargaining power based on monopsony power. Within the airplane industry, this is rather difficult due to the limited number of suppliers (mainly Boeing and Airbus for intercontinental services), but for environmental goods, it is different. Suppliers from Europe are being played each other due to the national organization of the EU. The aims of 12th Five-Year Plan will intensify the buying activities of the Chinese in the environmental goods market. Europe still has an advantage in these markets, but in this way, China can leapfrog the EU very soon if strategic renewal remains absent.

In fact, the above-mentioned approaches are market economy-based technology transfers. This is creative entrepreneurialism: creating your own economy base by learning, improving, and using creative market tactics. These tactics put China on the manufacturing map. Since the 1990s, ever-increasing export volumes created positive trade balance with many countries. But what is behind the impressive export figures? About 90 % of the exports are based upon processing and assembling with supplied materials from abroad (Cong Cao, 2004). Furthermore, export is based on low-cost and imported foreign technology or components. The Chinese assembly lines boil down to using high tech from abroad combined with low-tech domestic components. Economic characteristics are low-end product-oriented, low added value, and foreign investment dominated.

But in order to be a world player, China needs champions who can compete globally with the biggest multinationals. Innovation is the key to be a global player.

3.8.3 Phase 3: Innovation

The financial crisis showed the large dependency of the Chinese economy on exports. The transferred knowledge, the copying by Chinese firms, and the

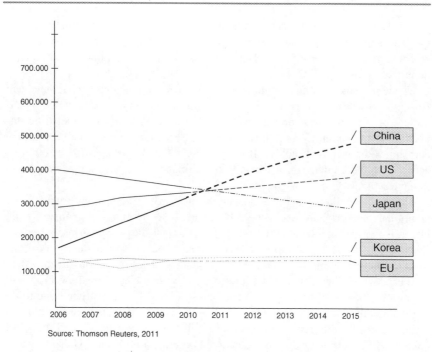

Source: Thomson Reuters, 2011

Fig. 3.5 Projected total patent application per region and projected growth

accumulated capital enable Chinese firms to extend their involvement in other functions of the value chain like R&D, design, and marketing.

From Fig. 3.5, it can be seen that the patents volume from China will rise sharply. In 2010, the patent offices of Japan, the USA, Europe, Republic of Korea, and China accounted for 77 % of all new invention patent applications published worldwide. Japan, Korea, and China alone accounted for 54.8 % of these. Japan shows a downward trend, and Korea is on the same level as Europe. In particular, the rise of Chinese patents is remarkable. The projection to the future is even more staggering. But it should be kept in mind that the number of patents says nothing about quality and scope of patents. Nevertheless, a tendency towards Asian-based patents can be seen.

In this respect, it is interesting to know how China performs on homegrown patents compared to other nations.

A closer look to the domestic invention patents provides insight into the progress of indigenous innovation. The notion invention patents exclude design and utility patents and therefore give a more precise view on the technical knowledge progress. Based on the figures given by the Chinese patent office named the State Intellectual Property Office (SIPO), it becomes clear that number of invention patents has increased substantially.

Moreover, Table 3.9 shows the total invention patents granted in the period from 2001 to 2010. The number of domestic patents has doubled. The share of domestic invention patents has risen from 33.11 % to nearly 59 %.

Table 3.9 Total patents and invention patents granted by SIPO (2001, 2006, and 2010)

Year	2001	2006	2010
Total patents granted	114,251	268,002	814,825
Total invention patents granted	16,296	57,786	135,510
Total domestic invention patents granted	5,395	25,077	79,767
Domestic invention patents as % of total patents	4.72 %	9.36 %	9.79 %
Domestic invention patents as % of total invention patents	33.11 %	43.40 %	58.86 %

Source: State Intellectual Property Office of the P.R.C., "Statistics," http://www.sipo.gov.cn/
sipo_English/statistics/

Based on these data, a few indications become clear about the aims and results of
the 11th Five-Year Plan mentioned in this chapter (cited from Thomson Reuters,
2011a, b):

- China has become the third largest patent office in the world after the USA and
  Japan by annual invention patent applications.
- Published applications have increased by 16.7 % per year over the period from
  171,000 in 2006 to nearly 314,000 in 2010. Thomson Reuters projects that China
  will publish 493,000 patent applications annually by 2015.
- Slow to expand globally: Chinese organizations are not protecting their
  inventions by filing patents globally at the same level as other innovation-
  minded countries. Currently, only 5.6 % of China's inventions are protected
  with global patent filings abroad, far less than the United States (48.8 %) and
  Japan (38.7 %).
- China's global ranking based on citations in international science papers has
  moved from 13th in 2006 to 8th in 2010.
- In 2008, China invested 457 billion RMB (US$65.8 billion) in R&D, or 1.52 %
  of its increasing GDP.

This performance looks impressive, and the 12th Five-Year Plan will continue
on this road. But only looking and being impressed by the statistics and jumping to
conclusions is dangerous. Just because the central planners in China go for more
innovation, the reaction is to increase the number of patents. Minor changes to
existing technologies will be submitted, thereby blowing up the number of patents.
Furthermore, there is more than R&D and patents.

The number of patents says nothing about total innovation output and the rate of
success of corporations based on nontechnical innovations or specific business
formats. Especially in the desired service sector, this is often the case where, for
example, customer intimacy decides about success and not technology.

Also with regard to citations and number of scientific publications the habit of
Chinese academicians is to involve more than an average number of coauthors.
When for another article a coauthor becomes lead author, he or she invites others to
join even if their contribution is minor. Hence, the number of contributions per
author and citations is rising.

Therefore, when looking behind the scenes, another picture emerges. It is no
surprise that China's global innovation index is still relatively low. To understand

this, we have to know the starting position of Innovative China and its development towards the future.

Why is innovation already now necessary, and why cannot the Chinese continue to be the low-cost high-quality manufacturers for the world? An example makes it clear. A Chinese DVD player exporter can make only $1 from each machine priced at $32, while $20 goes to the foreign patent owners. That is 60 % of the total value. And according to a former Minister of Commerce, China must export 100 million shoes or 800 million shirts in exchange for the value of one Boeing aircraft (China Daily 19.03.06).

Furthermore, due to rapidly rising labor costs, China loses its competitive advantage of the past decades. The current Chinese Mode of Production and its export- and investment-based economy are coming in the maturity phase. Only strategic innovations offer a way out to create and jump to a new growth curve. In order to participate in business activities with high profit margins, China has to move up in the value chain like design and branding and to create high added value products or services.

For this, new technology, knowledge, new business concepts, and widespread innovative entrepreneurialism are needed. But because of the emulation process— imitation, improvements, and innovation by competitors and new entrants—profit margins decrease in time. New innovations are needed. Western companies are forced to adopt the same solution of being innovative, but their problem is different. Western companies will not be able to compete on costs with their Chinese rivals. A competition on quality may still be won by the West, but that is only a short-term solution. Additionally, due to the outsourcing of the manufacturing function, product quality is already dependent on Chinese sources. Improved logistics and distribution will contribute to an efficient system of moving products around the world.

From the classical corporate functions, only design, branding, and marketing are the arenas left over to get a competitive advantage. But also in these areas, and together with high quality, China has the potential to leapfrog the West. A relatively new one is the urbanization trend and the megacities as separate economic entity. Megacities offer new opportunities for service sector like mobility and SMEs as required by the 12th Five-Year Plan. The only option on the long run for Western firms is to become and stay unique by developing innovations beyond the classical corporate functions with high speed.

The shortage of low cost labor is increasingly pulling the legs of the entrepreneurs in developed regions. The opportunities generated by the fast growing underdeveloped regions keep the young people home. But also the one child policy generate many small emperors who rather not work for small money. Moreover, laborers become more aware of their rights and are prepared to switch jobs if payment or circumstances elsewhere are better. The only way out is to innovate and to come up with unique designs and superior quality and to improve their social accountability.

The latter leads to another big issue: the balance between economic prosperity and social and ecological issues. Already Chinese customers in prosperous cities like Shanghai are very demanding and changing their preferences quickly. In future, with ongoing prosperity, other segments of the population will join and increase the demand. Also entering massively international Western markets forces Chinese firms to be innovative.

These are examples of a logical continued development in the third phase. But the continued high-speed developments do have a downside. Social tensions between the rich cities and regions versus the poor rural side appear. Also traditional values of the Chinese society like modesty and respect for people with high education and knowledge and taking care of elderly people come under pressure.

As soon as traditional values are influenced because of opening up in a relatively short period, a dangerous mixture of societal developments can occur. This is even increased because of ecological problems connected with adopting Western lifestyle. Imitating Western solutions for transport (carbon fuel-based cars) and high energy consumption because of PC, TV, and refrigerators, the issue of sustainable development will come to the forefront. Cheap but ecological detrimental production will at least slow down the prosperity of China.

The Chinese Central Committee announced in both their 11th Five Year for 2006–2010 and 12th Five-Year Plan for 2011–2015 to foster both inclusive growth and sustainable development.

The biggest challenge in the third phase is to develop and introduce innovations in order to satisfy international demand of end consumers and to solve new issues like sustainable development. Institutionalizing innovation in the academic world, institutions, and firms is the necessary next step. Here, Chinese companies have to create their own solutions.

In Europe, the European Commission is still trying to increase the R&D intensity to a level of 3 % of GDP in 2020 because the EU as a whole is lagging behind with regard to the innovation output. Moreover, many decades long, national governments in the EU have tried to improve the innovation capability without substantial result. Also small and large European firms do have their problems with getting grip on the innovation process.

Therefore, there are some interesting technologies left which will have undoubtedly the interest of the Chinese. But imitating an innovation system which shows little success and does not perform does not seem to be the intelligent solution. In the innovation phase, the once powerful strong single buyer position disappears, and global competition in a more oligopolistic market situation, i.e., more buyers and more sellers in the same market, will replace the monopsony. Being and staying unique together with smart industrial power play is the mantra for the innovative phase.

Together with attempt to foster innovation to increase wealth (GDP), also the goals of sustainability and even happiness have to be included. On People's Party Congress in 2007, Wen Jiabao suggested that national happiness should be the next focus. According to Prof. Hu Angang of Tsinghua University on top of the Human Development Index—measured by per capita GDP, life expectancy, and educational level—the Happiness Index should pay attention to governance, environmental quality, sense of security, social capital, and distribution of income (China Daily, 02.03.11).

This innovation phase marks a crossroad for China's policy makers and businesses. In this phase, the transformation to an innovative society requires the development of a national innovation system, Triple Helix structures, value circle, Chinese brands, creating Chinese business models, and above all bottom-up initiatives. Besides economies of scale, now the economies of scope are being tried to exploit to their maximum. Not only the move to other parts of the value chain but also the value circle is combining scope and economies of time.

3.8.4 Phase 4: Internationalization

The large amount of capital allows China to do foreign direct investments (FDI). These FDIs are in fact official policy of the Chinese central government. This "Go Out" strategy has been carried out for many years by many companies even before the official government policy.

Companies like Haier entered years ago the American market. They followed an old military principle of Sun Tzu. Haier did not target the main market of household refrigerators but the hotel room refrigerator market. This relatively small market segment enabled them to learn doing business with American customers and setting up distribution and service facilities. Also this market did not get much attention. After building up the capacity and competences to deliver, the attack on the household market will follow. Haier is now investing in Europe.

Car manufacturers followed soon, and the first Chinese models are being introduced to the European customers. Other direct investments are from the conglomerate Hutchison Whampoa. This company took a large share in the container terminal ECT in Rotterdam and also became owner of the Dutch druggist's retail chain Kruidvat. The consequence? Kruidvat became more aggressive and expanded with bigger stores and new business formats. Cosco, the second largest shipping firm of the world, wants to transform its activities from terminal-to-terminal towards door-to-door services. An alliance based on 50 % joint venture with TNT has been announced. Cosco brings in the distribution network of household machines and TNT systems for storage and distribution of natural resources and end products. In Germany, China is the second largest buyer after the USA of machinery leaving behind France, the UK, and Italy (Fletcher, 2005).

The main interest of the Chinese is to buy German patents and technical knowledge as a basis for the next step towards introducing Chinese brands. In the field of ICT and software development, in 2005, the Indian and Chinese central governments agreed to cooperate more closely. For both the home and international markets, Chinese firms now have to learn how to market products and to create famous brand names. Moreover, logistics has to be improved to have an effective and efficient distribution in (inter)national markets. International mergers and acquisitions will be now part of the game supported by central government.

Other issues are of course increasing the availability of sufficient energy and water resources and other natural resources. Here, also international cooperation between countries and firms is being set up to ensure supplies to China. Even large-scale M&A attempts have been made. China National Offshore Oil Corporation (CNOOC), a state company operating like a private firm, tried to take over the American oil company, the Union Oil Company of California (UNOCAL). The USA did sell oil to China and other countries before. The issue at stake with the takeover attempt was not the oil itself but the drilling and exploration rights owned by UNOCAL (Perurena, 2006).

China started these kinds of FDIs early. In 1995, China National Petroleum Corporation (CNPC) formed a joint venture with Sudanese government to produce oil together. CNPC invested $757 million in the $1.7 billion project and has a 40 % share in the joint company named Greater Nile Petroleum Operating Company. Other partners are Canadian, Sudanese, and Malaysian firms (Unctad (2003)). In another African country, Nigeria, the Shanghai Huayuan Group Corporation (SHGC) together with a Nigerian company acquired a textile company. SHGC invested $2.4 million and owned 80 % of the shares.

Chinese firms are taking advantage of grants by national countries to pull firms to their regions. These FDIs are stimulated not only by central government but also by local governments, like Guangdong and Shanghai, promoting their local businesses. Already in December 2002, China has signed bilateral treaties with 103 countries and double taxation treaties with 68 countries. China's approved FDI outflow in the period 1972 till 2002 grew from a very low $0.5 billion to about $35 billion in 2002. Nearly 7,000 approved outward investment projects by nonfinancial firms that total to $9.340 million.

The activities covered trade transportation, resources exploration, tourism and manufacturing, and other activities in over 160 countries. Asian countries have a cumulated investment of $5.482 million, a share of more than 60 %, North America about $1.270 million, Africa about $818 million, Latin America about $658 million, and Europe about $561 million (Unctad, 2003). In 2002, of all developing countries, 12 transnational firms from China belong to the top 50 largest transnational firms.

It indicates clearly that China is building a global network with minor and major stakes but with a firm grip on the resources needed. Their strategy follows another tactic of Sun Tzu called outflanking the enemy, i.e., the Western world. First, develop relations with neighbor states and strategic relevant but less high-profile countries before competing with the current dominant regions like the USA and Europe.

But Europe and the USA are increasingly confronted with Chinese M&A strategies. These M&A activities are in the beginning low profile by buying less known medium-sized firms. Only to give other examples: Shenyang Machine Tool Group bought East German-based Schiess, a 140-year-old maker of heavy-duty lathes and boring machines; TCL bought German Schneider Electronics; TCL merged the television and DVD operations with France's Thomson; and TCL has a majority position. In case of Schiess, the knife cuts on two sides. Shenyang's smaller machines to Europe will be marketed by Schiess, and Shenyang will use Schiess' expertise to produce large equipment for the Asian market. Schiess was already a bankrupt firm, and without the acquisition of Shenyang, the knowledge would have disappeared (Business Week, 21.02.05). Sometimes the Chinese are the savers of Western employment; sometimes they are taking it away when only patents have their interest.

Another field of quiet movements with long-term strategic effects is R&D. In the area of R&D, global alliances are being build up as well. Huawei Technologies and ZTE Corporation have both set up R&D facilities in Sweden. Guangdong Galanz Group has set up R&D in Seattle, Konka in Silicon Valley, Haier founded a R&D center in Germany. But also in design centers are being established. Haier has set up a design center in Boston and Kelon a design center in Japan.

The aim is not only to produce for export but also for an internal Chinese market. Vice premier Li Keqiang, said in Davos 2011: "We will focus on boosting domestic demand. The growth in domestic consumption in China will not only drive growth in China but also provide greater markets for the world." In this respect also the development of regional clusters and metropolitan areas are becoming relevant. The urbanization rate of China from 2010 to 2020 will go beyond the 50 % mark. Urbanization is an opportunity for domestic markets.

On a meso- and macro-level, the investment in foreign countries to get access to natural resources is meanwhile a well-known phenomenon. Again the tactics according to the 36 strategemes are used. Sudden weaknesses of countries due to the financial crisis like Greece and Portugal are used to buy them in bonds, ports, and other industries. China is buying worldwide resources like oil, technology, and recycle materials such as plastics, old PCs, and other metal scrap in any state it can get contracts. China is preparing for the world power play and lining up their industries. Central government took the initiative to concentrate industries in order to create powerhouses by increasing the economies of scale. This sometimes quiet conquest of relatively small activities is a stand-alone, not a problem. But taken together and accumulated over time, they form a worldwide network of activities in Chinese hands. Controlling the value chain and later on the value circle is the basis for future security of economic development. But then even more the ability to generate Chinese strategic innovations will become more relevant.

Several institutions support these FDI like the Export–Import Bank of China and preferential policies like income tax exemption. Also provinces are active with building worldwide cooperation treaties. For example, around 2010, the province of Hebei has over 52 official treaties with regions all over the world. About 12 have the higher status of friendship relation. You can imagine that like the private forms, the politicians and governors of the Western partners have to present their regions with maximum effort in order to win the competition with the other partners of Hebei.

Often Western governments and politicians do not realize their position in this global play. Celebrating their new treaty and photos in newspapers seems to be more important than making a strategic plan on how to develop a win–win situation. These illustrations show that step by step Chinese firms together with political support extend the activities from being world's manufacturer to a full service provider sometimes covering the whole value chain. It attacks the Western business model of Western business in the role of value chain manager. What is the answer of the Western world?

In China's history, they several times opened up their society for foreign influences, but as many times, they have withdrawn themselves from the international arena. In the sixteenth century, several voyages of armadas with ships as five times bigger than the largest European ships were sailing around the globe. Internal political problems made the Chinese government decide to let these ships return to China and not sail out anymore. Nowadays, small and big Chinese companies go to Eastern Europe to locate their manufacturing and distribution centers or to trade. In this way, the EU trade barriers can be avoided like the Japanese did with their car assembly locations. Hungary, Slovakia, and Poland fight for getting Chinese firms in their regions. Hisense, a Chinese state company, produces its televisions in West Hungary.

Nowadays, in the more intensively connected world and interdependencies of economies, a complete withdrawal is hardly possible anymore. But still a standstill or even collapse of the prosperous development is not unthinkable when current issues of sustainable development are not solved. The growing international Chinese activity is linked with wordlwide issues like sustainability. Within the 4I scheme, the phase of internationalization in Chinese eyes means economic expansion and market development.

3.9 The National Innovation System: Hell or Heaven?

A few general characteristics describe the current status of the Chinese innovation system around 2010.

1. In the low-tech industries, the Chinese demonstrated entrepreneurial activity to create and develop industries within China. They created jobs and contributed to gradual rise of GDP and salary levels. However, they were involved in low added value activities.
2. China profited from the outsourcing and offshoring decisions accompanied by FDI by many Western firms. It enabled China to develop a manufacturing base and grasp this part of the global value chain.
3. The export boom was largely based upon imported technologies and low labor cost. Although the export level measured in money is impressive, the added value for Chinese economy is relatively low. China has more or less involved low added value activities of the global value chain.
4. Foreign multinational companies dominate in several sectors the export volumes as well as the technological content protected by patents. Only a few Chinese firms are investing large sums into original R&D projects. But this pattern is going to change, and the scale and scope of enterprises involved in R&D are increasing.
5. For a long time, Chinese investments in R&D have been organized in governmental institutions and not firms. As a consequence, firms have a relatively low level of investment in R&D due to the allocation of governmental money but also because of investing their money in imports instead of own innovation

trajectories. Therefore, the current Chinese innovation system lacks accumulated knowledge and experience with institutionalized innovation.

6. Most individual Chinese-owned enterprises had no opportunity to accumulate knowledge and experiences with radical innovations. Most of them grew by imitation and improvement of imported technology and management principles. Moreover, they were part of the global value chain.

7. Cultural aspects interfere with the innovation performance of China. The new breed entrepreneurs do not have the patience as their ancestors had and want to earn money quickly, thereby stimulating technology imports. Another cultural aspect is trust. Innovation is partly based on sharing information and knowledge for which trust is needed. Exactly this aspect of trust is traditionally not very widespread in China when not the inner circle like family is involved. The low trust level and dependency on inner circles can hamper the innovation performance in particular when more than one party is involved. But the inner circle can initiate very fast innovative development due to the existent trust and quick mobilization of resources.

8. The existence of several Regional Innovation Systems (RIS) largely stimulated by central and local governments and partly foreign FDI fosters local creative and innovative entrepreneurialism.

9. The main focus in China is on technological innovations and R&D. Other categories of innovation are hardly discussed or part of the policies. Illustrative is the remark made by John Markoff (2006) who cites the director of Microsoft, Mr. Lee, in Zhongguancun. According to Mr. Lee, differences between American and Chinese Silicon Valley exist including culture, different types of talent, different definitions of innovation, different types of venture capital, and different involvement of academic institutions. Silicon Valley is featured by a market-driven innovation whereas in China, innovation is still largely driven by technology.

10. R&D is scattered around China and not coordinated due to competition between provinces and cities. Furthermore, global research and innovation networks and alliances with foreign institutes and enterprises are in their infancy but growing.

11. Triple Helix coordination between R&D institutes, business corporation, and government is largely absent and needs improvement. The main focus now is on the Double Helix between Chinese enterprises and government with regard to business development of copy–paste or improved technology.

12. Mercantilism describes the current economic system due to the leading role and strong support of government in selecting areas and new frontiers.

13. Technology is dominant focus of innovation content. Market and demand side get relatively less attention. The role of markets is to efficiently allocate the resources but apparently not to make the decisions where to invest. This is probably the most relevant element of the new path of innovation with Chinese characteristics.

14. The absolute venture capitalist investment in China is twofold of total EU investment. Compared with the USA, the venture capital investment per capita

of the population amounts to $100, in Israel it is $250, and in the EU, this indicator is on average $12–$15 and in Eurozone around $5 and China $3–$4.

15. Only original innovations and building innovative business models ignited by Chinese companies will enable China to belong to the winners of the emulation process.

16. The absolutely main strength of the Chinese innovation system is to formulate new policies and especially to mobilize the required resources for its implementation. The size of the resources enables not only to start large-scale projects but also to create new industries. However, plans are often uncoordinated, consequently leading to overcapacities.

17. Central planning does not mean that all plans are carried out as written on paper and declared by senior party leaders. Local governments and local leaders often have their own agenda and priorities. These interests can be opposite of the aim of the central government. For example, the greening of the energy sector by implementing renewable solutions in large cities like Shanghai is countervailed by the interests of large energy companies to build coal-fired plants. Other effects are overcapacity and risky financial investment and lending policies.

18. State planning cannot cover every aspect of innovation and ensure maximum results. Individual creativity, innovative actions, and a culture of innovation are at least as important, and these aspects are still largely underdeveloped.

19. On the level of individual firms, policies are largely absent, whereas it is necessary to develop Chinese strategic innovations including new business models. In each key sector, China plans to have at least two top world-class players. Key is to develop a Chinese way of institutionalized innovation system within and between organizations within the value chain and related organizations. Moreover, separate functions like branding, human resource management, procurement, and mergers and acquisitions need improvement.

20. At the same time, the weaknesses are part of this advantage. Policy and availability of resources do not necessarily lead to implementation. Also evaluation of derogations of policies are largely absent or not applied. Moreover, innovation is rather new, and little experience exists on how to deal with this relatively unknown field. For example, policy formulation and execution are in same organization. Besides coordination between both involved organizations but also between central and local government has room for improvement. This is enhanced by local aims and protection of own interests. The Chinese reaction is to announce coordination as a top priority. Other weaknesses are disinvestments occurring when top-down decision making dominates and check and balances are lacking. When individual companies are required to generate breakthrough technologies, a culture of freedom of invention and creation is needed. Simultaneously, a system of IP should be in force to protect homegrown inventions and innovations.

21. The search for flagship innovation projects and the quick buck has a potential detrimental effect on issues like safety, environment, and health. In these cases, Triple P and the circular economy are empty phrases. An example of earning

money quickly at the cost of public health is the milk powder scandal. Flagship projects like the incredibly fast construction of the bullet train network show the downside of speed. The Chinese copied train technology from other countries like Germany, France, and Japan but not the track-safety system for collision avoidance. The latter technology has been developed by China itself. After the deadly accident of the fast train in July 2011, it is feared that the economies of speed achieved in building up a large-scale high-speed train network neglected the economies of scope like safety aspects. Here, the execution of the innovation system comes into play. In case of the high-speed train, one of the relevant aspects is the procurement function. The manufacturing of the trains is sometimes outsourced to allied business partners in the network instead of choosing the partners fulfilling the proper QHSE (quality, health, safety, and environment) criteria. The underlying current business model and especially the failing necessary strategic innovations to shift the execution of the national innovation system programs towards a higher level are the main weaknesses of the current Chinese innovation system.

22. The Chinese road to independence and innovative society has some financial risky and ineffective elements. The banking sector and shadow banking (private loans) need a risk assessment system in order to be able to judge on a commercial basis the venture risks. Innovative China will learn that no country and no policy can circumvent the economic law of value conversion. Bad loans, risky investments, and investments in overcapacity can be hidden as long as growth is existent. But as soon as demand diminishes the windfall, profits will reverse the money-generating model. Furthermore, future Innovative China needs financial resources for other purposes like social security and health care, making industries dependent on government transfer money vulnerable. Industries, informal networks, and individual firms need to become self-sufficient and value conversion on a commercial basis. Only strategic innovation offers the way out.

23. The phase of imitation and improvement started the creation and accumulation of wealth. In the coming phases, the Chinese government will be confronted with defending the accumulated wealth and investing in systems to distribute the wealth to parts in the society not yet involved in the prosperity. China will not be able to avoid these classical challenges of maintaining and improving the new conquered world power position. Maintaining and defending require investments in health, social security, and pension plans, and improving requires national innovation system.

The national innovation system is a reflection of the national administration system (*tiao/kuai*) in which top-down governance dominates. This fits to the place of the individual entrepreneur discussed before. The national innovation structure is in first instance a top-down governed and coordinated system. The highest leading institution is the National Steering Group for S&T and Education in the State Council responsible for coordinating innovation between the ministries. But with the aim to achieve enterprise-centered innovation coupled with the road to a Chinese market system, decentralization is gaining momentum.

When China wants to achieve these ambitious goals and to get rid of "reverse engineering" and "import–assimilate–re-innovate" or imitation–improvement scheme, a new innovation culture is necessary. The biggest challenges are to coordinate innovation policies, innovation at single firms; to establish cooperation between innovation partners like enterprises, research institutes, and government (Triple Helix); and especially to increase the role and impact of SMEs. Till now the focus was on the MNEs, thereby neglecting SMEs. The identification of the service sector and the role of SMEs in this sector push the smaller companies more to the forefront. The focus of the strategic investments in the national innovation system is on horizontal R&D and governance issues. The investments in market-based innovation and creating an innovation culture are lagging behind.

3.10 Consequences for Western Firms

There are many notions that indicate what China really wants and how it wants to be achieved. The White Paper, the MLP, 11th Five-Year Plan, and the 12th Five-Year Plan are true examples of Confucian thinking. Harmony, balancing countervailing developments, indigenous innovation, and transformation of its economy are the key words that could have come from the big philosopher himself.

Illustrative for the consequences of the combination of several policies like indigenous innovation and public procurement (Buy China/Circular 618) for Western firms is the wind industry. Within a period of 6 years, Chinese domestic wind energy suppliers replaced the Western wind manufacturers.

The aim of the Chinese government is to keep unemployment rates low in order to minimize the chance of social unrest. Western companies account for 20 % of Chinese GDP, much higher than in Korea (8 %) or Japan (1 %). China will make corporations feel comfortable and at home in China. But China will always keep in mind how the West exploited China and in fact let Chinese lose face. Although it is more than a century ago but in the mind of Asian and in particular Chinese people, historical facts and events are as happened yesterday. For West European people and North Americans, these historical events are not relevant anymore, but for Chinese the time factor is very present in their decision making, behavior and interpretation of events.

This humiliation of China should never happen in the future again. This way of thinking is more than arguing on basis of rational commercial arguments. In fact, it is the cultural value and pride that are at stake. As soon as these kinds of deeply held beliefs and values are part of the game, then a very strong impetus to succeed is driving the aim of independent innovation. Already for this reason alone, China is seeking at all costs independency of Western technology, knowledge, and management competences. But first Western knowledge will have to be absorbed, copied, imitated, improved, and reengineered. The managerial and organizational vehicles will be cooperation between individuals, institutions, small and big firms, cities, regions, and countries.

But a domination of Western firms will not be tolerated. Already now, in some industries, the Chinese government observes a too high market share or even monopolistic dominance of Western multinational companies. For example, multinational companies possess more than 80 % of China's supermarkets, and other sectors like beer and skin-care products are nearly under foreign monopoly. China's premier Wen Jiabao has mentioned in his government work report, delivered on 5 March 2006 to nearly 3,000 deputies to the National People's Congress, that in opening wider to the outside world, China must "pay particular attention to safeguarding China's economic security." How will this safeguarding look like? Li Deshui, director of the National Bureau of Statistics and a member of the country's top political advisory body, says[4]: "Any sovereign state will not allow such a thing to happen... If we allow hostile takeovers to happen without limitations, we would gradually lose our domestic brands and innovation capability...The consequence is that China may become a link in international division of labor with the least profits. Most corporate profits will be taken away by transnational companies, leaving China with only nominal big GDP figures...Laws and regulations on business acquisitions by foreign companies should be made as quickly as possible in line with international practices...There should be severe measures to curb and punish hostile takeovers aiming to monopolize the Chinese market." The creation of both a home market with big Chinese players and a larger region in which China is the dominant player will be the path of China in the coming years.

The case of successful Yingli shows the dependency on foreign technology. Solar panels are originally an American invention. But Yingli has become the top 3 of solar panel manufacturers stimulated and subsidized by the Chinese government's Golden Sun Program. However, apart from allegations of dumping and financial governmental support, this could not be achieved without the required production machines provided by Western suppliers in the United States, Japan, Germany, and Switzerland. But the key question is how long these advantages and leads will be maintained. The remainder of this chapter gives a short overview of some of the main policies in the USA and the EU. This helps to understand the different approaches towards innovation and the different context of each region.

3.11 US Innovation Policy

In the past decades, the USA has been regarded as the motherland of innovation. Especially the IT innovations from leading companies like Microsoft and Apple and the often imitated Silicon Valley region come to one's mind. The innovative entrepreneur, the market-based innovations, powerful multinationals, and spin-offs from knowledge institutes characterize the US innovation system.

---

[4] "Chinese official warns of monopoly by foreign companies," http://www.hebiic.gov.cn, 07.03.06.

The history of US innovation is characterized much more by heroic individual entrepreneurs like Bill Gates and famous firms such as GE than by innovation policies. The USA had followed a similar 4I growth and development scheme as China. Manufacturing followed by innovation and globalization characterizes the rise of the Western superpower. In Table 3.10, a condensed overview of the history of American innovation is presented.

But are the American entrepreneurial heroes Americans? The research centers were filled with immigrants and scientists coming to the promised land and trying to make a career and live an American Dream. A recent study shows that more than 40 % of the 2010 Fortune 500 companies were founded by immigrants or their children (Partnership for a New American Economy (2011)). Examples are AT&T (2010 rank 7) founded by Alexander Graham Bell from Scotland, Procter & Gamble (2010 rank 22) by William Procter and James Gamble from England, United Technologies (2010 rank 37) by Igor Sikorski from Russia, and Intel (2010 rank 62) by Andrew Grove from Hungary. In Table 3.11, some remarkable achievement of immigrants is presented.

The reason is that the immigrants or their children are risk-taker and hard workers. These attitudes thrive innovation.

Furthermore, the US innovation system is featured by its large size, diversity, federal structure, and competitive nature (Shapira & Youtie, 2010). On average, around 2.8 % of GDP is spent on R&D. Private industry is the main driver of innovation. About 71 % of US R&D in 2006 comes from private sector, of which 76 % was development, 20 % was applied research, and only 4 % was basic research. Another factor fostering innovation is the military complex which has spin-off effects on many industrial sectors such as new materials, energy, logistics, and IT. About 50 % of federal R&D spending is allocated to defense-related organizations.

The American innovation system is founded on the dream of establishing something new and become rich. The social security system allows American citizens to survive, but being entrepreneurial is the much better option. Innovative entrepreneurs are supported by some excellent often private universities and venture capitalist infrastructure. In the American view, commercialization of innovation is a primary task of the private sector in cooperation with universities and laboratories. The role of government is to support and facilitate the interaction between the organizations. But sometimes US government intervenes by issuing laws and regulations.

The American policies are primarily addressing commercialization, and the less frequent mission-like policies can be found in the sectors like space, health, and military. Recent framework innovation policies focused on intellectual property, tax, and procurement. But there are also some policies directly linked with innovation by means of funding and technical support. Most of them are focused on SMEs and university-based consortia. Another relevant area is the enhancement of innovation capabilities of humans and institutions and underdeveloped regions and coordination of decentralized research. However, contrary to China, the federal government plays only a minor role in the stimulation of regions or states. That is a state responsibility.

Table 3.10 The 4I emulation process of the USA

Phase Issues	Imitation *American manufacturing*	Improvement *Applied innovation*	Innovation *Invented in USA*	Internationalization *Super innovation power*
Period	–1940	1865–1930	1920–1950	1945–2020
Knowledge	Copying Learning Diffusion	Developing home market Adoption European Know How Influx of knowledge workers	Technical innovatons Developing new industries Scientific approach	Frontier knowledge
Organization	Private ventures	Applied knowldege Low interfrence of government	Basic reseaerch and applied science Multinational companies	Outsourcing manufacturing
Time dimension	Short term No history	Short term and flexibility Rapid accumulation and diffusion ofmanufacturing principles	Short term Accumulation	Competitive home market Foreign markets
Economic engine	American Mode of Production Economies of scale	Domestic increasing income levels Economies of scale and scope	Economies of scale and scope Strong financial sector	Market-based Innovation Export and domestic consumption
People	Pioneers	American Dream Entrepreneurship Immigrants as entreprenuers and knowledge workers	Innovative entrepreneurship Development of MNE and SME Fix it and do it metality	Focus on America Global political and economic leadership
Business Model	Production orientation Low cost high volume manufacturing	Quality improvement Logistics Product and process innovations	End user orientation Enhancing involvement in all value chain segments Triple Helix development M&A	Market innovations
Main ways of Innovation	Exploitation of scale Standardization	Cost reduction by improvements Low quality/high volume segment Product and process improvement	Radical innovations Technology orientation Innovation in management	Global presence of MNEs IT driven sectors most succesful
Barriers	Scientific base Local activities	Basic research	Ignoring long-term consequences	Cross-cultural management Triple P business Sustainability issues

Table 3.11 Contribution of immigrants or their children to Fortune 500 companies

Issue	Contribution
Founders/ entrepreneurs	18 % of Fortune 500 founded by immigrants 23 % founded by children of immigrants (Total: 41 %)
Industry	In almost every industry, immigrants started new business e.g., 45 % of high tech firms, 50 % of medical equipment or devices
Brands	7 of the 10 most valuable and recognizable brands in the world
Employment	3.6 million workers world wide
Economic force	The combined revenues of "New American" Fortune 500 companies would constitute the 3rd largest economy outside the United States

Source: Partnership for a new American Economy, The "New American" Fortune 500, 2011

It can be concluded that the USA has a bottom-up market-based innovation system. It explains the close cooperation between private firms, research institutions, local government, cities, venture capitalists, and universities.

But recently some flaws of the American system come to the surface. Nation-wide issues like infrastructure, sustainability, renewable energy, natural resources sourcing, disappearance of manufacturing, and rise of China question the ability of the market-based innovation system to solve these challenges.

Being dependent on American ingenuity appeared not to be sufficient anymore. President Obama took action. In 2008, followed by an update in 2011, America's administration issued a "Strategy for American Innovation." In his State of the Union in 2010, he said the USA needed a Sputnik moment, and in the State of the Union in 2011, he announced several blueprint policies for homemade energy, manufacturing, and college affordability. The policies are summarized in Table 3.12.

Blueprints in a market-based innovation context? According to the American administration, the background is that for decades the outsourcing of manufacturing has eroded the financial security of the middle class. Are the blueprints comparable to the Chinese five-year plans? Are the "strategy for innovation" and the blueprints replacing the American market capitalism consist of the innovative entrepreneur and innovative firms? The general conclusion is that the innovation strategy and the blueprints are not identical to the Chinese five-year plans because the state organization to translate central government dreams into concrete action plans is absent. The nature of the two biggest challenges—rise of China and sustainability—require coordinated federal strategies. Furthermore, the allocated capital to implement the blueprints is minor compared to China. But like Chinese policies, the trend is towards becoming more independent and a traditional national American focus.

3.12 Innovation Policy in the EU

3.12.1 Breeze and Ripples

The history of Europe is one full of gales and occasionally high waves but more in a political than an economic sense due to the many wars in the old world. In the recent years, the economic gales have been reduced in strength, and the waves have

Table 3.12 Recent US innovation policies

Policies	Aim
Strategy for American innovation	1. Invest in the building blocks of American innovation 2. Promote market-based innovation 3. Catalyze breakthroughs for national priorities
Blueprint for an America to last	1. Manufacturing: create new jobs Here In America, discourage outsourcing, and encourage insourcing 2. Skills: give hardworking, responsible Americans a fair shot 3. Energy: make the most of America's energy resources 4. Values: ensure every American plays by the same set of rules and pays their fair share

become ripples. The 4I emulation scheme also applies for Europe, but we have to keep in mind that in fact a unified Europe does not exist. It is more a history of different countries and individual firms and entrepreneurs. Table 3.13 gives some snapshots.

The size and power of the USA and China dwarfs the successes of the single member states. The European Union does not exist as a unity or nation compared to the USA and China. The recent European big innovation policies are the Lisbon Strategy and Europe 2020 as summarized in Table 3.14.

Statistics show that in nowadays EU, no gales and waves exist but breeze and ripples. On a world scale, the average R&D input is on a lower level than in many other countries in the world. The EU average of R&D spending as percentage of GDP over many years fluctuates around 1.7–1.9 %. Over many years, the EU scores lower than the USA (2.6 %) and Japan (3.4 %), and recently even China is catching up (in 2009 R&D spending was 1.7 % of GDP). Of course, China has started on a lower level, but it is indication that innovation is now taken seriously. In 2009, the growth rate of R&D spending by Chinese companies was around 40 % (EU R&D Scoreboard 2009).

But at the same time the EU Lisbon Strategy launched in 2000 has failed. We know this for almost a decade already, but R&D investments and outcome are on average compared to other regions still lagging behind. Paradoxically, at the same time in the past 20 years, the EU and its member states put innovation at the core of their policies. In 2010, the Lisbon Strategy has been replaced by a new strategy called "Europe 2020: a European strategy for smart, sustainable and inclusive growth."

Besides the big picture policies, the EU has formulated a large bunch of different policies on a lower level. These small policies can be as effective as the big picture policies, but it all depends on execution and implementation. In Fig. 3.6, some of the innovation policies of the past 20 years are listed.

Table 3.15 shows a regular change in nature and scope of policies. Europe's policies are more a succession of hypes than comprehensive policies reinforcing each other. On average, each 4–5 years, a new policy pops up without a full implementation of previous policies. Of course, each new hype-based policy gave the impression of working on the innovation edge. The contrary was true. It kept the

Table 3.13 4I emulation process in the EU

Phase Issues	Imitation and improvement	First Innovation wave *Industrial Revolution*	Second Innovation wave *Scientific and applied knowledge*	Internationalization
Period	–1720	1720–1870	1870–1950	1950–2020
Knowledge	Agriculture and trading Adopting from other cultures	Technical innovations	Technical innovations Developing new industries Scientific approach	Member state based
Organization	Dominance of royal and clerical ventures	Private ventures	Basic research and applied science Multinational companies	European Union
Time dimension	Short term	Long-term investments	Accumulation of wealth	Slow integration
Economic engine	Local economies Early international expansion	Domestic increasing income levels International expansion	Economies of scale and scope New industries	Internal market Export based but depending on member state
People	Bound by institutions like church	UK main driver Labor becomes atomized and commodity	Rise of Germany as state and economic power	European does not exist in mind Member state nationalities Entrepreneurship less important than employee status
Business model	Trade and local economies Guild system Colonization	Capital intensive industries	Scientific research and basic research	Internal market and export based Member states are still dominant
Main ways of innovation	Agricultural and logistics	Process, product, technology	Radical innovations Technology orientation	Global presence of MNEs IT driven sectors most successful
Barriers	Institutions	Basic research Exploiting labor	Failing internal market	Social security system Employee rights more important than entrepreneurial spirit Low innovation output Demographic development

employment rate of civil servants and research institutions high, but it did hardly improve the innovation capacity or value-creating capacity. This is typical for almost every governmental institution, but it does not help to increase the innovation output or performance. For example, the implementation of the EU

Table 3.14 European innovation policies

Policies	Aim
Lisbon Strategy 2010	1. Spending 3 % of GDP on R&D in 2010 2. Becoming most competitive region in the world by 2010
Europe 2020	1. Smart growth: developing an economy based on knowledge and innovation 2. Sustainable growth: promoting a more resource-efficient, greener, and more competitive economy 3. Inclusive growth: fostering a high-employment economy delivering social and territorial cohesion 4. 75 % of the population aged 20–64 should be employed 5. 3 % of the EU's GDP should be invested in R&D 6. The "20/20/20" climate/energy targets should be met (including an increase to 30 % of emissions reduction if the conditions are right) 7. The share of early school leavers should be under 10 % and at least 40 % of the younger generation should have a tertiary degree 8. 20 million less people should be at risk of poverty

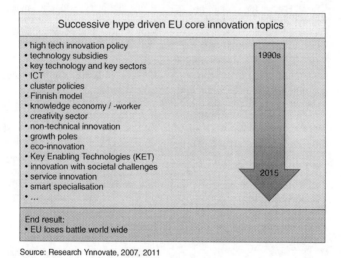

Source: Research Ynnovate, 2007, 2011

Fig. 3.6 Hype-driven EU innovation topic-related innovation policies

programs is similar to a forced top-down program in which consultants and knowledge institutes have to convince private business to participate. Dissemination of knowledge is organized by network meetings and used as a scapegoat for Pan-European diffusion of innovation. For the intermediary organizations, the EU is a Walhalla.

The general statements and aims are not very attractive for Europe's businesses and in particular the SMEs. As a consequence, the result of all policies is marginal. The average level of R&D as percentage of GDP stabilizes around 2 %.

It can be concluded that the main message and aim of Europe 2020 Strategy does not differ much from the Lisbon Strategy. The main shifts are the attention to

Table 3.15 Strengths and weaknesses of innovation policies of China, the USA, and the EU

	Strengths	Weaknesses
China	Long history in strategic state planning	Missing history in individual enterprise innovation
	Relatively strong link between macro-planning and implementation on meso-and micro-level	Micro-level of individual initiatives is weakest developed link
	World perspective on innovation and means of knowledge transfer	Focus on technology
		Bottom-up initiatives underutilized
		Government is strongest link in Quadruple Helix
USA	Focus on innovative entrepreneurialism	Lack of China strategy and focus on autarkic US
	Triple Helix works on local level	
	Private sector and R&D are strongest link in Triple Helix	Lack of history in central planned macro-innovation policies
		Context of market-based bottom-up innovation does not fit to central planned macro-policies
		Political priorities determine agenda instead of industrial strategy
EU	Local string cultural embedded innovation policies	Lack of China strategy and Eurocentric world view
	Local strong innovation performance without innovation policy	Priority to local and global social security leading to insufficient innovative entrepreneurialism
		Policy hypes instead of industrial strategies
		Lack of link between macro-policies and implementation power on meso- and micro-level
		Lack of Pan-European strategy and coordination between member states and rivalry dominates
		Lack of Quadruple Helix
		Comitology decides about innovation strategy

sustainability, education, and youth and the acknowledgement that developing countries (read: China) will become more important. On the macro-level, the EU's bottom-up approach is in European speak comitology or in normal speak lobbying. Comitology reflects the decision process about European regulations. According to Guéguen (2010, p. 5), "…it conveys the sense of a higher mysterious and non-transparent power." In the whole process of proposal, adoption, and execution, the central place belongs to the management committees who represent comitology. Comitology is involved in 98 % of all European regulatory activity and in fact controlled by the Commission (Guéguen (2010, p. 29). The real power is in Brussels, but specialists (lobbyists) are needed to identify the right persons who really determine the regulative decisions. In Brussels, wide implementation is not an issue; it is a responsibility of the member states.

Besides the official EU 2020 Strategy, all the member states formulate their own policies on innovation, knowledge economy, energy policy, and industrial and regional development. Moreover, these policies differ to a great extent between

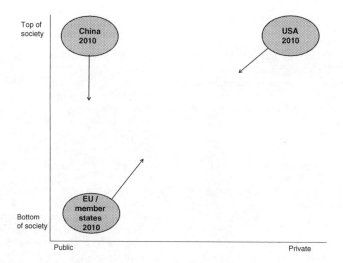

Fig. 3.7 Private and public investments in top or bottom of society by China, the USA, and the EU

the member states due to history, institutional structures, culture, and innovative competence of knowledge organizations and private businesses.

3.12.2 EU Invests in Bottom of Society and Not in Top of Society

The European macro-interpretation is that the weak in the society are not able to take care of themselves and should be protected, subsidized, and supported. This is the basis of the welfare states in most European member states, and each country chooses its own priorities and implementation. The major difference with the USA and China is presented in Fig. 3.7.

Figure 3.7 shows the existing positions of China, the USA, and the EU. Most European countries have a decades old tradition of investing in social system such as social security and rights of employees. The philosophy is that a prosperous region such as Europe is not measured against its earning capacity or richness but how the poor are treated. This is a noble and human aim, but with the rise of China and the competing power of the USA, the picture is now changing. But the question is who is weak and who is not. The good cause of helping poor and disabled people is often misused, and the accumulation of rules and aid programs created a monster of social security.

China follows the philosophy that first the economy has to be developed in order to create industrial activity and job opportunities for the hundreds of millions of Chinese who have not yet participated in the economic bonanza of the recent past. China invests in the top of the society by creating top sectors, economic development programs, and Chinese entrepreneurialism. However, the ecological problems and increasing social inequality force China to move into the direction of investing in social security. One of the triggers is the Foxconn labor circumstances as a supplier for Apple and most other IT product sellers.

The USA also invests in the top of the society but not as in China by means of governmental policies and programs but bottom-up market innovations. But the need for, e.g., investments, in infrastructure and sustainability requires more federal or local spending.

The arrows show in which direction the China and the USA is moving. Figure 3.7 makes clear that Europe should move too. The debt crisis, the high debts of governments, the diminishing earning capacity, and the overinvestment in social security require new thinking. An inversion from investing in the bottom of the society towards the top of the society with involvement of private sector is necessary. The argument that European Nordic countries with their high commitment to social welfare and their top position for R&D does not hold on the long term. Their earning capacity has got some fierce blows such as the bankruptcy of Saab, the takeover of Volvo by the Chinese Geely, and the problems of Nokia in the mobile phone market which are strong signals of changing market conditions.

3.12.3 The Social Security Iceberg

Chinese and US Americans seek for opportunities to become a famous entrepreneur and get rich. Europeans seek for job security, a company car, a pension plan, and holidays. The European economy is a social market economy in which meanwhile the social dimension dominates the society. Our institutional structures are based on maintaining welfare and redistributing earned money. It is about employers versus unions, taxing high-income fee earners, securing employees' rights, protecting the poor, and fostering and investing in less educated people.

The USA and China show that investing in the best leads to economic success and not the other way round. But also China is paying more attention to the social dimension of their Triple P. But Europe has paid too much attention to the social dimension and too less on the economic dimension and specifically to the future earning capacity for a shrinking and aging population. Keeping up welfare is a luxury which Europe cannot afford anymore unless new earning capacity is created.

The European welfare state is a money transfer and wealth distribution machine instead of a wealth-creating machine. According to the European Commission (2010), the expenditures for social securities in the EU, with differences per member state, will increase from 27.5 % to 30.8 % of the EU's GDP between 2007 and 2010. In this respect, the notion of European transfer union gets two linked interpretations. On the micro-level, money is transferred from the working to the nonworking. On the meso-level, the rich northern part of the EU should pay for the poorer southern part. On the macro-level, money is transferred to developing countries. But a transfer union only can be kept alive when the earning capacity is being renewed.

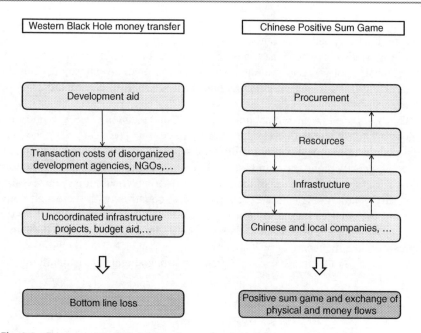

Fig. 3.8 Chinese and the EU vision on international relations

3.12.4 The Development Aid Black Hole

The attitude of transferring tax money to the so-called weak is also visible in the international relations. Europe has a long history of giving aid to underdeveloped countries. This has been done because of real pathetic feelings with poor people in areas of low prosperity, post-colonization payback time, or areas hit by natural disasters. In the Netherlands only, as of 2010, already 67 care organizations have received subsidies totaling 2.1 billion € for a period of 5 years. For example, Oxfam Novib receives 421 million € and Cordaid 402 million. Governmental aid programs, pop stars, and famous actors who collect money in government-supported large-scale events to give to poor people are a typical European interpretation of being social.

The European vision on international relations is focused on the social dimension of the Triple P, whereas China focuses on the economic dimension of the Triple P. Figure 3.8 shows the striking different approaches.

The European foreign policy for developing countries had its roots in compensating former colonial times. As of the 1970s, former colonies and developing countries were supported by development aid. Lager sums of money were transferred and allocated to projects without knowing the effects. Besides some successes, the majority of the aid resulted in uncoordinated projects and absence of added value. There is no relation between investment and purpose. National campaigns supported by artists like Geldof collected aid money. Western aid is a black hole money transfer system. Only recently, a change towards economic diplomacy can be witnessed with the aim to participate private companies in the development aid budgets.

The Chinese interpretation of helping emerging countries is that social market economy means that everybody should be enabled to participate in the value creation process based on his or her own capabilities or to be developed capabilities. Self-interest is at the center.

Providing fish or learning to fish is the summary of the different views. The Chinese way of helping other regions is not by giving aid but making clever deals which are profitable for both sides. But the core idea of Western aid is still to help the others. This is in sharp the contrast with the Chinese idea to help itself. Partly the background is in Chinese culture where self-reliance, self-support, and faith determine your role in the world. Therefore, if the developing countries do not help themselves by hard work and exploiting the richness of their home country, others cannot be blamed to do it for them. The Chinese approach focused on resource security and smart deals is very commercial and has the potential of neglecting social and ecological consequences. Therefore, at least for the Chinese, it is a positive sum game but not the ideal model either.

3.13 Evaluation of Innovation Policies

The strengths and weaknesses of the Chinese, American, and European innovation policies are summarized in Table 3.15.

The USA excels in market-based innovation, whereas macro top-down innovation policies do not fit into their bottom-up innovative entrepreneurial dynamism. Trying to beat China with grand innovation strategies and blueprints will not be successful. However, issues like sustainability do need nationwide approaches. European firms have a long successful history in innovation; European firms have a huge knowledge base, but the use and exploitation is on a low level, and European managers have relevant management competences and experiences. Illustrative are the remarks made by John Markoff (2006) about a Silicon Valley initiative in Beijing's Zhongguancun: "And though they work half a world away from the world's better-known high-technology mecca, this group of graduate students is in many ways closer to the authentic entrepreneurial spirit that drives Silicon Valley than many of the ersatz Silicon Deserts, Mountains, Glens and Forests, which are most frequently the public relations products of overzealous economic development agencies. 'It has been remarkable to me how similar the entrepreneurial high-tech Chinese are to their American counterparts,' said Kai-Fu Lee, an American-educated computer scientist who is director of a research laboratory that Microsoft has established in Zhongguancun." Although the Chinese central top-down macro-policies are being implemented, their multiple duplication on the provincial level leads to overcapacity and inefficiencies.

The innovation policies of China, the USA, and the EU clearly demonstrate that policies alone are insufficient and market organizations are needed to realize aims. Table 3.16 presents a summary of the findings of the main current innovation policies.

Table 3.16 Static view on current innovation policies

	China	US	EU
Ambitions	Building an innovation-oriented country The leading country of the twenty-first century Adhering to innovation in ideas and systems Reliance on foreign technology declines to 30 % or less in 2020 Raise R&D level to 2.5 % of GDP in 2020 2020 science and technology will contribute at least 60 % to the country's development Building a harmonious society and a circular economy	Revival of America's strength US-based economy, less dependency on foreign energy sources and manufacturing capabilities Increase innovation capability Strengthen fundamental research leadership Restore American values	EU will be the sustainable and innovative region in 2020 Raise R&D level to 3.0 % of GDP in 2020 Building a sustainable and a knowledge economy
Strategy	From fast follower to leading innovator	Reviving market-based innovations	Stimulating innovation
Finance	Central and local investment in top sectors Private sector investment	Primarily Triple Helix private investments Defense R&D dominates federal spending	Private sector and relatively low contribution by EU and member state
Key dimensions	Top-down sector policies Technological research Breakthrough in key technologies/flag hip Improvement of laws and technological plans Involving Western knowledge, firms, and institutions Raising innovation capability/ingenious innovation	Bottom-up market-based innovations Promote innovative, open, and competitive markets Discouraging outsourcing and encouraging insourcing Clean energy revolution Creation of a world class workforce Immigration of skilled and unskilled workers	Uncoordinated mix of bottom-up private sector and EU top-down Stimulating technology and R&D Focus on knowledge creation Stimulating entrepreneurship Increasing the application of knowledge Creating system of intellectual property rights
Key actors	Government leads scientific and technological innovation High risk taking entrepreneurs, private firms, and institutions decide on direction and allocation of resources Market has role of allocating scientific and technological resources Building up advanced	US state-based Triple Helix of US firms, research institutions, and educational organizations Federal government has low key roles of coordinator and facilitator High growth and innovation-based entrepreneurship	EU and national governments only support and create favorable circumstances Private firms but differences among member states

(continued)

Table 3.16 (continued)

	China	US	EU
	scientist groups, research, institutions, and enterprises Individual firms are increasingly involved		
Programs	• Selection of key technologies, sectors • Selection of industries, institutions, and firms • Promote service industries and SMEs • Blueprints for technological development • Knowledge transfer from Western players	Innovation strategy Blueprint for a future America built to last Industry programs for certain industries such as health, space, nano, bio, and advanced manufacturing	Decided by key actors in private sector R&D programs supported by EU Stimulation of SMEs, growth pole policy National member states innovation program
Main obstacles	Low level of original innovation More top-down than bottom-up Financial resources especially for SME IPR protection regulation Shortage of skilled workers and innovation capabilities Lack of institutional, social, and educational context fostering innovation	Long-term investment in infrastructure and sustainable economy Lack of transparent clear goals Renewal of governmental institutions is absent Policies lack implementation plan and sufficient resources Transformation of financial sector	Manager and employee culture instead of entrepreneurial spirit High investments in social security Low level of R&D expenditures Low level of entrepreneurial activity Lack of cooperation between institutes and private firms Inadequate appliance of knowledge Lack of integrated European innovation system

Instead of these updates of Western capitalistic systems, it is better to have a close eye on the rise of a specific Chinese system. The reason for this discussion is shown in Fig. 3.9. All the discussed policies are summarized in Fig. 3.9, but the dynamic view reveals the convergence of innovation systems.

The direction of the EU is towards a sustainable innovative growth region. In the European Commission, a shift is taking place from industrial policies towards macro-perspectives without implementation plan. The US government strives for the same aims, but the private sector is the real driving force of any change. The direction of the Chinese policies is from the macro-perspective such as striving for a circular economy to individual firms and even happiness of the people on the individual level. Paradoxically enough, the Western policies, and the European policies in particular, follow exactly the opposite direction, from entrepreneurial and individual support by means of subsidies to a top-down visionary macro-policies.

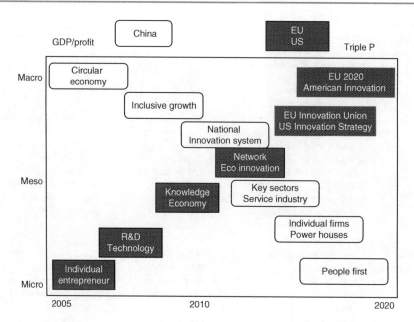

Fig. 3.9 Dynamic view on innovation policies

By 2020, the policies of China, the USA, and the EU have converged. They all cover the whole spectrum of macro to micro, thereby including complete national innovation systems to support for industries and individual firms or even individuals. But we have demonstrated in this chapter that governmental policies or even government itself need strategic innovation. But even then policies alone are insufficient.

In this setting, the scale, scope, and speed of implementation and execution power decide about effectiveness of the policies.

In this respect, China has moved away from communistic state planning to more effective short- and long-term strategic growth and development plans. Moreover, for the strategic sectors, the symbiosis between government and private sector in many cases till now proves to be successful alliance.

The US counts and hopes on technological breakthroughs by the private sector and policies are not regarded to be pivotal for future success and prosperity.

The EU lags behind in effective policy making and especially implementation. The policies are hypes instead of coherent successive policies often made ineffective by national state member policies. The European Commission identifies strategic issues, whereas many member states follow strategic top sector approach. Moreover, coordination between top sectors or issue-driven policies are lacking.

China is increasingly dependent on the ability to carry out the aims and policies in the field of innovation by the state-owned and private firms. The West is also dependent on the innovation performance of their private sector and public organizations. Strategic innovation is the key.

By 2020, China, the USA, and the EU will have covered almost every topic of innovation. Sometimes the policies and aims are identical. The winner of the race will be decided not by the policy but implementation power and realization of aims. In this respect, success is dependent on innovative entrepreneurship, innovation culture, private firms, bottom-up processes, symbiosis between private and public sector, and nontechnical innovations.

But now the first bombshell, the most striking feature of both the European and US policies, is that they are formulated in a world in which China does not seem to exist. Both the US and the EU policies are focused on their own limited world. Both the USA and the EU neglect the clearly stated Chinese policies to strive for being a leading innovation country, to become independent of Western technology, to develop and invest in almost every industry, to create future powerhouses, to foster sustainability, and to conquer global markets. Of course, not all Chinese policies have been realized in the past, but by now, we should know that the Chinese governmental leaders and policy makers are very serious about making the best out of it and to realize as much as possible. They need an answer from Western governments.

The second bombshell is that innovation policy makers in the USA, the EU, and China are struggling with bottom-line results. Both top-down innovation and government-stimulated bottom-up innovation policies do not work. Therefore, it is time to pay attention to the market participants. And what strategic approaches do they use? The next chapter reveals what the fields of strategy and innovation have to offer to realize the dreams of the leaders of China, the USA, and the EU. In Chap. 5, some practical business cases reveal the way Western and Chinese enterprises apply innovation and develop Chinese markets.

References

Chen, J., & Xu, Q.-R. (2000). Innovation strategy for building indigenous technological innovation capability in China. *Journal of Zhejiang University Science, 1*(2), 229–232.

Cong Cao. (2004). Challenges for technological development in China's industry foreign investors are the main providers of technology. *Perspectives chinoises, 54.*

The 2009 EU industrial R&D investment Scoreboard, Joint Research Centre, Directorate General Research, European Commission, European Communities, November 2009.

European Commission. (2010). *Cohesion policy: Strategic Report 2010 on the implementation of the programmes 2007-2013, SEC(2010)360.* Communication from the Commission to the European parliament, The Council, The European Economic and Social Committee and the Committee of the regions, 31.03.2010, COM(2010)110 final.

Fletcher, A. (2005, February). *Chinese firms tapping into potential of EU market.* Retrieved from http://www.Foodproductiondaily.com

Gu, S., & Lundvall, B.-Å. (2006). China's innovation system and the move toward harmonious growth and endogenous innovation. *Innovation: Management, Policy & Practice, April* (Spl Issue).

Guéguen, D. (2010). *Comitology. Hijacking European power?* Brussels: European Training Institute.

Markoff, J. (2006, August). *Silicon Valley's primal spirit lives, in a Part of Beijing.* Retrieved from http://www.bebeyond.com

Motohashi, K., & Yun, X. (2005). *China's innovation reform and growing industry and science linkages* (RIETI Discussion Paper Series 05-E-011). Tokyo: RIETI Research Institute of Economy, Trade and Industry.

Partnership for a New American Economy. (2011, June). *The new American Fortune 500.*

Perurena, G. (2006, February). Chinese oil can help American Capitalism. *The Collegian Online.* Retrieved from http://www.utulsa.edu

Shapira, P., & Youtie, J. (2010). The innovation system and innovation policy in the United States. In R. Frietsch & M. Schüller (Eds.), Preprint of chapter published in: *Competing for Global Innovation Leadership: Innovation Systems and Policies in the USA, EU and Asia* (Chap. 2; pp. 5–29). Stuttgart: Fraunhofer IRB.

Thomson Reuters. (2011a). *Chinese patenting. Report on the current state of innovation in China, Belgium.* Brussels: Thomson Reuters.

Thomson Reuters. (2011b, December). *Trademarks in China* (Special Report). Brussels: Thomson Reuters.

Unctad. (2003, December 4). *China: an emerging FDI outward investor* (E-brief).

van Someren, T. C. R. (1991, June). Innovatie, Emulatie en Tijd. De rol van de organisatorische vernieuwingen in het economische proces. *Tinbergen Institute Research Series, 9.*

van Someren, T. C. R. (2005). *Strategische Innovationen. So machen Sie Ihr Unternehmen einzigartig.* Wiesbaden: Gabler.

van Someren, T. C. R., & Someren-Wang, S. (2012). *Green China.* Heidelberg: Springer.

Xu, Q., & Wang, Y. E. A. P. (2000, April). *A new paradigm of technological innovation in China's enterprises: Innovation portfolio.* Report Memorandum #01-05, based on a presentation by Xu Qingrui and Wang Yi at the Sino-U.S. Conference on Technological Innovation, Beijing.

Demystifying Strategic Innovation

4

Both the current strategy and innovation concepts are insufficient to give an answer to the future challenges. Both fields of corporate strategy and innovation are characterized by the search for the Holy Grail. Although a lot of insight has been gathered, the core future issues in the fields of strategy and innovation are not connected to the rise of China. This rise is accompanied with new policies, new roles of private and public organizations, new industries, new market rules, new norms and values, and different interpretations of time. Consequently, Western management approaches of dealing with the future have to be changed. Current concepts of corporate strategy, innovation, and transition management are obsolete. Popular notions like open innovation, network organization, and knowledge economy do not fit to real market situations. A new approach is necessary. The strategic innovation theory offers a new approach to decide about in which direction to go on the crossroad. Several basic elements of the strategic innovation theory like non-technical innovations, creating a context for innovation beyond business models, a new profit definition, cross-cultural aspects, and the factor time are pivotal for the future success of China, the USA, and the EU. Paradoxically, Innovative China is more dependent on strategic innovations than on new technologies.

4.1 Transformation in Time

The rise of China requires a redefinition of Western thinking about strategy and innovation. The USA, the EU, and China are on a crossroad and the next decades will decide about winners and losers. China's growing power is also a clash of different systems. For our purpose we need to identify the core and general principles of the market economy in order to be able to formulate a strategic answer to the rise of China. In Fig. 4.1 some well-known or even popular views on innovation are presented but also some alternative views.

The alternative views form the basis of the future innovation processes in China, the USA, and the EU. They are an answer on the rise of China and the accompanying core issues of sustainability changing our world order. Moreover,

T.C.R. van Someren and S. van Someren-Wang, *Innovative China*,
Management for Professionals, DOI 10.1007/978-3-642-36237-8_4,
© Springer-Verlag Berlin Heidelberg 2013

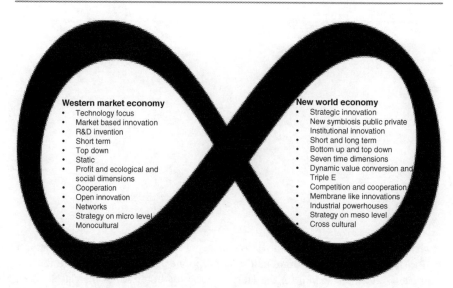

Fig. 4.1 Transformation in time

the Western market economy does not exist because many interpretations and many different appliances of some principles exist. The market economy in France is different from the USA. Furthermore, the market economy is in a constant flux and not static at all.

In our view, the Western market success depends on the appliance of four economic principles: division of labor (Adam Smith), accumulation (Marx), and innovation (Schumpeter). The division of labor and accumulation of capital supported by the rise of the international finance industry enabled entrepreneurs to set up large-scale factories and also to make a start with globalization. It was the start of pure capitalism represented by, e.g., big textile and consumer good factories. This market system allowed the entry of China with their low-cost manufacturing. According to Marx, the seamless endless accumulation of capital in hands of a few capitalists at cost of the factory worker would at the end lead to its downfall. However, even with the several finance as well as sustainability crises, the end of capitalism did not happen. There was a third factor which renewed the capitalistic system. Schumpeter showed that because of innovation the endless accumulation was replaced by new activities preventing in fact the downfall. The free-market system focused on the renewal capacity of its market organizations under conditions of market regulation like antidumping laws, tax laws, and antimonopoly laws. But what is the fourth factor? Knowledge was regarded to be the new production factor of the future. But a more fundamental factor is at work. The connection and underlying factor between the principle of labor division, accumulation, and innovation is time (van Someren, 1991). Corporate success depends on aspects of time like the right timing, organization of accumulation of knowledge, capital and experience of a certain time period, cycle time of new product development, and dealing with uncertainty. In this respect knowledge is nothing else than the accumulation of (creative) labor, natural resources, and capital over time. Knowledge is dead capital until innovative entrepreneurs come into action.

Time is the most crucial dimension of the economy. Amazingly enough, time as the fourth dimension is not integrated in mainstream economics and management studies. The time dimensions are the source for the market process consisting of competition and cooperation resulting in bottom-line results.

The Western free-market system was regarded to be the best model for development, growth, and prosperity. But the rise of China is accompanied by alternative forms of industrial organization.

In this respect, the different market systems developed in the EU, the USA, and China are on a crossroad now. The crossroad of the EU, the USA, and China needs an answer in which direction the world order will develop. But where does the answer come from? Policy makers and leaders of enterprises need to find new and strategic answers on how to contribute and participate in creating or adapting to a new world. In the previous chapter, the strategic innovation policies have been evaluated. The main conclusion is that policies itself cannot create renewal and prosperity. Individual and corporate innovative entrepreneurialism are the missing link. Now we turn our attention to the world of enterprises and innovation. Both private and semipublic organizations will be included.

There are two main management fields which are most promising in providing the answer. The first is strategy and the second innovation. In the next sections these two fields will be examined in their potential contribution for giving an answer on our crossroad challenge. The conclusion will be that these mainstream approaches do not provide the instruments for a strategic answer to the rise of Innovative China. A new approach is necessary.

4.2 Strategy, Sense or Senseless?

4.2.1 The Overview

On average, in the West, board meetings spend 90 % of their time on evaluating performance and targets and only 5 % on strategy and 5 % on the right to exist in markets. Why? Because financial experts dominate the discussion. Especially in times of crises and fundamental change such as the rise of China, the time spent on strategic renewal should dominate the board meeting. Instead, the focus is often on short-term operational issues. The managers are held responsible and the focus is inward looking. Inside problems overshadow developments in the outside world. But when are the core issues discussed what the role and contribution of the enterprise is to society?

To paraphrase John F. Kennedy: ask not what your board can do for your EBITDA, ask what your enterprise can do for society. Most strategy concepts are based on the first and not on the second part of the paraphrase. The first focuses on cost reduction and improvement programs, whereas the second requires to interpret trends into future needs and customer demand and to prepare the enterprise for the future. That is what strategy is about.

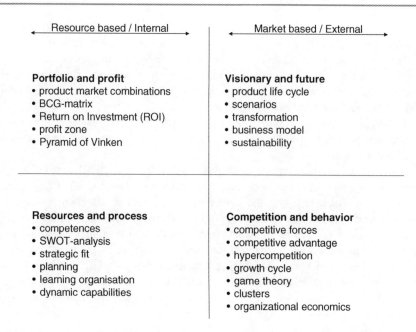

Fig. 4.2 Overview of the field of strategy

Strategy can be senseless or even dangerous for an organization when it is dead paper without innovative capability to renew. The rise of China challenges the Western way of dealing with strategy. China is trying to stimulate innovative economy. Chinese companies are earning money with improving or combining Western technologies. Some Western companies cannot earn money because they do not have a China strategy. But many failed because they have a wrong China strategy without adapting to the Chinese situation. On the one hand, if the West does not catch up, the Western companies will be threatened inside and outside China. On the other hand, the success stories in China mostly have a strategic background of considering Chinese paradoxes like private and public, long term and short term, culture identity and diversity, and steadiness and innovation.

Below, a very short summary of the main characteristics of the different approaches is presented. In the field of strategy, the main controversy is between the resource-based view (RBV) and the market view to which the majority of all different strategic concepts belong.

Figure 4.2 shows the overview of the main strategy approaches.

The overview presented in Fig. 4.2 shows that the Holy Grail of strategy has not been found yet. There is not a single dominant approach. It is more a supermarket of concepts and everybody can take what he likes. The academics have their fundamental discussion about RBV versus market approach, the businesses and consultants focused mainly on providing tactical instruments to create an operational strategy.

The current approaches were sufficient to formulate outsourcing strategies, but they are incapable of giving an answer to the long-term industrial development strategies of

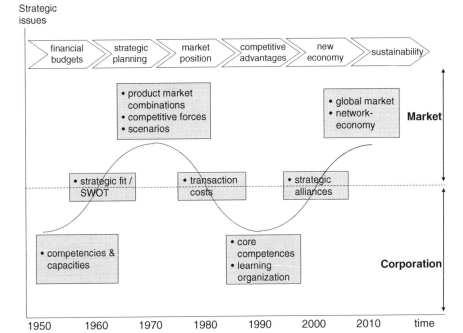

Fig. 4.3 Dynamic view on evolution of strategy

Chinese government and industries. Western corporate strategies fail against Chinese 4I emulation strategy supported directly or indirectly by the government.

4.2.2 Dynamic View on Strategy

To understand the field of strategy, a dynamic view is necessary. The respected textbook writer on strategy, Grant (2007), identified a succession in strategy topics through time. The successive topics were financial budgeting (1950s), corporate planning (1960s), strategy as positioning (1970s), competitive advantage (1990s), new economy (2000), and sustainability (2010). Within the boardroom, an evolution of certain dominant topics has taken place.

But we have to go one step further. Within the time line of strategy evolution, the fundamental discussion between the RBV and market approach becomes clear. Figure 4.3 makes this clear.

Figure 4.3 clearly shows that all the main strategy approaches discussed before follow an action–reaction pattern within the boundaries of the market and RBV. It can indeed be expected that as of 2010 the global market, sustainability, and network economy will be the future topics of strategy. Furthermore, when extrapolating the curve, the focus rather returns to individual firms and other RBV-related concepts than on market approach.

Any corporate strategy should be based on both a market (external) and resource (internal) view. The dominant strategy concepts focus on only one of these both views.

But the challenge of China blows this pattern of strategy development and its boundaries of market and RBV to pieces. There are four main reasons. First, the strategies used by Chinese organizations are beyond the boundaries of Western corporate strategic thinking. The role of government in global sourcing and creating new markets and new corporations requires fundamental new thinking in the field of strategy. Second, although innovation is in several strategy approaches a central part, it does not belong to the core of strategic thinking. Third, cross-cultural differences in creating, interpreting, and using strategy concepts are mostly ignored. Fourth, although strategy is theoretically connected with long-term view, in practice the short term dominates due to the pressure of stock markets and other financial institutions. Therefore, in the next sections, the contribution of innovation approaches has to be discussed.

4.3   Innovation

4.3.1   The Overview

For understanding and creating alternative roads to a sustainable innovative society, we need to know some key notions of innovations.

The field of innovation is as comprehensive as the field of strategy. Therefore, we use the same approach as in the previous section by only presenting the main contributions. Figure 4.4 shows a matrix with several innovation approaches.

Like in the field of strategy, the innovation approaches are also in search of the Holy Grail. The matrix in Fig 4.4 shows some mainstream approaches. All these approaches mainly focus on product, process innovation, and technology output. The rise of China requires a strategic answer beyond the classical boundaries of the firm. Two alternatives are transition management and system renewal which will be elaborated below.

Transition management and innovation system renewal are attempts to integrate the before-mentioned fields of development and process and to focus on changing the whole innovation system.[1] However, this dominant thinking in innovation theories does not reflect the renewal processes in practice.[2]

The goal of an entrepreneur is not to change a complete innovation system, but it is to introduce strategic innovations which offer a new or cheaper quality to customers or other innovations which improve life and benefit society and which generate an added value for the entrepreneur. Both innovation system renewal and transition management largely neglect the element of uncertainty, which is inherent to innovation. Therefore, because the innovative entrepreneur and a modus operandi

---

[1] See for example van den Bosch, 2010.

[2] See van Someren, 1991, 2005; Van de Ven & Poole, 1995; Birkinshaw, Hamel & Mol, 2008, van Someren & Nijhof, 2010, van Someren & van Someren-Wang, 2010.

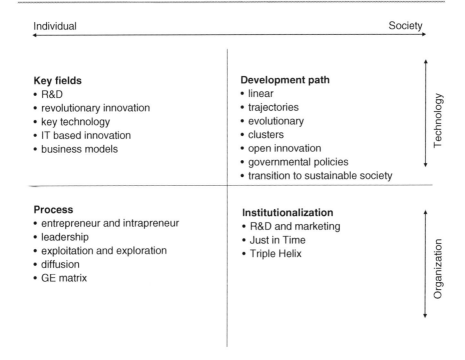

Individual   Society

Key fields
- R&D
- revolutionary innovation
- key technology
- IT based innovation
- business models

Development path
- linear
- trajectories
- evolutionary
- clusters
- open innovation
- governmental policies
- transition to sustainable society

Technology

Process
- entrepreneur and intrapreneur
- leadership
- exploitation and exploration
- diffusion
- GE matrix

Institutionalization
- R&D and marketing
- Just in Time
- Triple Helix

Organization

Fig. 4.4 Innovation approaches

are failing, transition management will not be used to support enterprises to provide an answer to the rise of Innovative China.

4.3.2 Dynamic View on Innovation

When the innovation concepts are compared to the strategy field, there are two relevant differences. First, the scope is much wider. On the one hand, individual innovative entrepreneurs play a far greater role in the field of innovation than in the field of strategy. On the other hand, the society at large sets the boundary of technology like with GM food. It is believed that technology changes society such as the idea of paradigm shift or sustainability demonstrate. Moreover, national innovation programs exist but national corporate strategy programs are absent.

Secondly, the role of governmental policies in the field of innovation is often much bigger than in corporate strategy. Governments do directly stimulate certain technologies, innovative regions, and national innovation policies. With regard to strategy, governments only formulate boundaries such as giving concessions for mining activities or regulations for mergers and acquisitions but hardly have a direct influence on corporate strategy.

The dynamic view on innovation is presented in Fig. 4.5.

In the past decades, a succession of core innovation issues has characterized the time line of innovation. The individual sometimes heroic entrepreneur has been

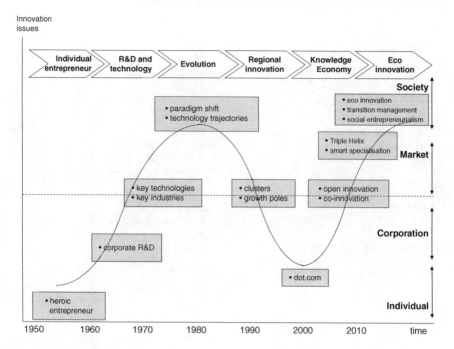

Fig. 4.5 Dynamic view on innovation

followed up by corporate innovation (1960s), the key technologies together with key industries shifted the focus to the industry level and soon by the level of the whole society based on paradigm shifts (1980s), concentration of innovation such as clusters and growth poles turned attention to regional innovation (1990s), the knowledge economy hype featured by the Internet and dot.com companies put the creative individual entrepreneur at the center again (2000), the cooperation in networks put cooperation and co-innovation at the core, and the problems of sustainability asked for a societal perspective on innovation (2010). Transition management is a concept of everything without a modus operandi and doomed to fail.

In this respect the idea of cooperation and networks combined with entrepreneurialism created the notion of social entrepreneurialism. Social entrepreneurialism is the opposite of profit-seeking individual entrepreneurs. It fits to the hype and single issue innovation topic of societal relevant innovations and eco-innovations discussed earlier. It is supposed to be more or less the opposite of commercial entrepreneurship. Social entrepreneurialism means a post-materialism entrepreneurship aiming at realizing social or ecological projects with benefits for the society at large. Social entrepreneurialism is carried out in the context of larger societal interests and working together with stakeholders defending the sustainability issues. But with the rise of China, the profit-seeking entrepreneur dominates the market scene to contribute to his own wallet and the growth of China. Therefore, the interpretation of the paraphrase what you can do for society differs depending on the market situation and context.

Like in the field of strategy, the successive notions and concepts of innovation show a pendulum movement. With regard to innovation, the pendulum of approaches moves between the individual and the society which go beyond the strategic pendulum between market and the corporation, respectively. A simple extrapolation of the innovation issues as presented in Fig. 4.5 will not offer the required solutions to deal with the rise of China. Just as in case of the strategy field, the rise of China asks for a different perspective. The different role of the government, the different interpretation of innovation due to cross-cultural issues, the institutionalization of innovation, and the time factor are few differences in the approach to innovation.

Taken together and accumulated in time, the continuous innovations have a tremendous influence on any strategy of a private or public organization. In fact, all those innovations have the potential to undermine any corporate strategy. This is the reason to name them strategic innovations.

4.4 Strategic Innovation Theory Is the Future

The strategic innovations will at the end lead to a new world order. It is now time to show the power of strategic innovations and its relevance for Innovative China. World societal development as well as progress is dependent on continuous innovation not only in market economy. Sustainability is one such a societal development.

As shown in the previous sections, there are four mainstream approaches to deal with creating a new future. These are scenario analysis, transition management including innovation system renewal, strategy, and innovation. It was concluded that all approaches are insufficient and follow a pattern in time of hypes. Table 4.1 presents the main differences between these approaches.

Van Someren (1990, 1991a, b, 1992a, b, 1998a, b, 2005, 2006) has showed that the influence of nontechnical innovations, the context of innovation, the time dimensions, the role of government, the cross-cultural influence on formulation, and the implementation of both strategy and innovation require a complete new approach. This strategic innovation theory (SIT) is an alternative for the fields of corporate strategy including scenario analysis, and innovation including transition management. This approach can be applied on sustainability in both Western countries and China. In Fig. 4.6 the different views on relevant management themes are presented.

The strategic innovation approach is triggered by three drivers: nontechnical innovation, the relation to business models, and the emulation process including the time dimensions. The modus operandi of value conversion determined by economies of scale, scope, and time is pivotal (van Someren, 1991a, b).

For the main topic of this book, the rise of Innovative China, it is however necessary to highlight a few new basic foundations based on the economic laws and management principles described in the SIT fitting to the new world order as mentioned in Fig. 4.6. In this book we only highlight the several issues relevant for understanding Innovative China. For the theoretical foundation and its interconnectivity, we refer to the literature (van Someren, 1991a, b, 1995a, b, 2005). For its appliance on the creation of a sustainable society in China, we refer to van Someren & van Someren-Wang (2007a, b, c, 2009a, b, c, d, 2011, 2012). In the sections below, new notions and basic concepts

Table 4.1 Four main approaches dealing with the future

Strategic innovation	Scenario analysis	Transition management	Corporate strategy/ innovation strategy
Focus on aspiration	Focus on training	Focus on system	Focus on vision, mission and budgets
Creating the corporation of the future	Create possible futures	Creating new total system	Survive existing competition
Focus on creating context for innovation and business models	Different situations	Focus on change	Focus on R&D, products and services
Divergence by means of market creation	Different combinations of dominant trends and drivers	A single future	Benchmark with rivals leading to convergence
Focus on dynamic value conversion	No specific performance indicator	Depends on situation	Focus on profit
Creating both short term improvements as well as long term new growth curves	Long term	Long term	Short term improvements
Focus on non-technical innovation leading to non-imitable and unique solutions	Selected technologies or other drivers	Focus on change in all levels (political, institutional,...)	Focus on technology which can be copied fast
Leader's role is to create context for innovation leading to long term value conversion	Coherent scenarios	Moderator	Leader's role is to create shareholder value
Continuous cycle of innovation	Ad hoc	Backcasting	Ad hoc process
Scale, scope and time lead to dynamic emulation	No modus operandi	No modus operandi	Static scale and scope lead to new status quo
Dependency on national culture	National culture plays no role	National culture plays no role	National culture plays no role
Micro-/meso-/macro-level	Macro-level	Macro-level	Micro-/meso-level

will be developed which are needed to describe, understand, and predict the developments of the new world order and its new growth curve. To these new basic concepts belong emulation instead of invention–innovation–diffusion, dynamic value conversion instead of profit (Triple P), cross-cultural innovation instead of monocultural innovation, institutionalized innovation instead of technology push or market-driven innovation, Quadruple Helix instead of Triple Helix, industrial governance instead of corporate governance, public–private symbiosis instead of separation between private and public, membrane innovations instead of open–closed innovations, and value circle instead of value chain.

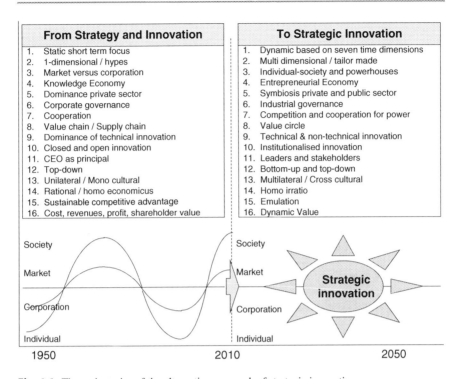

From Strategy and Innovation	To Strategic Innovation
1. Static short term focus	1. Dynamic based on seven time dimensions
2. 1-dimensional / hypes	2. Multi dimensional / tailor made
3. Market versus corporation	3. Individual-society and powerhouses
4. Knowledge Economy	4. Entrepreneurial Economy
5. Dominance private sector	5. Symbiosis private and public sector
6. Corporate governance	6. Industrial governance
7. Cooperation	7. Competition and cooperation for power
8. Value chain / Supply chain	8. Value circle
9. Dominance of technical innovation	9. Technical & non-technical innovation
10. Closed and open innovation	10. Institutionalised innovation
11. CEO as principal	11. Leaders and stakeholders
12. Top-down	12. Bottom-up and top-down
13. Unilateral / Mono cultural	13. Multilateral / Cross cultural
14. Rational / homo economicus	14. Homo irratio
15. Sustainable competitive advantage	15. Emulation
16. Cost, revenues, profit, shareholder value	16. Dynamic Value

Fig. 4.6 The main topics of the alternative approach of strategic innovation

In Fig. 4.7 these subjects are categorized along the so-called 4 C's of strategic innovation: conditions, context, creativity, and content.

Each of these subjects will be elaborated in the next sections.

4.5 Conditions

4.5.1 New Growth Curves and Emulation

From a market perspective, there are two options with regard to existing business: to improve or to innovate. Improvement implies to make the existing growth curve or business model better or cheaper. In fact, the lifetime of the existing business model is being extended. Chinese firms are masters in improving and adapting the product specification to Chinese demand and introduce optimization improvements in primary and secondary business processes. The majority of firms, smaller and bigger ones, behave in this way. But in the end, improvements are insufficient to sustain development and growth, and the corporate life cycle can be ended by bankruptcy, takeover, or termination of business. But there can be gained more than only improvements.

Strategic innovation implies to create a new growth curve generating new business. In this perspective, strategic innovation is in fact the central task of

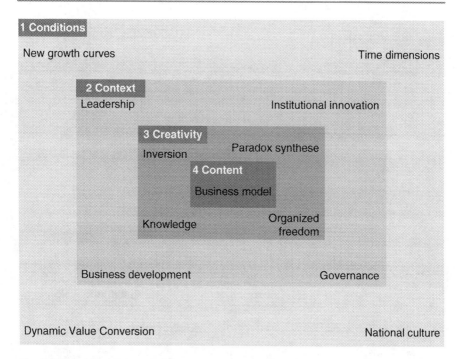

Fig. 4.7 The 4 C's of strategic innovation

entrepreneurs and top management. It shows the pivotal role of strategic innovation for any business being part of the process of emulation.

Emulation refers to the (market) process of trying to surpass others by cheaper or better imitation, innovation, the will to be better than others, and going for the best. Both countries and firms emulate each other. The principles of emulation are worldwide and the same, but they are applied differently because of cultural differences. Understanding this process of emulation offers the opportunity for the competitors from the East and the West to create their own chances.

Therefore, emulation has clear distinctions to current dominant mainstream thoughts about innovation. First, emulation includes the behavior to be the best and to win. Second, innovation is not only about cooperation as is advocated nowadays but also about competition. Third, by including the time element, emulation stresses the dynamic side of societal development. Traditionally, innovation was thought to start with R&D followed by a prototype before its first commercial launch in market and end by diffusion. Emulation opposes this linear approach and stresses the cyclic character of innovation. Therefore, emulation replaces both the linear R&D–invention–innovation pattern and the innovation–diffusion pattern (van Someren, 1991b).

But it is important to understand this process of emulation in the context of the Chinese economy. Since the existence of human being and animals, learning and becoming the best starts with imitation. The competitive advantages are embodied in these managerial, organizational, ethical, and cultural inner workings and not in technology alone.

The innovation–internationalization phase in the 4I emulation scheme replaces the imitation–improvement phase and represents the start of a new growth curve. For example, Shenzhen is the core of Guangdong's manufacturing center and has the densest cluster of toy manufacturers. Already since early 2000, occasionally, exports declined due to increasing prices for materials, rising labor costs (about 20 % in two years), and cutthroat competition (China Daily, 22.12.05). The result was razor-thin profit margins. In Guangdong, shortages of labor supply are not an exception anymore. Particularly, the category of young women between 18 and 25 years— preferred because of their small and quick fingers—is decreasing due to the one-child policy. Moreover, laborers become more aware of their rights and are prepared to switch jobs if payment or circumstances elsewhere are better. The only way out is to innovate and to come up with unique and superior quality designs and to improve their social accountability.

The latter leads to another big issue: the balance between economic prosperity and social and ecological issues. Already Chinese customers in prosperous cities like Shanghai are very demanding and changing their preferences quickly. In future, with ongoing prosperity, other segments of the population will join and increase the demand. Also entering massively, international Western markets force Chinese firms to be innovative.

Therefore, technological leadership is not the only dimension to become number one. To be number one or at least a top global player, other elements like organizational innovations will decide who will be the winner. In or outside China, every business will be confronted with Chinese companies or business activity. Chinese firms in Europe like Haier, Huawei, and ZTE want to deliver quality, and they will do everything to prove that.

But the case of Taiwanese HTC shows how difficult these easy-stated aims are to realize. Founded in 1997, HTC managed to earn a market position in the mobile phone market. However, with regard to the competition with Apple and Samsung in the market of smart phones, HTC loses on being innovative, especially in customer service. Problems with their technical platform, low economies of scope with regard to product range, unsatisfied customers and lacking after-sales service, and the threat of rising competition in Chinese market from Huawei and ZTE lead to lower profit margins. Winning on technical aspects from Apple or Samsung will be nearly impossible on the short term, and therefore, the relation with the customer offers best opportunity to emulate. But offering excellent service is precisely the weakest link in the HTC chain.

China was successful with the first two stages of imitation and improvement to emulate the West measured in total value created. The main advantages were the lower labor costs; imitating and improving existing knowledge, products, processes, and services; and fast decision-making process. But the next two stages of the 4I emulation scheme, innovation and internationalization, require a circular innovation process.

Through time, societies evolve and after the stage of copying, now China enters the stage of innovation. The behavior of copying, adapting, improving, and surpassing characterizes the process of growth and development in China. The Chinese prefer the step-by-step approach which fits to emulation. This is contrary to American approach of fast radical innovation and heroic achievements. A step-by-step approach does not mean the ambitions are low. On the contrary, the process of emulation enables to win trust between partners, to lower the risk, and to learn and to find out what the opportunities are. Many Chinese firms that once started with cost advantages are gradually entering the phase of making process and product improvements.

Generally, the Chinese like to win and to be the best. Already the Chinese educational system forces young children to compete for the best universities. Parents support and stimulate their children to study hard and to give their parents face by excellent results. Brilliant results pave the way to study in Western countries and even to get better and to increase the chances on a good career. Businessmen show the same behavior. Every businessman wants to be the best and have success. Hence, imitating and buying foreign technology gives at least the opportunity to be in competition at all. But this strive for success has been based for a long time on copycat behavior and reproduction of knowledge.

The aim of China to increase R&D input and to foster innovation output is to achieve indigenous innovation. From Chap. 3 we know that China's R&D and patent applications are increasing rapidly compared to other countries. The first sign shows that China has indeed started to climb this mountain of homegrown innovation which is presented in Table 4.2. Table 4.2 shows the number of domestic applicants compared to the total number of applicants.

It becomes clear that the growth of the number of domestic invention patent applicants has risen more than the total number. Domestic invention applications have risen more than total including foreign applicants. But it should be kept in mind that the numbers do not show the quality or how new the contained knowledge in the filed patents really is. Nevertheless, in 2010, within the business sector, two Chinese firms belonged to the top patent applicants. Panasonic from Japan is number one followed by ZTE as number two and Huawei Technologies ranked fourth (WIPO, 2011).

In Europe the total number of patent filings clearly shows a trend to an increased Chinese activity. In general the majority (62 %) of European filings in 2011 came from non-European countries (61 % in 2010). The European Patent Office (EPO) notices that a shift to Asia is the trend. The share of the USA remains dropped slightly from 26 % (2010) to 24 % in 2011. The share of Europe remained unchanged but the share of China and Japan increased from 5 % to 7 % and from 18 % to 19 %, respectively. Also, the number of Chinese filings in Europe has substantially increased as Table 4.3 shows.

Table 4.3 confirms the trend of a knowledge transfer in the direction of China and the increase of the stock of knowledge. The question is of course whether they are able to exploit and commercialize it. Based on their entrepreneurial spirit, the answer is yes but based on the current market successes, a long road lies ahead.

Table 4.2 Total patent applications and applications for invention patents filed with SIPO (2001, 2006, and 2010)

Year	2001	2006	2010
Total patent applications	203.573	573.178	1.222.286
Total applications for invention patents	63.204	210.490	391.177
Total domestic applications for invention patents	30.038	122.318	293.066
Domestic invention applications as % of total applications	14.76 %	21.34 %	24.00 %
Domestic invention applications as % of total invention applications	47.53 %	58.11 %	74.92 %

Source: State Intellectual Property Office of the P.R.C., "Statistics", http://www.sipo.gov.cn/sipo_English/statistics/

Table 4.3 Total European filings in 2011

Country of origin	2011 Count	Versus 2010	Rank 2011
United States	59.089	−2.5 %	1
Japan	46.934	+12 %	2
Germany	33.289	+0.5 %	3
PR China	16.153	+27.2 %	4
Rep Korea	13.324	+8 %	5
France	11.862	+1.5 %	6
Switzerland	7.745	−1.6 %	7
United Kingdom	6.484	−9.4 %	8
Netherlands	6.176	−13.2 %	9
Italy	4.970	+0.4 %	10
...			
Total	242.642	+2.6 %	

Source: European Patent Office, 2011

The trend is towards sharp increased application but one has to consider the difference in single and multi-application.[3] Some offices allow for more than one design per product. The USA and China offices are single design system. The nonresident number of applications in China is below 6.5 %, indicating a large homegrown design application content (Fig. 4.8).

Buying original foreign brands is a sign of wealth and personal prosperity. But future China in accordance has to develop own brands. This move upward from manufacturing to branding and trademarks and selling is shown in Fig. 4.9.

With regard to absolute quantitative numbers, China is emulating other nations and regions in the world in trademark applications. But also here, one of the key questions is whether the trademark registrations are homegrown or not.

According to statistics, the office in China has received more than eight times the number of trademark applications as in, e.g., Germany. Definitely, the homegrown

---

[3] See for detailed analyses, World Intellectual Property Organization (WIPO), 2011, World Intellectual Property Indicators, Geneva.

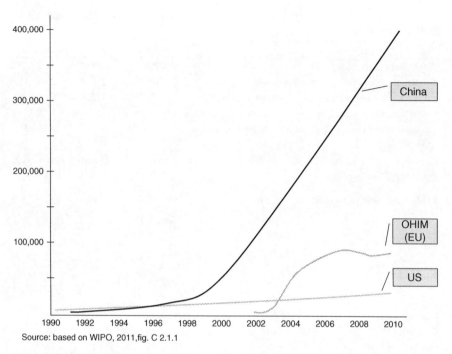

Source: based on WIPO, 2011,fig. C 2.1.1

Fig. 4.8 Trends in design applications in top offices: China, USA, and OHIM (EU)

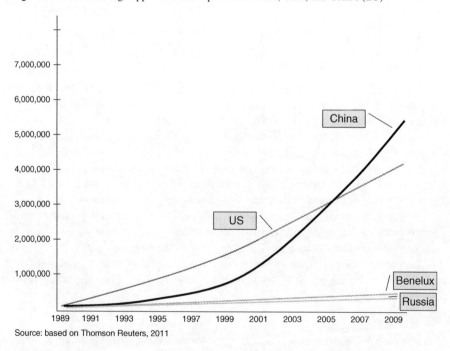

Source: based on Thomson Reuters, 2011

Fig. 4.9 Trends in cumulative trademark growth in various countries (1989–2009)

trademarks are rising, but the steep increase is also caused by the Chinese single-class filing system requiring multiple registrations for the same application opposed to multi-class filing in other countries requiring only a single registration. Similar to R&D and design, also here, a clear trend of homegrown trademarks and brands is existent. However, registering new brands and trademarks is one thing; the other thing is whether the Chinese businessmen are able to make from local known brands, Chinese brands, and later on famous world brands.

4.5.2   Power of Time Dimensions

Time is an underestimated factor in relation to innovation but of crucial relevance in relation to China. First of all, time is the basic source of risk and uncertainty. Second, innovation is about the future. Any innovation creates new uncertainty for the others. Third, time is the measure of business as Francis Bacon already said. Success in business is about being able to do the things on time. Third, and may be even more important, are the time dimensions hidden but at the core of strategic innovations. Fourth, Chinese interpretation and use of time differ from the West.

Therefore, time is more than clock time. In Table 4.4 seven time dimensions are being identified (van Someren, 1990, 1991a, b, 2005).

As Table 4.4 shows, time comes back in economic life in many often hidden appearances. For example, with regard to economies of time, the Western discussion of work–life balance is in Asian culture seen with amazement. As the founder of BYD says (Financial Times, 11.05.09), "Maybe in the Western world, life is number one and work is number two... But in China, work is number one and life is number two."

The seven time dimensions as part of the strategic innovation theory are crucial for understanding Chinese behavior. The role of time in Chinese society is crucial and it substantially differs from Western time notions. The Chinese believe in very long time periods about 12,000 years in which everything repeats itself in a new context.

Time is circular and not linear as in the West. For this reason, despite enormous environmental problems China is facing, the notion of sustainability fits very well to Chinese ways of thinking and deeply held beliefs, paradoxically more than in Western society.

In the same line of thinking, the Chinese also think in stages or certain time periods with specific characteristics. This can be found back in all the different time periods with emperors called dynasties. Also the 5-year plans are an expression of period thinking. Another aspect of time is the short- and long-term thinking. For Westerners, short- and long-term thinking are opposites.

For the Chinese short and long term, in conformity with Taoism, belong to the same notion of looking forward, but depending on the situation, one or the other is more important. Governmental planners and businessmen can make plans and vision for the long term in which long term is sometimes 20, 50, or even 100 years. For example, China's dream and aim is to be the leading technology nation as of

Table 4.4 The seven time dimensions

Time dimension	Appearance	Economic relevance	Innovative China (examples)
1 Time culture	Past and future; constructive and destroying	Influence of time on behavior and decision taking	In the long run China will regain its natural Number One position
2 Time arrow	Progress, linear and circular, presence and future	Forward or backwards thinking, context for innovation	Forward thinking, future orientated but proud on history
3 Time control	Time as an institution; coordination; individual versus organization	Instrument of industrial power	Government and plans decide about timing of new activities
4 Timing	Moment of decision; first mover or follower	Optimal/maximal point in time	From fast follower to first mover
5 Time duration	Accumulation, learning; flexibility; short and long term; life cycle; building trust	Dynamic nature of time (more periods not one period)	Accumulation of Western experience, short and long term; building trust
6 Time consumption	Productivity, emotional experiences	Value of time for user	Life time working
7 Time intensity	Speed; frequency; evolution and revolution	Amount of turbulence and uncertainty	Frequent long term evolutionary change

Source: van Someren, 1991b, 2005

2050. But at the same time, they can react extremely quickly when new opportunities arise. Buying a competitor in trouble with cash is not a problem for well-embedded firms in a privately financed network because no formal bank loan procedures have to be followed. Chinese strategic behavior is characterized by both long-term and short-term time lines.

Time changes everything and therefore flexibility is of utmost importance to survive. Time as an instrument for being flexible is often used by businessmen to gain an additional advantage. Changing market conditions are used by Chinese businessmen to renegotiate contracts and deals. Earlier-signed agreements are like photos; they are true situations of moments in the past without relevance for new current situations.

The time dimension of accumulation of knowledge and experiences is in the Chinese context coupled with entering new stages of development. The introduction of IP laws shows that these are introduced to please Western complaints of but to prepare for the next stage of innovation. Also, Chinese organizations will become dependent on protection of their knowledge. But here, new dilemmas are being created for Western firms. In case of alliances between Western and Chinese firms, the IP laws will be used to get the Western knowledge and to claim it for the joint venture mostly dominated by Chinese.

Also, for Innovative China, the time dimensions have great impact on the way strategic innovations are being created and implemented. In the next section, we will show that in the future time will lead to a new performance measurement criterion: the dynamic value conversion.

4.5.3 Dynamic Value Conversion

The ultimate purpose of strategic innovation is value conversion (De Jong 1989, van Someren, 1991a,b, 2005). Value conversion is a very old economic principle, but in time its content or, better, its interpretation has changed drastically. In the West value conversion has transformed in profit or even the aim of maximum profits. In some cases maximum revenues and an acceptable profit level together with a certain sales level were different interpretations of value conversion. After stock exchanges and banks played a pivotal role in capital supplies, the notion of value conversion was replaced by the notion of profits. Even worse, short-term profits were preferred above long-term profits.

Because of sustainability, it has been suggested that the classical profit criterion should be replaced by the Triple P (People, Profit, Planet) criterion. Depending on the scope of the definition, different approaches to Triple P value creation exist such as value proposition (generating the idea) and value capturing (securing the value). Another variety is shared value creation, which indicates stakeholder involvement. These concepts rather reflect the organization of the value-creating process than the bottom-line value in time. Although the Triple P criterion is principally right, its use is dependent on the time-based attitude of market participants. As long as Western market behavior prefers short-term results stimulated by annual bonus systems, stock prices, and short-term ROI project results, Triple P will be overshadowed by the classical profit dimension.

Dealing with the two biggest challenges of the current century, the rise of China and sustainability, requires a new value concept. The classical profit criterion is focused on short term, whereas the Triple P is focused on the long term. The 4I emulation scheme of China reflects the equal importance of short-term profit and (very) long-term value conversion. Moreover, learning and accumulation effects together with a strategic trade-off between short-term profit and long-term market dominance characterize Chinese industrial behavior.

For this purpose, the dynamic value conversion has been developed as the modus operandi of strategic innovation. The two spirals of negative and positive dynamic value conversion illustrate the two basic inner workings of the dynamic value conversion.

Chasing short-term profit ignites a negative spiral of value conversion as shown in Fig. 4.10.

The negative spiral of dynamic value conversion fits to extending the growth cycle by improvements. The short-term focus reinforces improvements of the existing activities and strengthens the exploitation culture and removes the strive for exploration and creation of strategic innovation. The economic modus operandi will be dominated by economies of scale and cost lowering. This is not a sufficient perspective for strategic innovations.

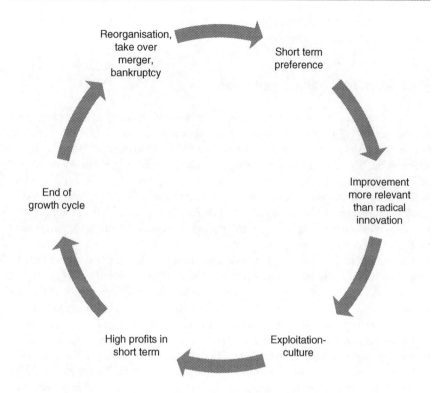

Fig. 4.10 The negative spiral of dynamic value conversion

The economic modus operandi for strategic innovation in creating new growth cycles is the Triple E. The Triple E consists of economies of scale, economies of scope, and economies of time (van Someren, 1991a, b, 2005). For example, in the 1980s and 1990s, Western car manufacturers have chosen to expand the scale of operation, thereby forgetting the diseconomies of time effect. Toyota showed that with the organizational innovation of Just-In-Time, a smaller scale is possible (economies of scale) with higher quality, less defects, faster production, lower delays (economies of time), and higher variety (economies of scope).

Very often, the expected profits or value conversion of innovations are under-estimated. The uncertain future profits of innovation are discounted with the net present value method or internal ROI. Hence, within larger corporations, only very promising innovations will be accepted by the management. This is the reason that SMEs have the opportunity to fill the gap and take the risk to develop something completely new. But due to the Triple E effects, the potential value conversion lies higher than classic profit estimation. The economies of time effects of, for example, a right timing, the accumulation of knowledge and experience, longer lifetime of materials and products, learning, and trust building with suppliers have a multiplier effect on classical profit expectations. Often, incumbent firms are surprised by the apparently sudden breakthrough of innovations. The experience of a sudden unexpected breakthrough is the time and

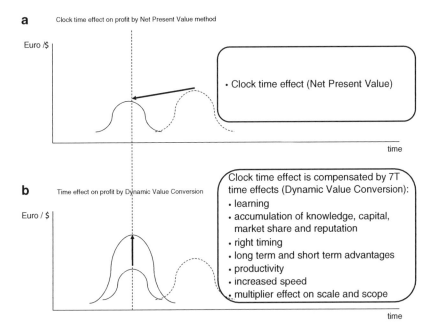

a   Clock time effect on profit by Net Present Value method

Euro /$

• Clock time effect (Net Present Value)

time

b   Time effect on profit by Dynamic Value Conversion

Euro / $

Clock time effect is compensated by 7T time effects (Dynamic Value Conversion):
• learning
• accumulation of knowledge, capital, market share and reputation
• right timing
• long term and short term advantages
• productivity
• increased speed
• multiplier effect on scale and scope

time

Fig. 4.11 Multiplier effect of economies of time

multiplier effect of economies of time. This situation is graphically represented in Fig. 4.11.

Future profits have always a lower present value, but this clock time effect is more than compensated by other time effects such as right timing, accumulation, and multiplier effects. Clock time has a negative influence whereas other time dimensions have a positive effect on value conversion. The net present value can be higher due to better timing and/or accumulation effects. That is why innovative David's can beat conservative risk, avoiding Goliath's. As soon as the MNEs discover the potential, it can be too late or too costly to participate or emulate the innovative challenger. The Triple E creates a positive dynamic value conversion as shown in Fig. 4.12.

Now, the time effects such as starting as a first mover and accumulating knowledge and experience or a fast-follower strategy have a multiplier effect on economies of scale and scope. The simultaneous exploitation and exploration culture supports the institutionalized innovation function, thereby creating further dynamic value conversion opportunities. The growth and development of new growth cycles is ensured. Therefore, Triple E is the modus operandi of strategic innovations. These Triple E effects are always part of any strategic innovation, but they have to be created and are often hidden treasures.

The Triple E will determine the underlying economic–strategic foundation of future business models. Some private and public corporate strategies are slowly replacing their performance criterion profit or shareholder value creation towards a form of Triple P criterion. The current (short term) stock market, overvalues and

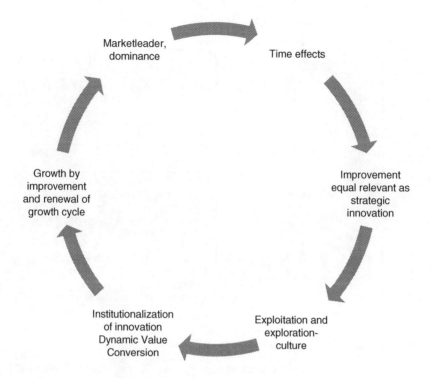

Fig. 4.12 The positive spiral of dynamic value conversion

enhances short term results and underestimates value of Triple P due to the absence of multiplier effects, whereas the dynamic value conversion will force to take into account the long-term effects, the positive spiral effects and its multiplier effects as well. In Table 4.5 the four principal performance criterions are compared.

For this reason the dynamic value conversion criterion has been developed.

Table 4.6 reveals that the dynamic value conversion fits to organizations and societies focusing on the long-term success. For organizations and societies focusing on the short-term success, the dynamic value conversion demonstrates the untapped long-term benefits. In fact Chinese government and organizations apply the dynamic value conversion criterion.

In China, the notion of profit has a different role than in the West. Before the opening of China, the communistic aim of production levels was dominant. After the opening, remnants of this way of thinking still dominated the economy. In order to gain face and acquire esteem or prestige, becoming the biggest or number one is more often a goal of entrepreneurs than maximizing profits. Furthermore, accounting the profits in Chinese organizations is not as developed in Western organizations. The reason is the rather underdeveloped accounting system and the different financing system and stakes of government in the organization. Moreover, on a regular basis within a single organization different accounting and book keeping systems are applied to decrease transparancy of financial results.

Table 4.5 The new performance indicator dynamic value conversion compared to profit, shareholder value, and Triple P

	Profit	Shareholder	Triple P	Dynamic Value conversion
Content	Annual revenues minus costs EBIT/EBITDA is inclusive clock time effects	Net present value of future profits	Profit or net present value and ecological and social performance	Future value conversion including Triple E and Triple P
Time	Short term Static only clock time	Short term Static (only clock time)	Long tern Static (only clock time)	Short term and long term Dynamic by including 7 T effects
Goal	Profit maximization	Maximization of shareholder value Profit per share	Acceptable profit level and realisation aims of stakeholders Added value for business and wider society	Creation of sustainable value Economizing innovation and business development
Advantages	Transparant Underestimation of innovative projects Fits to Anglo Saxon capitalistic system	Current business most relevant and short term new projects with direct commercial value Clear Shareholder most relevant interest group Underestimation of innovative projects Fits to Anglo Saxon capitalistic system	All stakeholders are relevant Underestimation of innovative projects Fits to Rhineland market system	Future orientated Multiplier time effects increase value of innovation (exploration) without neglecting exploitation Combining short and long term orientation Captures real value of innovative ventures Fits to both Western and Chinese market system
Disadvantages	History is dominant Dominance of short term Integration of sustainability impossible	1-dimensional Corporation is money machine Dominance of short term Sustainability only if commerical viable Chance on articifial vaue creation on stock exchange	Relatively qualitative performance measures Triple P do not have common denominator Trade off not transparent Connected or shared value development focusses on involvement of stakeholders (= process not content)	Requires long term thinking and measuring multiplier effects

Table 4.6 Old value creation versus dynamic value conversion

	Old	New
Value creation	Maximizing shareholder value Maximizing profit per share Minimization of costs and transaction costs	Dynamic Value Conversion Value conversion on short and long term 7 T time and multiplier effects on value are considered
Players	CEO is leader and decider for strategy and innovation ('principal') (top-down approach) Managers are executers ('agent') Network of organizations Multi-stakeholder approach (bottom-up approach)	"Principal-agent" scheme is abandoned Entrepreneurs are value creators Stakeholders are provider, creator and executors of strategic innovation CEO keeps end responsibility but main task is creation of context besides strategy formulation (top-down and bottom-up) Symbiosis of private and public organizations can foster long term perspective
Business development	Efficiency and cost savings Growth by adding activities with higher financial value Financial value is more relevant than value conversion	Growth by innovative entrepreneurship Simultaneous efficient exploitation and innovative exploration Dynamic value conversion is more relevant than financial value
Time	Time as clock time Linear time Short time focus and static (1-period)	Value creation by applying time dimensions and multiplier effects Linear and cycle time Long term and short term and dynamic (multiple periods)

But despite the absence of a transparent profit notion, Chinese organizations, supported by long-term aims of the government, do have a short-term and long-term perspective. The short term is about grasping new emerging opportunities and survival in often highly competitive markets. The long-term perspective opens up the opportunity to create strategic innovations and strive for value conversion. Remember the aim of becoming a leading technology country by 2050 (Chap. 3). The 4I emulation process demonstrates the long development of high volume, low profit manufacturing to higher added value activities by improvements in product and process. By learning and accumulation of knowledge and experience, slowly but decisively new innovative industries are being established. The case of the wind and solar industry is illustrative. The Chinese copied and applied proven technology to emulate Western competitors. The fast imitation combined with cost-reducing manufacturing measures created additional economies of scale effects.

Moreover, Chinese factories work 24/7, giving other economies of time advantage. The postponement (economies of time) of radical technology development, the low flexibility of some rivals, and work around the clock gave the Chinese another time advantages. These are the true effects of Triple E leading to low-cost manufacturing.

For this reason the Chinese are already able to produce high-quality products with low prices without subsidies. Taken together, these Triple E advantages together with cooperation with Chinese government are more relevant than the

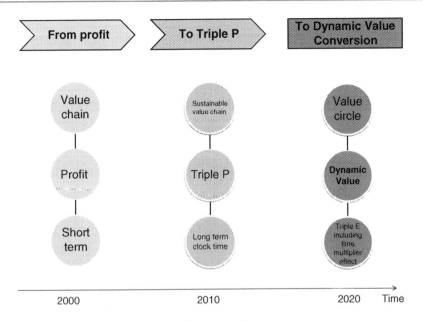

Fig. 4.13 The development in time of performance indicators

argument of cheap capital and dumping. Strategic innovation is more necessary than ever.

The conclusion is that the criterion of Triple P is insufficient to deal with the economic development of Innovative China. The Triple P and/or shared value creation has to be replaced by the dynamic value conversion criterion as presented in Fig 4.13.

The classical value criterion is profit linked to short-term behavior in the whole value chain. The time effects only include the clock time used to calculate net present value.

Moreover, the value chain instead of the value circle is still dominating the market. Furthermore, also here the time effects are dominated by the clock time effect.

The dynamic value criterion includes the seven time effects, and depending on the situation, short or long term are preferred. Due to long-term effects, it is possible to use the value circle as the primary concept for markets.

As demonstrated before, the seven time (7 T) effects have the potential to increase the value conversion. The multiplier effect takes into account the long-term and other time-based effects.

In fact, the Chinese follow the dynamic value conversion principle. For example, the loss of profit due to sharing agreements of alliances with Western firms is compensated by acquiring knowledge and long-term increased market power. However, the biggest challenge with regard to creating dynamic value conversion for the Chinese is lying ahead: how to realize value conversion with strategic innovations?

But Western firms have to apply the dynamic value conversion principle as well for two main reasons. First, the challenge of strategic innovations is evenly great for China as for the West. Second, applying the dynamic value conversion criterion on the alliances between Western and Chinese firms throws another light on the value for Western firms. In the short run, exchanging profits for technology as most Western firms do might be profitable. But on the long run, the dynamic value conversion will be negative due to imitation and low chances on a continuation of cooperation destroying the time needed to earn money. Therefore, a long-term perspective and a China strategy are necessary.

4.5.4 Cross Culture Impact on Innovation

In Chap. 2 the potential devastating and stimulating influences of Chinese culture on innovation have been illustrated. In this section it is tried to concretize and generalize the cultural influence within the strategic innovation theory. Innovation is not the same as innovation. Ask a German what an innovation is and the answer goes in the direction of a new technical product or chemical process. Ask a Chinese what an innovation is and the answer goes in the direction of new technology or large complex mega projects like the Three Gorges Dam or the Olympic Bird's nest in Beijing. Both a German and a Chinese will not so often answer that a new service or a quality system is an innovation as well.

National cultures influence the notion of innovation. With the increasing globalization of innovation function due to dispersed knowledge and research centers, the influence of national culture becomes extremely important.

The increasing globalization increases the influence of different national cultures on the process of innovation. In particular multinational firms who have foreign laboratories, have local R&D facilities, or are thinking about outsourcing innovation functions abroad have to take into account intercultural differences. Behavior, strategy, and organization of the innovation process established in other countries are very likely to be adapted in order to meet the expectations.

An international survey of the leading expert on international cultural differences, Prof. Hofstede (2001) gives insight into the dimensions of what determines a national culture. It must be kept in mind that the results are generalizations on a country level and not on a firm level. In his research five dimensions are considered: power distance, individualism, long-term pragmatic, masculinity, and uncertainty avoidance.

When we apply two of dimensions on innovation, the following illustration is insightful for understanding Innovative China. Of the five dimensions, the individualism and uncertainty avoidance are chosen to have the relevant influence on the intercultural differences on innovation. But one should remind that other cultural issues can interfere with the outcome of these two dimensions. Nevertheless, it gives insight into the power of cultural issues on innovation.

Individualism is important for the way innovation processes are organized. A more individualistic country will have more individual entrepreneurship and competition between firms than in a cooperative country. Uncertainty avoidance is

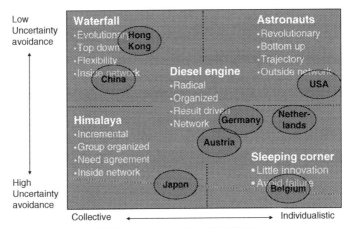

Source: van Someren, 2005, Strategische Innovationen, Gabler Verlag,

Fig. 4.14 National innovation culture

a very good indicator for entrepreneurship. High uncertainty avoidance indicates that innovative initiatives will be relatively low.

Based on these two dimensions giving an indication of the level of entrepreneurship and institutional organization, countries can be grouped along characteristic innovation clusters as shown in Fig. 4.14.

The national innovation culture clearly shows the difference between China and, for example, the USA. Whereas in the USA individual entrepreneurs like Bill Gates can become heroes out of nothing, the Chinese entrepreneur is more dependent on its long-term developed network. An innovation process in a society with low uncertainty avoidance and a high collectivism index, innovation will be evolutionary, top-down oriented, flexible, and very often carried out in a network. The collective dimension in innovation leads to cooperative forms or networks. On the one hand, the collective dimension tempers the revolutionary approach which could disrupt too much the inner workings of the network. On the other hand, the low uncertainty index, which can be interpreted as an entrepreneurial spirit, will look for flexibility. For an extensive analysis of the national culture, see van Someren (2005).

4.6 Context

4.6.1 Twenty-First-Century Leadership

The most important task of top management is not to control shareholder value but to create a context for strategic innovation. The nontechnical and less sexy measures are more important than stimulating a fancy R&D project. It is the most difficult task of any leader to create such an environment. Moreover, the international aspect of doing business also holds for generating and capturing the value of knowledge.

Boards are caught in daily operations. Paradoxically, the core focus of CEOs and boardroom members is not to formulate a strategy, not even a business model. Their core task is twofold: first to mobilize entrepreneurship, creativity, and knowledge or intellectual capital and, second, to build a context in which (cross-cultural) institutional innovation is being created within or between the organizations.

In a research in 2005, 900 human resource managers and 4,500 leaders in other corporate departments across 42 countries and 36 industries were asked the following question[4]: "In your organization, which of the following leader qualities get the most respect?" The results were remarkable. From the Chinese HR managers, 72 % thought creativity and innovation to be important against 39 % of North American HR managers. Working across other cultures and countries was important to 26 % of Chinese managers and only 19 % of the American HR managers. On all questions related to innovation as a leadersip quality giving respect, the American managers scored lower than their Chinese conterparts. The most important ability for both the American non-HR and Chinese non-HR managers was the ability to bring in the numbers (financial targets). With regard to innovation, 16 % of the Chinese answered it to be the most important issue in their organization, but only 4 % of the American leaders shared this opinion.

Explanations are that performance systems do not reward innovations but instead reward operational efficiency, reducing costs or increasing sales. Managers want ideas that work and assurance that it pays off. Innovation cannot bring that. Top leaders did not take high risks during their career; it would have delayed or even closed off their way to the top. Chinese leaders are more prepared to take risks and to experiment, and they have the eagerness to learn. Sometimes they become gamblers. Sometimes they jump on the bandwagon of governmental policies to reduce risk and increase speed and raise their chances as shown in Chap. 2.

The first core task ensures a flood of ideas, improvements, innovations, and revolutionary concepts. In every organization, there are some employees who have a high innovative potential and ideas about creating a next growth wave for the organization. But within the existing power relations, these innovative employees have little or no chance to get their ideas through the new project criteria and formal and informal decision making.

This leads to the second core task to create organizational forms which canalize all these ideas to increase their chances to survive and to offer a methodology which turns the ideas into value conversion. It ensures creating new products and services or even business models for global and local markets on time. Only then managers and employees will be focused on new trends and innovations for the market and the Chinese market in particular. Investing more in R&D and technology is only a small part of managing innovation.

---

[4] Innovation: Why the Short Shrift?, http://www.my.opera.com/devil_inside 21.02.06

These management tasks have to be implemented in order to get ready for the innovation battle soon. There is no time to lose. Leadership in general and specific with regard to innovation is different in China.

Therefore, leaders need a world intelligence to identify, grasp, and exploit the worldwide opportunities. Business leaders need to prepare for the jump from ad hoc innovation projects to institutionalized innovation. The role of top leaders boils down to:

- Formulate tailor-made conditions and assumptions for institutionalized innovation which fits to the organization and their previous experiences.
- Create a team which takes into account criteria such as younger and elderly persons, man and women, diversity in cultural background, experiences inside and outside industry, and employees and other stakeholders.
- Fostering entrepreneurship implying individuals and team to start businesses within the company or together with business partners.
- Stimulating bottom-up processes for innovative initiatives.
- Set up a reward system for successful innovation.
- Allow failures but at the same time organize lessons learned.

For the majority of current business leaders, the above-mentioned tasks are far away from their daily business. If they still believe that any revolution starts at the top, they can reform their own behavior and agenda.

4.6.2 Institutional Innovation

4.6.2.1 Chinese Forms of Institutionalization

Institutional innovation means embedding the innovation function internally or between organizations. This is more than a R&D facility. It implies an organization generating improvements, radical innovations, new possible business models, alliances with other stakeholders, and so on (van Someren, 2005, Fig. 9.15).

China started to formulate their own innovation principles at the beginning of this millennium not only on the macro-level of central government with notions like indigenous innovation and the circular economy but also on the micro-level of the individual organizations.

Chinese firms are masters in copying, improving, and adapting to the requirements of their customers or the needs of the Chinese demand in general. The main current virtue of Chinese entrepreneurs is not basic or revolutionary innovation but rapid adaption to changing (market) conditions and customer preferences. It is a smart strategy to turn knowledge and foresight into cash. A well-known example is the use of Haier's washing machines for cleaning potatoes instead of clothing in the rural areas of China. Initially, the washing machines were not designed for this purpose and broke down on many occasions. Not the marketing department was ordered to communicate that this was not the purpose of the machine but instead the engineers were ordered to adapt the machine able to fulfill the customer's need as cleaning machine for vegetables. Haier adapted its design and technical specifications for the use as vegetable cleaning machine. In fact it was Haier and many other SMEs who developed the

Chinese system of innovation. This Chinese version of dealing with innovation is since 2004 known as Total Innovation Management or TIM (Xu, Jiang & Yang, 2004).

Long before Chinese government came up with an innovation policy, the founder and CEO of Haier Zhang Ruimin had clear ideas about the path of development of Haier. When founded in 1984, a continuous process of improvement and taking chances and realizing opportunities has been implemented from the beginning. Haier started with manufacturing refrigerators but soon diversified in other product groups such as air conditioners, washing machines, televisions, water heaters, personal computers, mobile phones, and kitchen appliances. Haier is now the 4th largest manufacturer of the world.

With hindsight four development stages can be identified: brand building, diversification, internationalization, and global brand. By the way, we leave aside the organizational stages: hierarchical and functional structure (1984–1991), business unit structure (1992–1999), and flatted and process-based network structure (1999–now). In all of the development stages, Chinese self-formulated management principles guided its development. For example, when entering the globalization phase sayings like "where there is a market there must be factory," "we are not selling goods but goodwill," "making new cake," and "winning the added value instead of price war" accompanied the new stage of development (Tao Haier, 2003).

The strategy of Haier was first to learn and improve products by importing technology, to introduce an innovation system, and to expand business in new areas. In all phases two general business principles were applied: differentiation and speed. With differentiation market segments were created but more importantly every product was modified to specific needs of each segment. For example, in rural areas a washing machine was used to clean vegetables which required technical adaptations to meet this appliance.

Furthermore, speed characterized the primary process of satisfying the demand of customers as fast as possible. Although its strategy is built around technical innovations, the main foundation of its success is based on a combination of several strategic innovations. The idea of continuous innovation has been adopted from the beginning. The reason behind is that never delay work that can be done today and a 1 % improvement every day leads to a doubling of performance in 70 days.

These ideas formed the foundation of two organizational innovations: Overall Every Control and Clear (OEC) Management, and market chain and people first. OEC means overall control and supervision of every employee every day. Market chain is based on IT and corporate culture of improvement to generate an efficient and fast flow of goods to customer. During the globalization phase, it also refers to local design, local manufacturing, and local marketing, leading to increased productivity and new business development. With regard to human resource management, Haier recognized that people are core to their success. Employees are compensated based on team performance, but more importantly, everyone is thought to be an innovator.

With regard to innovation, Haier developed Total Innovation Management (TIM). Core of TIM is a technical innovation platform supported by innovations for market, strategy, and organization. Haier's approach represents already in the early 2000s indigenous innovation, thereby breaking through the pattern of imitation

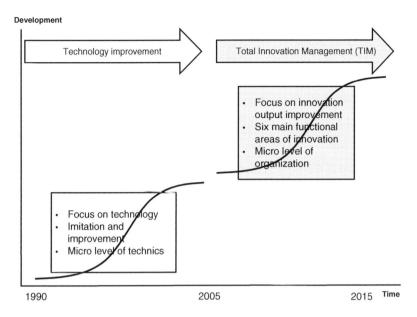

Development

Technology improvement

Total Innovation Management (TIM)

- Focus on innovation output improvement
- Six main functional areas of innovation
- Micro level of organization

- Focus on technology
- Imitation and improvement
- Micro level of technics

1990   2005   2015 Time

Fig. 4.15 Chinese version of innovation: Total Innovation Management

and improving and improving again. Haier's approach enabled the enterprise to become a world-class manufacturer. The aim is to create added value and accumulate and improve core competency. According to Liang, Zheng and Xu (2003), TIM strategy innovation delivers blueprint, culture innovation is precondition, management innovation is operational base and organizational innovation is structural pledge, institution innovation is stimulator, market innovation is orientation, and innovation synergy is approach. Meanwhile, Haier has set up an international innovation network with spending around 6 % of revenues in R&D.

As Fig. 4.15 shows, compared to the improvement principles, Total Innovation Management is focusing not only on technology but on nontechnical aspects as well. The predominat focus on technics ahs been replaced by six areas of innovation, a stakeholder as innovator approach and the individual firm is the most relevant level of innovation.

By lack of own technological breakthroughs, Haier felt back on the old Chinese tradition of focusing on nontechnical innovations (see Chap. 2). This case also shows that, initially, Haier did not follow the massive preference of government for technology, but it did make use of the allowance of government to develop business outside of China. Haier's leaders did it their way. That is also possible in China.

TIM is the Chinese version of a systems approach to innovation which fits to the holistic characteristic of thinking and developing new concepts. The main elements of TIM are the following: strategic innovation, technologic innovation, marketing innovation, cultural innovation, organizational innovation, and mechanism innovation. These notions do not have the same content as in the West. Moreover, the focus on innovation and nontechnical innovation does not mean that the bias for technology has been disappeared. The notion of non-technological innovation is dominantly used, also in the West, to improve and foster technological development. Furthermore, the elements of TIM are all functional areas of innovation or different angles of perspective. In the Western hemisphere, similar partition of the innovation area has been introduced like financials innovation, eco-innovation, and social innovation.

With regard to the current stage of the Chinese economy, TIM indeed offers an improvement to the imitation strategies. For the Chinese it fits to their culture of trying to grasp the whole picture, and it supports organizations to make their innovation system better. But the TIM approach is not very widely used and widespread management tool among the majority of Chinese organizations. But diffusion and appliance will not take very long.

4.6.2.2 Mobilization of Entrepreneurship, Knowledge, and Creativity

Passion for innovation has to be reinvented. It requires the mobilization of entre-preneurship, knowledge, and creativity within the organization or between related business partners (van Someren, 2005). This notion comprises more than the now-adays popular notion of social innovation. Social innovation in the classical definition deals with empowerment and bottom-up processes within the enterprise. Mobilization goes beyond the border of the enterprise and involves entrepreneurship as well; otherwise, only information and knowledge is collected without a sound business plan. Moreover, as we will see, bottom-up is not sufficient, and top-down remains part of governing innovation processes.

In most instances, corporate strategy and innovations are decided in board meetings, sometimes with support of external consultants. The chosen strategy is then communicated and the implementation is the responsibility of middle management. Periodically, often once a year, strategy sessions are planned to evaluate and adapt existing aims. Often these meetings are characterized by fights between managers about defending own interests and budget allocation.

As a result, the available entrepreneurship, knowledge, and creativity are hardly used to create a corporate strategy or a bold innovation plan. Moreover, the same holds for the active involvement of clients, suppliers, or even general public. Nowadays, with help of Internet, new possibilities like crowd sourcing arise to get valuable input.

Therefore, the gold mine of own employees or external parties is largely neglected by many top managers. It requires a complete different role from the board. Instead of being responsible for the content of the strategy and innovation, they should get responsible for the mobilization of their gold mine consisting of stakeholders representing entrepreneurship, knowledge, and creativity. It also implies giving away power. Paradoxically, it requires very strong and confident leaders, involving others to contribute to creating strategic innovation. But when ideas from employees are used, the implementation is not an issue anymore because one gets the opportunity to implement your own ideas. Furthermore, top managers are now asked to be in charge of the bottom-up and top-down process. In Table 4.7 the advantages and challenges of such an organized bottom-up–top-down strategic innovation process are presented.

Table 4.7 Advantages and challenges of organized bottom-up–top-down strategic innovation process

Advantages	Challenges
Mining and exploitation of golden ideas	Top leadership required
Stimulating intrapreneurship	Absence of pre-fab solutions
Unexpected insights and opportunties	Judging far out of the box ideas requires entrepreneurship and not ROI criteria
Large scope of output from improvements to renewal of business	Courage needed to implement new solutions
Maximum motivation of employees and other stakeholders	Not a once in a life time event
Empowerment in practice	Dealing with top-down cultures
Less problems with implementation	Time invested in internal resources and time versus pays back time by new business opportunities, motivation and employability
No invasion of consultants needed	First step to institutional innovation
Cheaper and more effective	Use of stakeholders, social media, crowd sourcing requires strategic planning and excellent communication
Fun factor number one	

Source: van Someren, 2005

When the leaders of such a strategic innovation process meet the requirements and challenges, then the advantages dwarf the efforts and challenges to overcome.

For Chinese organizations, the challenge to work along a combined bottom-up–top-down strategic innovation process will be a huge challenge. In Chap. 2, it has demonstrated that the requirements of a combined top-down bottom approach do not always fit to a culture used to strong leaders most often acting top-down. But these kinds of approaches are necessary to realize their dream of becoming an innovative society.

A special case of the mobilization of human resources is the worldwide dispersed Chinese. It is estimated that more than 40 million Chinese are living outside China. It is the greatest diaspora of any people in the world. Moreover, these Chinese feel connected with their home country, and in fact they are the largest investors in mainland China. They are locally connected because of forming their own guanxi within family and in the China towns. Some of the overseas Chinese are well connected, well educated, entrepreneurial, and often on the forefront of new developments. For China, the Chinese diaspora is a global goldmine which is increasingly discovered by Chinese governmental leaders.

4.6.2.3 Bottom-Up and Top-Down Governance

The requirement for institutional innovation is to allow bottom-up innovation combined with top-down governance. But in practice the right mixture of bottom-up and top-down is a real challenge and master test for top management. The good news is that it is one of the most rewarding and necessary organizational innovations to achieve institutional innovation. In a Western context, the core of strategic innovation is the renewal of existing business practices bottom up, in which entrepreneurial activity is key to success (van Someren, 1991b, 2005, Wolcott & Lippitz, 2010). This focus on bottom-up business models created under uncertainty is a crucial difference with the totally system-oriented, largely top-down transition management and innovation system renewals, which has clearly defined goals and sometimes projected technologies.

For Chinese top leaders, it would require a fundamental other approach to their leadership model. Instead of being the boss and giving hierarchical orders, the more supporting and serving role to foster innovation becomes the central role.

4.6.3 Business Development

4.6.3.1 Risk Perception

The risk perception within an organization determines the organization and scope of the institutionalization of innovation. Innovation is not about being open or closed but about the trade-off between sharing risks and costs and grasping the benefits. This is dependent on uncertainty of available technologies, uncertainty about market expectations, and scale including deep pockets of your business.

Chinese business strategies are characterized by grasping almost every opportunity. As shown in Chap. 2, the entrepreneurial attitude together with the historic window of opportunity given in the past decades to develop business, the market opportunities, and to be acknowledged in society gives Chinese business people wings. From Western perspective, they do not fit in mainstream strategy thinking which tries to limit strategic development along two main lines: cost (cost leadership) and differentiation (focus and niches). In the 1960s Western business world, the organizational form of conglomerates was regarded to be one of the options to reduce business risks. Nowadays, lacking a focus is regarded to be nonstrategic behavior. MNEs, also pushed by the interest of their shareholders, are supposed to have a clear focus implying low economies of scope.

Asian organizational structures show a contrary movement: in Japan we encountered zaibatsus and keiretsus, and in Korea we have the chaebols. These often family-based conglomerates reflect the networking and grasping opportunities behavior. Asian strategic eyes are different than Western strategic eyes. In China the governmental supported firms seem to have no limits, and every opportunity is added to companies' activities. This behavior can be explained by the vast unlimited opportunities in a growing economy. But it also belongs to the Asian culture of which the networks have a relevant role. In the West corporations are relatively stand-alone and uncertainties have to be reduced by limiting focus on short term or creating conglomerates, thereby hedging internal risks of different business activities.

In Asian countries the business risks are dispersed along the partners of the whole network and not a single corporation. Moreover, the governmental support reduces the business risk. But the social cohesion based on network ties is changing in Asia. Within families and family businesses the social security of children taking care of parents, respectively, lifelong job security is eroding. In Japanese keiretsus and Korean chaebols, these old traditions are under pressure due to market forces.

Government should take over the role of family by investing in social programs and state-owned firms.

Finally, Chinese strategic thinking is also based on big holistic view of the future to keep it in one hand and under control. The old dream of any entrepreneur is to be a monopolist or at least a powerful tycoon. As a result strategies do have a complete different content and direction and description. However, this fits in Chinese thinking of long-term aims and extreme flexibility to react on new market circumstances and adapting business activities accordingly. The takeovers of IBM's PC division and Swedish Volvo by Chinese firms illustrate the speed of handling as soon as opportunities arise.

As a consequence of these characteristics, several companies follow the same strategy of grasping the same opportunities. The result is a fast buildup of supply followed by cutthroat price competition due to overcapacity. This situation can be seen in the industries for shoes, toys, electronics, solar panels, and cars. Another feature of Chinese businessmen pops up as soon as grasping opportunities is mingled with high-risk behavior. This cocktail leads to gambling behavior which can be often seen in Chinese society. The eagerness to create indigenous innovation often leads to gambling behavior as soon as new technology policies are issued.

4.6.4 Governance

All these aspects demonstrate that fostering strategic innovation comprises more than the current hype of social innovation. The Western hype of social innovation is an important aspect but only a relatively small part of the total picture. Strategic or market governance will become more relevant than corporate governance or social innovation in the future. Strategic governance comprises issues like new symbiosis between private and public organizations, Quadruple Helix, membrane innovation, cooperation, and the illusion of network organizations as dominating organizational forms of the twenty-first century.

4.6.4.1 New Symbiosis Between Private and Public Organizations

The governance of your organization or network also determines the process of value creation. The replacement of the profit criterion by Triple P is an example. But also the different forms of cooperation between the public and private sector forces to integrate private and public interests beyond profit. In Western countries, a common organizational form of cooperation is the public–private partnership (PPP). However, these PPP constructions often have a loose and single project-based form of cooperation compared to state-owned companies in China. The strong symbiosis between governmental organizations and business organizations in China shows successful outcomes. But this is not the only and best solution. Other solutions can work as long as they are carried out consistently. But in Western free-market situation, these forms of symbiosis prove to be very difficult and uncommon. In case of Airbus, the EU was able to set up a successful alliance between governments and business.

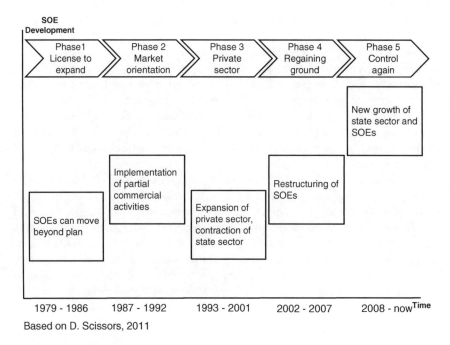

Fig. 4.16 Fall and rise of SOEs

The future challenges like creating an innovative society or sustainability are not only huge from a physical perspective but also from a financial perspective. The financials are not only costs but much more investments in a new sustainable economy, resulting in revenues for successful firms. Simultaneously, there is a power side as well.

Western governments and policy makers were blinded by their idea of a knowledge economy in which knowledge, intangible capital supported by ICT, would be the main production factor. Natural resources were completely out of sight and were regarded to be something for factor markets and stock exchanges. The exception is of course oil and gas. But all our products and especially services are dependent on materials. Computers and batteries are partly made of scarce materials. Capturing those markets is a lifeline for future economies. China has discovered this already in the mid-1990s and started to make a strategic resource plan assuring materials flow to their factories. Getting access to natural resources needs big large-scale firms supported by the government. Not only natural resources need governmental support but also the development of new industries is often depending on governmental support. Also here, the Chinese government supports in different ways favored firms which become the growth and development vehicle for future prosperity and market presence.

Therefore, the role of government is not to transfer subsidies or be the owner of the venture but to ensure long-term commitment by, for example, opening new markets and supporting global expansion.

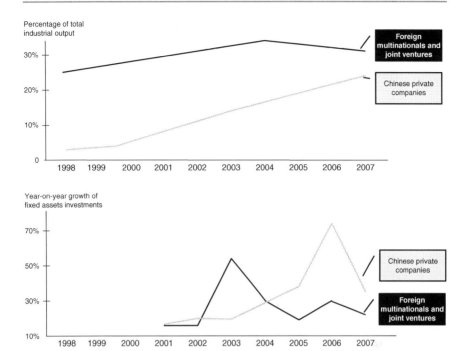

Fig. 4.17 Chinese-versus foreign-owned private-owned companies (POEs)

Governmental support for ventures is a common behavior in centralistic governed societies. Recent history is a huge transition from pure central planning to a mixed system of central and bounded free enterprising. Figure 4.16 shows the different successive policies regarding the state and private companies.

Bounded free enterprising means that even private firms have to watch closely and carefully central and local governmental policies and aims. The rise and fall of SOEs and private ventures is largely explained more by central governmental policies instead of market forces. Furthermore, the economic development and growth by central planning and selecting key and strategic sectors requires organizations under full control and regulatory protection of the government. Contrary to Western governmental policies, the Chinese governmental boundaries often more represent opportunities and chances than limitations. Only the ones who have excellent ties with the government are able to turn the opportunity into cash and profit.

But compared to the non-Chinese (foreign) private companies and joint venture, the private Chinese companies are gaining influence as Fig. 4.17 indicates.

In Fig. 4.17 the danger of becoming too dependent on Chinese markets is becoming clear. Whereas share of Chinese revenues in total revenues of Western enterprises is increasing, the investments and industrial output of Chinese rivals are

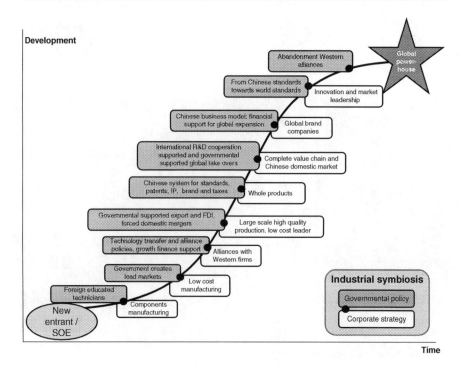

Fig. 4.18 China's growth strategy: from corporate governance towards industrial governance

surging. As soon as the Chinese rival is also capable to create their own innovations, Western firms have to prepare for difficult times and intensified competition.

Although the private-owned enterprises (POEs) are steadily gaining influence, the role of the central and local governments is in China still substantial. For both SOEs and POEs, the governmental policies are often leading for their strategic actions and aims. In Fig 4.18 this is illustrated.

China's industrial strategy is broadening the notion of corporate governance towards industrial governance. Along the whole growth curve and the jump to a new growth curve, the link between private business and government is relatively close. To the governmental support along the growth curve belong actions like the selection of key sectors, preferred companies, governmental organizations as launching customers, cheap credit facilities, and support for global expansion. In this respect, sometimes the central government in conformity with industrial strategic policies tries to influence the industry structure. For this reason the notion of symbiosis is used. This symbiosis is on the level of the industry and the macro-interest of China as a nation. State companies have to adapt to market circumstances; strategic sectors have to be protected and guided into a new era of global competition and securing interests of China. These interests are linked to industries like natural resources, agro food, finance, and technology sectors.

In this situation, Chinese organizations have to be supported to gain access into worldwide markets. In strategic sectors, selected companies get indeed financial

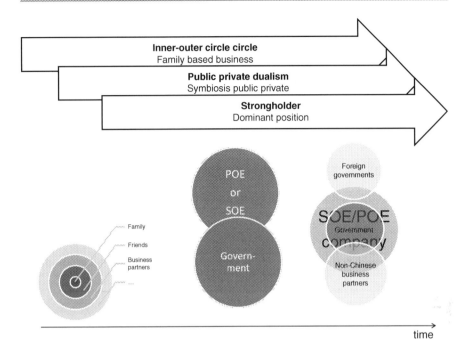

Fig. 4.19 The main players in the strategic governance

governmental support to secure interests. Governmental support does not only come from the central government; local governments are also involved. The end result is often overcapacity and intensive competition on Chinese market.

China is counterattacking the Western growth of market shares by means of both private businesses and the revival of SOEs. The Western business strategies of business as usual and China as a new important market are insufficient to survive in the long term.

Furthermore, there are a lot of cases in which, due to governmental support, technical installations have been build, but they are not operative. The reason is that competences to operate the installations are absent. Governmental support has a preference for eye-catching technical equipment, leading to overcapacity or inefficient technical installations. They are examples of ghost cities and idle windmill parks. One strategic way out is to enter worldwide markets as is the case for solar panels. For many Chinese firms, foreign markets are more profitable than home market. Governmental support allows low prices, sometimes even dumping, giving Western firms difficult times. But there is also another side. China has a tradition of entrepreneurship and private business. In Fig. 4.19 the parallel developments of family business, the symbiotic relation between private and government, and the strive to dominate the world by means of strongholders are presented.

In every relation between individuals and organizations, the inner–outer circle determines the behavior and result of the enterprise. This inner–outer circle idea comes back in any other form of strategic governance. The private-owned enterprises

(POEs) have a long tradition in China, but at the same time, the state-owned enterprises (SOEs) have become more and more based on capitalistic principles.

In the symbiotic relation between private and government, the mutual dependency and overlap of interests are larger than in the West. With the globalization of Chinese business, the foreign partners are formally linked up with the POEs and SOEs. But in most instances, and even with short-term successes, the non-Chinese partners will always be part of the outer circle. The foreign partners are used to catapult the Chinese enterprise into world market, but they will never be involved in the real strategic plans of the main Chinese partner.

Central government is aware of the behavior of Chinese entrepreneurs and local governments to imitate not only successful Western companies but also successful Chinese firms. The result of cutthroat competition and overcapacity is no surprise. However, cutthroat competition and overcapacity is a threat for the Chinese capitalistic system and hinders the realization of the aims mentioned in the 5-year plans. It is regarded to be an unhealthy economic situation, and governmental interference is necessary. One of the instruments is forced mergers and acquisitions to restore a perceived ideal or healthy supply structure. In the wind sector, this measure has been used to influence industrial structure. But deals and investments are also used to acquire the necessary technical knowledge, securing resources or access to markets.

In 2001 Chinese enterprises spent $ 1.5 billion buying Western firms, and in 2011, it has increased to $ 47 billion (Het Financieele Dagblad, 22.03.12). It becomes clear that merger and acquisition deals are an important instrument to realize the expansion from pure manufacturing towards mastering the whole value chain or value circle. It demonstrates the relevance of getting access to new markets besides acquiring new R&D, technology, and resources. But in both strategies, Chinese firms have to learn a lot before the Chinese Dragons lose their innocence. A quote from a Chinese Minister Wang on overseas acquisitions says all (China Daily, 13.09.10): "Just because you can doesn't mean you should." Wang then added, "Many Chinese companies have strong balance sheets and are looking to make acquisitions overseas. Think of how many Western multinationals are truly successful in China. There are not many. And they've been here for 30 years." For Chinese companies to be successful overseas, he said, they need to understand local markets, be patient, and have strong business plans. "Financing deals are easy but integrating operations, managing very different cultures and people are issues that are extremely difficult to solve." Therefore, the Chinese road for the future innovative dragons will be long as well.

In China, the number of private businesses is exceeding state-owned companies. These family-owned businesses are financed by family members or network members. Meanwhile, these growing firms form a growing class of SMEs and sometimes become a MNE. They operate independent of banks and make them very fast moving and flexible. They will become the backbone besides the SOEs or government-supported enterprises of future Chinese economy like the German Mittelstand (SMEs). But then they will have to be as innovative and get away from earning the quick buck.

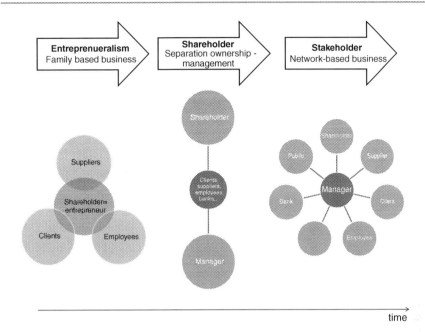

Fig. 4.20 Main players in strategic governance

4.6.4.2 Quadruple Helix

The cooperation between private corporations, knowledge institutes, and government is one of dealing with increasing the innovation output. Particularly, the commercialization is in Europe a big bottleneck. This form of cooperation known as Triple Helix is, in the EU despite governmental stimulation, still untapped. Of course many successful examples can be found; some of those have a large tradition like the contribution of, for example, the Fraunhofer Institute to their commercial clients. Also in Belgium, Flemish examples show an increase in successful commercialization of research results. But the emulation principle is already at work. China has shown as that with their earned money and with hard work, they now finance new activities. Government investments are increasing in all kind of areas like securing natural resources, backing favored companies, building new industries, buying strategic positions in bonds, ports and take overs of firms. Because of the huge sums involved and the scope of this finance instrument, this new phenomenon might be called the Quadruple Helix as a solution to the Innovation Valley of Death. The Quadruple Helix is a very tight and close cooperation between private or public corporations, knowledge institutes, government, and Finance department.

Figure 4.20 presents the main development of strategic governance with regard to influence of stakeholders on strategic course of the organization.

The family business with own-invested money can only survive when client needs are being identified and satisfied, a good relation with suppliers guarantees the timely delivery of required quality input, and motivated employees contribute in the long run to the business. Family businesses have a very close, tight, and long-

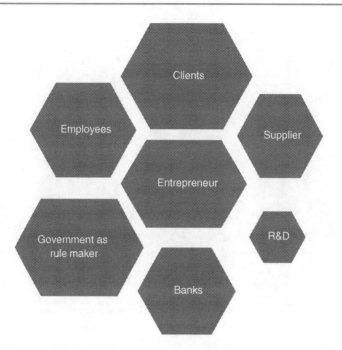

Fig. 4.21 Loose network in the EU

term relation with their closest stakeholders. The integration of ownership and management (better: entrepreneurialism) contributes to a market conform growth and development of the business.

The separation between ownership and management has long been regarded to be key to unlimited growth. However, with the power struggle between management and shareholders, the long-term focus of client satisfaction and value conversion has been replaced by short-term profit behavior. Creating shareholder value became the new mantra. With the rise of sustainability and the return of entrepreneurialism, the stakeholder approach regained relevance in determining the strategic course of the corporation. But the potential of stakeholders being involved in the strategic innovation process is still underdeveloped. The perceived network society is believed to be based on knowledge sharing, cocreating, and open innovation. Weighing all the interests distracts from the actual business of strategic innovation, creating new value propositions in a real world of intensified rivalry and claiming resources and knowledge. But differences between the EU and the USA exist as Figs. 4.21 and 4.22 reveal.

In the EU, the characteristic of the networks boils down to ad hoc unorganized or not coordinated spider webs without spider. It is often a loose network organization without clear leader or leader structures. Equality and less power distance lead to bottom-up and less acceptance of strong leadership. But innovation requires strong top-down leadership as well.

Compared to the EU, the USA has stronger ties between the innovative entrepreneur and the knowledge institutions, government, and its financiers. In the USA

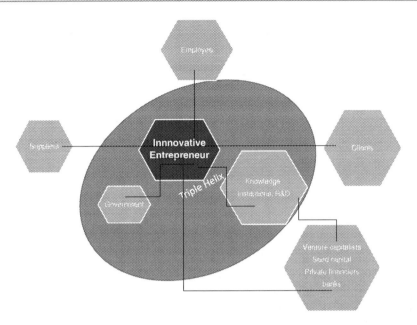

Fig. 4.22 Strong ties network with the USA

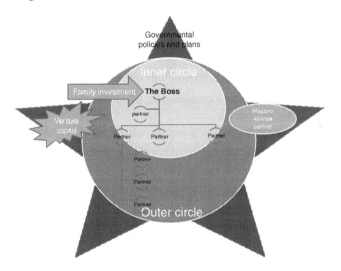

Fig. 4.23 Clear leadership and hierarchical structures in Chinese network

the innovative entrepreneur acts as a spider in the center. Also, multinational companies like Nike or Apple act like a spider in the web. But these two companies are exceptional and not representative for every industry.

In many cases, Triple Helix as supporting organization can be identified, although the role of local US government is often limited to creating favorable situations for industries. However, the fancy Triple Helix structure hides the persistent characteristic of short-term focus and difficulties of long-term strategic plans.

Based upon the inner–outer circle, the relationship building, and harmony, the center piece in China's economy is the network. In Fig. 4.23 the clear role of the boss and the hierarchical relations in the formal and informal network demonstrates a different network organization than in the EU and the USA.

Whereas in the USA the innovative entrepreneur is the spider in the web, the Chinese entrepreneur has to act within more complex structures. Although the Chinese boss can act as the boss, he or she has to take into account the interests of the inner circle and all other partners. Bosses can turn into spiders. Business partners can turn into rivals. In the former case, the risk of missing innovation opportunities and disregarding bottom-up initiatives increase. In the latter case, the risk of being emulated is high.

But the selection criteria are not always performance or innovation output related but network related. Eventual underperformance is compensated by both substantial support and protection by government, enabling the enterprise to catch up backlogs.

With regard to financing, Chinese entrepreneurs prefer investments by family due to the trust between family members. When demand for capital exceeds the family resources, other sources come into play such as venture capitalists. Increasingly, the Chinese venture capitalists are not only providers of capital but they are like viruses. The virus tries to get hold of the enterprise by infecting top management and get direct control. This is different from an arm's length governance by Western investors.

In the background the governmental policies and plans always play a decisive role in investments and business development. As shown in Chap. 3, the role of the Chinese government cannot be neglected, and they act as the invisible hand and sometimes visible hand.

Furthermore, the role of the Western alliance partner is almost without exception at the borderline and seldom in the inner circle. Blinded by Chinese hospitality and efforts to build up close relationships, Western managers often seem to forget their real place in Chinese network.

From an economic perspective, the main participants in this network are the family, business relations, and the government. The consequence is that formulating a corporate strategy or an innovation program has to involve all the consequences for the network and not only the individual firm. Because of the close family ties and early relationships within school, military, and university, the Chinese network is closer and more long-term orientated than the Western networks. This requires different thinking and applying different context for making strategic decisions and creating and implementing strategic innovations.

4.6.4.3 Membrane Innovation Instead of Closed and Open Innovations
Nowadays, thinking about innovation is dominated by the notions of cooperation and open innovation (Chesbrough, 2006). Open innovation is opposite of closed innovation. These concepts are not wrong but they represent a very myopic view and one of the latest hypes in innovation theory rather than the real world of the innovative entrepreneur and organizations.

Strategic innovation theory offers a different view and solution. The defenders of open innovation state that cooperation is needed because of the so-called network society and the involvement of many private and public parties inside and outside the value chain. The focus is on cooperation with regard to the creation of the innovation because no single organization can develop the large quantity of R&D and technical opportunities. From a dynamic view, this is only relevant at a certain short period in time, due to five typical situations.

First, it is not clear which new potential technologies or nontechnical innovations will break through. Second, R&D costs are extremely high due to absolute volume and/or duration of investment. Third, the risks or costs of failure are high. Fourth, essential knowledge is not available. It is a time period in which the absolute value conversion is relatively low because of initial investments, low revenues, and high risks. Fifth, the trend towards an integration of enterprises instead of a loose open network is also stimulated by the economies of time effect based on faster innovation rates (e.g., new product development) and reduced uncertainty resulting in increased economies of scale or scope effect. A loose network can develop into, first, an alliance by means of swap of shares or investments followed by, second, a full integration by merger.

Therefore, the dynamic value conversion principle predicts that on the short run open innovation might be wise to do. But as soon as the dominant technology emerges, risks are lowered, critical knowledge is available, scale and speed of development become crucial, and costs are lower closed, innovation will be preferred in order to be able to capture and accumulate profits in the long run within a single enterprise. This enterprise becomes the new powerhouse based on applying the dynamic value conversion principle and "closed" innovation. Therefore, open and closed, although fancy, are not the right notions to describe the economic reality.

The strategic behavior in practice by enterprises and knowledge institutes is better described by membrane innovations instead of open or closed innovation. Therefore, the key question is not whether innovation should be open or closed but to foresee new developments, to react flexibly and on time, to accumulate knowledge faster than others, and to build up a new power base (van Someren, 2005). Some knowledge is shared and some is kept top secret. Electronics represent one of the main areas of competition for creating a unique value of the automotive sector in the future, and closed innovation is the result.

In time, open innovation becomes interesting only when some knowledge is not available, common knowledge which can be shared between competitors or depreciates very quickly in value because of volatile markets and fast innovation rates. Other forms of innovation development include the use of suppliers, customers, or other stakeholders to support and contribute to innovations. This kind of innovation management has already been applied by many firms, especially small- and medium-sized enterprises and family businesses. Nowadays, it is rediscovered and labeled open innovation. From a dynamic point of view, the mantra of open innovation reflects a static and one-sided world view.

However, open and closed innovation is a simplification of the realistic world of firms and entrepreneurs. Much more important is the creative entrepreneur who identifies and uses information and knowledge in and outside of his own firm and transforms it into new products, services, and business models. Every time the aim is to create something unique in which open innovation has its limits and does not fit the true aim of entrepreneurial activity. No system of open innovation can beat the availability and creativity of such an entrepreneur.

The innovative entrepreneur does not think in terms of open and closed innovations, transition management, system change, and any other notion used by academics and policy makers. The innovative entrepreneur thinks but, even more, acts in terms of new trends combined with existing bottlenecks in the existing business model and opportunities emerging from this situation. It is a continuous process of entrepreneurial acting in time under highly uncertain conditions.

4.6.4.4 Competition Versus Cooperation

Linked with open and closed innovation is the topic of competition versus cooperation. Internet and IT enables the atomization of businesses and the creation of network firms. Many trend watchers and management gurus predict the end of big corporation and the start of the network economy based in small innovative firms. Cooperation has the future. Additionally, the open innovation concept reinforces the idea of alliances and cooperation between partners to create new products and services. The knowledge economy will consist of a worldwide network of organizations dependent on cooperation.

But what about competition? Will competition be something of the past? Of course not. The future global economy will show an intensified competition. In particular, when the aim of China is to become the number one and be independent of Western technology, then the only outcome will be more competition. The SIT predicts that cooperation and allowing open innovation between business partners will only be continued as long as uncertainty about new technologies remains and risks and costs sharing is profitable for involved partners. A soon as a new dominant technology becomes apparent, the open innovation and cooperation will transform in closed innovation and competition (van Someren, 2005). This is exactly what the Chinese firms often do with their Western partners.

Therefore, emulation consists of both cooperation and competition. From a Western perspective, applying hypes like cooperation and open innovation will not be successful in dealing with Innovative China. From a dynamic angle, the current uncertainties and unknowns about winning technologies, new large markets, production factors, the shift of political and economic power away from Western countries, and many more lead to intermediate stage of cooperation. This intermediate stage is necessary to await for the breakthrough of dominant innovation in fields like biotech, nanotech, Internet business models, batteries, healthcare organization, integrated logistics, and so on.

Many Chinese firms follow the above-described dynamic view on market development. As long as Chinese R&D, technology, business formats, and international experience are insufficient compared to Western organizations, alliances and cooperation agreements will be preferred. At the moment the technology or business format has reached Western standards, the time has come to abandon Western partners and develop a Global Chinese Dragon Power player. Again, the dynamic value conversion is at work: Western alliance partners are promised midterm profits for which short-term technology transfer has to be paid for market entrance and development. When midterm profit moment in time has arrived, the Chinese enterprises have accumulated the knowledge and developed business. Only when alliance partners own new technology or other advantages, the cooperation will be continued.

Also a new world order is being shaped by China by creating their closed network of domestic interests. Recently, in European policies the notion of being smart is often used when innovative solutions are being sought for. What smart in practice means is not explained anywhere; it is an empty word. Nobody dears to ask what possibly could be meant by being smart; asking it would show apparently the opposite. By their worldwide FDI, the Chinese show how smart policies could look like. This shows that as soon as the dominant developments become clear, large integrated firms will be organized in order to dominate their trade. Google, COSCO, and Haier show this. For example, Inner Mongolia Baotou Steel Rare-Earth (Group) Hi-Tech Co Ltd. is the country's largest light rare earth producer. This company will further consolidate companies from Fujian and Jiangxi provinces in order to control mining but also distribution of rare metals. China provides 90 % of rare earth minerals global supply, but China's reserves are only 30 % of global total (China Daily, 080311). This is the Chinese interpretation of sustainability and circular economy.

4.6.4.5 The Future Domination of Network Organizations Is an Illusion

According to the current mainstream management thought leaders, network organizations and business models based on network will replace integrated or single hierarchical operating organizations. The main reason to their opinion is that information technologies and open innovation allows to have diffused activities and ownership is not relevant anymore. The future belongs to cooperation based on sharing information and knowledge, leading to mutual prosperity of the network partners.

The strategic innovation theory (SIT) offers an alternative view (van Someren, 2005). Current popular notions like co-innovation and sharing knowledge within network of firms are only temporarily answers in times of high uncertainty about dominant technologies and markets. As a result, risk can be spread by spreading technology development among several payers and alliances. As soon as a certain technology or business format becomes dominant, the networks will disappear and (vertically) integrated firms will take over. Therefore, along the growth curve, cooperation and competition alternate depending on the market situation.

As soon as improvements and radical rival solutions come to market, the need for competition and closed innovation increases and the role and interests of cooperation partners can change dramatically as well (see also van Someren, 1991b, 2005).

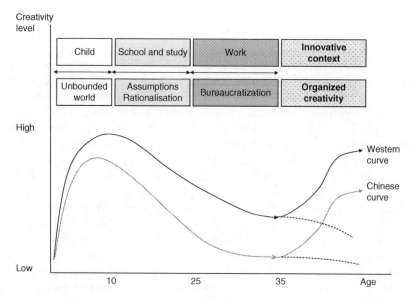

Fig. 4.24 Innovative context creates U-turn in creativity output

4.7   Organized Creativity

It is the task of top management to create an innovative context with organized freedom in which creativity can flourish. The rationale behind these core tasks is presented in Fig. 4.24.

The creativity curve demonstrates that the current system of education and organization does not support the desired indigenous innovation. Moreover, the historical background and appliance of philosophy within the context of the institutional setting of dynasties, as discussed in Chap. 2, do not foster creativity and innovation. This does not mean that the old philosophies are abundant; they should be applied in a different manner in a different context. Within the Chinese paradoxical world, this is possible and a recipe for survival.

Children live in an unbounded world with a maximum freedom of creativity because they are not hindered by knowledge, institutional boundaries, and bureaucratic rules. But as soon as children go to school, grow up, follow a study, and start as an employee, the creativity level decreases. We learn about the world how it is, why only a certain answer is right, and we follow orders and we act because the organization has always acted like that. Assumptions and rationalization make our truth. The space for creativity is very low. Therefore, creating new products, services, and business models requires a certain context to flourish. The implementation of an innovative context creates a U-turn in the creativity output. Only the CEO and his board can achieve this. But also when raising children and during studies, the U-turn can be made earlier by creating an innovative context.

Creative entrepreneurs are the main drivers of strategic innovation, although the initial move can be made by new policies, e.g., the zero emission laws in California state. Entrepreneurs start various initiatives, small and big ones and local and global ones, now and later in time; the total effects of which taken together may in hindsight be called a transition or paradigm shift.

As encountered in earlier chapters, the Chinese way of raising children and the education system based on knowledge reproduction create the opposite of an innovative context. In recent history there exists a dividing line between the traditional ways of raising and educating the Chinese people. As Chap. 2 showed, the Confucian tradition skilled and trained people in knowledge reproduction, and the main attention was on "soft" studies such as poetry and arts.

Moreover, the whole Chinese society put a pressure on children to follow the desired system of reproduction instead of studying societal studies paying attention to, for example, societal organization or popular Western studies like politics. As a result "safe" studies such as languages, arts, and history were popular. But the opening of China by Deng caused a dividing line with the past and tradition.

Besides education and Confucian tradition, the top-down organization, and the dominant position of the boss in Chinese organization, the potential creativity is bounded or even limited. The positive effects of the low uncertainty avoidance combined with the collective dimension of the national culture, as discussed earlier in this chapter, are lowered by the internal organization and the role of the boss based on Confucian heritage. But the Confucian tradition is not only a drawback; it can be turned into an advantage.

At the moment that the power of the people and the role of the boss are used to commit themselves to a defined road to innovation, Chinese enterprises can be hard to beat. But the prerequisite is to find a Chinese way of mobilization of entrepreneurship, knowledge, and creativity without the boss losing face.

Accidental or not, the opening of China coincided with the zenith of technical innovation theories in the Western scientific literature as shown in the beginning of this chapter. New safe studies on the other side of the scientific spectrum came into reach such as biotechnology and chemistry. A shift from extreme soft studies to extreme hard studies occurred. Again, the yard stick was the Western stock of knowledge of technical studies which initially were reproduced. The behavior or attitude to critically analyze stock of knowledge or to create new disciplines was largely absent.

Therefore, the copy–paste mentality is not born from laziness or improper behavior but from long-term historical institutional development of the founding philosophy and educational system. Changing the copycat behavior towards indigenous innovation requires going back to the basis of raising and educating people. Moreover, it is a very time-consuming process to implement, and its effects will take even at least a generation.

For these reasons the Chinese creativity curve is lower than in the West. As soon as these people arrive in private or public organizations, the aim of indigenous innovation will be very hard to achieve. It will be very hard to turn around the Chinese attitude of innovation and creativity due to earlier periods of life and education. Therefore, creating an innovative context in China not only requires innovative firms but also a transformation of the educational system. Only then the creativity curve can equal or even surpass the Western curve.

From research (Leung, Maddux, Galinsky & Ciu, 2008), it is known that multicultural experiences enhance creativity. In this respect the earlier-mentioned Chinese diaspora of over 50 million people represents a huge opportunity to improve and lift the creativity curve. Furthermore, as discussed in Chap. 3, another study showed that 40 % of the 2010 Fortune 500 companies were founded by immigrants or their children.

The positive influence of cross-cultural activity on creativity and entrepreneurship is a reason enough to rethink governmental immigration policies and diversity policies within private and public organizations. China's leaders recognized this and adopted new policies to stimulate the return of Chinese to their homeland. These so-called sea turtles ("hai gui") enhance the entrepreneurial and innovative capability of China. For the West this is an extra challenge.

4.8   Content

The content of strategic innovation is in principle unpredictable due to the nature of innovation. Strategic innovations have to be created. However, besides creating new products, new processes, and new services, the business model forces to think about how to earn money in changing conditions and environments. Therefore, the business model is put at the core of the content knowing that it is only one of the many opportunities. This view fits to the jumping of the growth curves model discussed earlier.

4.8.1   Business Model

A business model innovation is a combination of different single innovations, leading to a complete new way of doing business (van Someren, 2005). New business models have the potential to create a new industry. On the one hand, Chinese markets require new business models and, on the other hand, Chinese firms entering Western markets will introduce new business models. However, in the latter case, the new business models will go beyond the level of the business model itself and introduce strategic innovations such as public–private symbiosis. Moreover, the 4C approach shows that formulating a business model is dependent on many more factors than the format for creating a business model.

4.8.2   Value Circle

The main principle of these Western business models is along the industrial era scheme of input–throughput–output. Western input–throughput–output follows the same basic lines as the Christianity scheme of birth–life–death. The time line is one dimensional and linear and its economic equivalent is the value chain as shown in Fig. 4.25.

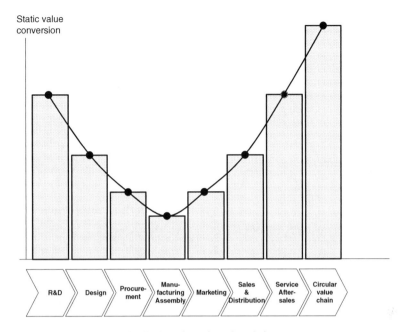

Fig. 4.25 Static added value distribution along the value chain

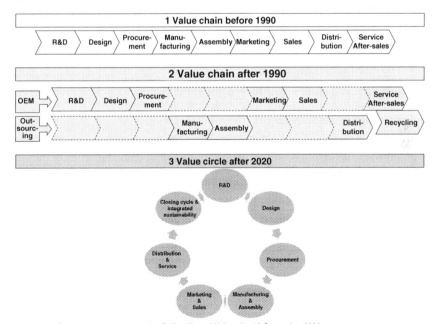

Source: van Someren, Lecture Automotive Beijing Normal University, 12 September 2006 t

Fig. 4.26 From value chain to value circle

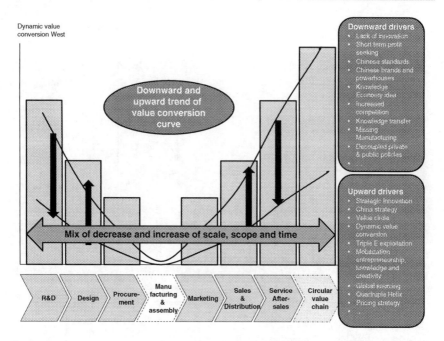

Fig. 4.27 Downward and upward trend on value conversion along value chain

The main driver is getting bigger and only growth is rewarded by stock markets. For non-listed companies, mainly family businesses, the quest for growth is less pressuring, but even there as soon as bank loans partly finance the venture, growth is essential. Not only financial markets ask for growth, also own employees have to be offered challenging jobs for which growth is essential.

For this inner pressure, it was important to know not only the cost levels of each stage in the value chain but also its added value. With regard to this inner drive, the value chains are not static but evolve in time. Figure 4.26 shows the three main stages of the value chain.

The total integrated value chain or coordination by markets is replaced by a value chain based on outsourcing. Due to sustainability issues, the value chain will be replaced by the value circle. Contrary to outsourcing and splitting the value chains, the value circle requires true strategic innovations. On top of the value circle, the rise of China has an influence by the emergence of Chinese companies and the growing importance of China as market.

With the rise of China, for the producing sector, the manufacturing link was now concentrated in China. But the last decades with the rise of other regions, gradually, also other functions are being transferred. Especially the R&D function is shifting and rising in Asiatic and other world regions. In 2011 Dutch DSM announced that it want to increase tenfold its number of researchers in China with the aim to gain from the growing Chinese middle class (Het Financieele Dagblad, 24.02.11). The strategy of outsourcing the manufacturing function was based on classical short-

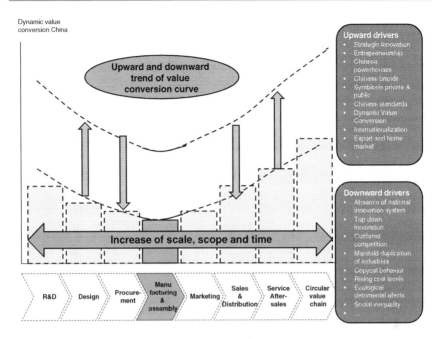

Fig. 4.28 Upward and upward trend of value conversion curve

term cost reduction arguments. Outsourcing is nothing else but an improvement strategy of existing business.

Two main dynamic value conversion effects were neglected. First, a long-term buildup of your own Chinese competitors was fully neglected by the shareholder maximization principle. The manufacturing base offered the opportunity to develop other value chain activities. Even worse, from a Western perspective, the accumulative improvements to products and process enabled many Chinese manufacturers to offer equal high-quality products against lower prices. The hurdles for Chinese to take are to develop own brands and trademarks to grasp premium prices. Second, based on the wrong promises of the knowledge economy, the elimination of the manufacturing function has adverse long-term effects. As a result a downward effect on the added value in the whole value chain forces Western corporations to create strategic innovations. Figure 4.27 shows this effect.

Only solutions like strategic innovations and an adequate China strategy have the power and potential to reverse the downward trend.

Why is innovation already now necessary and why cannot the Chinese continue to be the low-cost high-quality manufacturers for the world? Three developments forces China to act: first, profits are plummeting due to upcoming other low cost countries and detoriating exports, second, more highly educated Chinese people need high end jobs, third, pollution intensive industry encountered the carrying capacity of the planet. In order to participate in business activities with high-profit margins, China has to move up in the value chain like design and branding and to create high added value products or services. This is reflected in Fig. 4.28.

China is increasingly integrating all elements of the value chain including setting up the value circle and trying to grasp the higher profit margins. However, in China, cutthroat competition very quickly reduces profit margins. The only way out is to introduce strategic innovations including new business models.

Are there Chinese business models? Yes there are and Chinese business models follow their own trajectory of development, content, and pace. Already about a decade ago, the first discussions started to think about creating Chinese strategic innovations including tailor-made business models.

To the opinion of the Taiwanese Prof. David Liang, Taiwan is too manufacturing oriented and needs to make more effort to understand consumers. He says (China Daily, 12.06.05), "In Taiwan, ODM has come to stand for 'Own Development Manufacturing'—they don't understand how to focus on users...We have to understand the culture, the society and what people really need. Innovative design should be based on user-oriented product strategy. R&D technology can do everything, but if you don't understand people's needs, then it's nothing." According to Ben Tsiang, executive vice-president of China's leading portal website Sina.com, many innovations are necessary to fit a business model to a local market like China. It requires much more than copycat behavior. Tsiang says (China Daily, 12.06.05), "You see so many great companies coming out of the US and Chinese companies seem to be copying all their great ideas. But if you look at it deeper, there's a whole lot of context in terms of localization. We develop a unique feel and look for the China market."

For example, Chinese labor costs will rise as well and they will get the same issues as the West in future. During the 2011 NPC China's top legislator Wu Ba said that (China Daily, 10.03.11) "A socialist system of laws with Chinese characteristics has been established 'on schedule' in China." The laws include all areas of sustainability: "There are laws to cover every area of economic, political, cultural, social and ecological development in the country"...and.... It is also a legal system that embodies the innovations and praxes of socialism with Chinese characteristics and a legal guarantee for the prosperity and development of socialism with Chinese characteristics.

Another sign of Chinese characteristics is the remark made by Premier Wen Jiabao during the 11th NPC that China will follow a sustainable strategy by increasing the imports from less developed countries and from those with which it has a trade deficit (China Daily, 060311). In fact what he says is that China will continue to import and secure natural resources and buy high-tech environmental goods from the EU and the USA. This is internationalization with Chinese characteristics.

The current models are still based on ancient but highly respected philosophies and ways of business behavior. Chinese business models are still highly influenced by these old ways of behavior but are increasingly mixed with Western behavior and practices. At the end, new Chinese business models will evolve from traditional

Table 4.8 Sino-Western perspectives

Western perspective on innovation	Chinese perspective on innovation
Private firms and institutes are the drivers of innovation; governments do not understand innovation and should not be entrepreneurs	Both governments initiate and govern innovation and private firms
Innovation is needed to become unique and secures the long term survival	Imitation, improvement and buying embodied innovation knowledge leads to richness fast
Innovation is a high risk venture and therefore a barrier	Business is about taking risks
Both SME and MNE innovative	Becoming a MNE is a dream because of power not because of innovation capability
Design and creativity relevant	Technology dominates over non-technological innovations
Innovation is dependent on individuals and corporate leaders fostering innovation. Institutionalization is largely absent due to risk aversion and short term focus of (top) management	Innovation is dependent on governmental programs and increasingly firms. The long term focus offers the basis for basic as well as applied research
Trade in knowledge is based on mutual benefit (win win)	Trade in knowledge is based on two principles when one wins the other loses and when you give me something you owe me something
Learn in the West keep in the West	Learn in the West surpass in the East

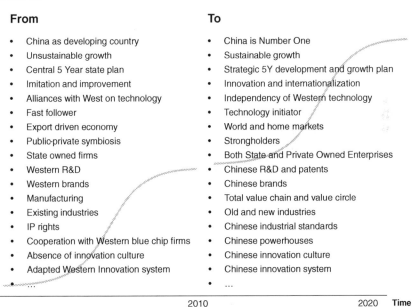

Fig. 4.29 New Chinese growth curve elements

norms and values, history of innovation system, ways of doing business, new influences from outside particularly the West, and the aims of government and own organization. A few examples of differences in thinking about innovation are given in Table 4.8.

The differences only are a few snapshots but they have a historical–cultural background as seen in Chap. 2. When all these centerpieces of Chinese development are taken together, it explains the sometimes very fast growth of new-established firms like Yingli. In Fig. 4.29 a few relevant shifts towards the future are summarized.

Each of the topics is a tremendous challenge for China, and taken together, the totality and accumulation of issues demonstrate the huge task of future governmental and business leaders in China. With the elaboration on the background of Chinese economic development and innovation management, the right context has been shaped to understand better some of the Chinese innovation cases. In the next chapter, we show several cases where the discussed aspects of strategic innovation are the focal point in creating a new business universe and the appliance of the conceptual framework discussed in this chapter.

References

Birkinshaw, J., Hamel, G., & Mol, M. (2008). Management innovation. *Academy of Management Review, 33*(4), 825–845.

Chesbrough, H. W. (2006). *Open innovation, the new imperative for creating and profiting from technology.* Boston, MA: Harvard Business School Press.

Grant, R. M. (2007). *Contemporary strategy analysis. Concepts techniques, applications* (4th ed.). Malden, MA: Blackwell.

Hofstede, G. (2001). *Cultural consequences. Comparing values, behaviors, institutions and organizations across nations* (2nd ed.). Thousand Oaks, CA: Sage.

Jong, H. W. de. (1989). Dynamische Markttheorie, Stenfert Kroese, Leiden.

Leung, A. K., Maddux, W. W., Galinsky, A. D., & Ciu, C. (2008). Multicultural experience enhances creativity. *American Psychologist, 63*(3), 169–181.

Liang, X., Zheng, G., Xu, Q. (2003). *Engineering Management Conference. IEMC '03. Managing Technologically Driven Organizations: The Human Side of Innovation and Change.* Albany, NY.

Scissors, D. (2011). The Heritage Foundation, 01.04.2011. Chinese State-Owned Enterprises and U.S.–China Economic Relations.

Van de Ven, A., & Poole, M. S. (1995). Explaining development and change in organisations. *Academy of Management Review, 20*, 510–540.

van den Bosch, S. (2010). *Transition experiments. Exploring societal changes towards sustainability* (Doctoral thesis, Erasmus University Rotterdam, 2010).

van Someren, T. C. R. (1990). Organisational innovation. *Tinbergen Institute Research Bulletin, 2*(1), 65–73.

van Someren, T. C. R. (1991a). Emulation and organisational change. In M. Perlman & F. M. Scherer (Eds.), *Entrepreneurship, technological innovation, and economic growth.* Ann Arbor, MI: The University of Michigan Press.

van Someren, T. C. R. (1991b). Innovatie, Emulatie en Tijd. De rol van de organisatorische vernieuwingen in het economische proces. *Tinbergen Institute Research Series*, no. 9, June 1991 (diss.).

van Someren, T. C. R. (1992a). "Vernieuwingen en de Factor Tijd". In: T. C. R. van Someren (Ed.), *Maandblad voor accountancy en Bedrijfseconomie* (pp. 293–299).

van Someren, T. C. R. (1992b). *"Innovatie, Emulatie en Strategisch Milieumanagement"*, Strategisch Milieu Management, MBA-course, Department Scientific Institute for Environmental Management, University of Amsterdam, Amersfoort, Netherlands, June 1992.

van Someren, T. C. R. (1995a). Sustainable development and the firm: organisational innovations and environmental strategy. *Business Strategy and The Environment, 4*(1), 23–33.

van Someren, T. C. R. (1995b, November 9). *"Umwelt-Cost-Controlling"*, Volkswagen Seminar Umweltcontrolling. Braunschweig, Germany.

van Someren, T. C. R. (1998a, September 17) *Strategies for sustainable profits*. International BMW Seminar, Dietramszell.

van Someren, T. C. R. (1998b, 7th December). *"Strategies for Sustainable Profits", International Shell Seminar Managing HSE in the Business*. Noordwijkerhout, The Netherlands.

van Someren, T. C. R. (2005). *Strategische Innovationen. So machen Sie Ihr Unternehmen einzigartig*. Wiesbaden: Gabler.

van Someren, T. C. R. (2006). Innovation stratégique: une question de leadership. *Business Digest, 162*, 9–10.

van Someren, T. C. R., & Nijhof, A. (2010). *Triple P business development in the Dutch agro-food sector*. Assen, The Netherlands: Van Gorcum.

van Someren, T. C. R., & van Someren-Wang, S. (2007b). Innoveren in China. *SER Bulletin*, maart, 14–17.

van Someren, T. C. R., & van Someren-Wang, S. (2007b). Quel Style de leadership pour réussir en Chine. *Business Digest, 171*, 16–18.

van Someren, T. C. R., & van Someren-Wang, S. (2007c, June). Strategic eco-innovations. In *Proceedings of the first Water Conference Province of Hebei*, China.

van Someren, T. C. R., & van Someren-Wang, S. (2009a). La pyramide inverse L'innovation stratégique par l'encadrement Intermédiaire. *Business Digest, 196*.

van Someren, T. C. R., & van Someren-Wang, S. (2009b). Opgeheven wijsvinger of opgestroopte mouwen? *Milieu, 7*, 28–29.

van Someren, T. C. R., & van Someren-Wang, S. (2009c, December 9). Klimaattop? Welnee, er wordt een markt verdeeld. *Trouw* (p. 29).

van Someren, T. C. R., & van Someren-Wang, S. (2009d, December). Controleur wordt createur. *Controllers Magazine*, 20–23.

van Someren, T. C. R., & van Someren-Wang, S. (2010). Revolutioneer het Transitiebeleid. *Milieu, 1*, 8–10.

van Someren, T. C. R., & van Someren-Wang, S. (2011). *Building new business models for sustainable growth and development* (B. Kh. Krasnopolsky, Trans. English). "Spatial economics" (ISSN 1815-9834), #3 (27), 2011, Russia, Khabarovsk, pp. 40–55.

van Someren, T. C. R., & Someren-Wang, S. (2012). Green China. Heidelberg: Springer.

Wolcott, R. C., & Lippitz, M. J. (2010). *Grow from within. Mastering corporate entrepreneurship and innovation*. New York: McGraw Hill.

WIPO. (2011). *World Intellectual Property Indicators*. Geneva: World Intellectual Property Organization.

Xu, Q., Jiang, J., & Yang, T. (2004). Analysis on management mode towards total innovation management. *Science of Science and Management of S&D, Zhejiang University, 21*(10), 20–23 (in Chinese).

Strategic Innovation in Practice

5

The race between China, the USA, and the EU will be decided by strategic innovations and not by business models. Due to the rise of China and other non-Western countries, it is necessary to increase the scope of renewal beyond the micro-level of business models. The several Chinese and Western cases presented in this chapter reveal totally different approaches and interpretations of strategic innovation. The issues connected to leadership, institutional innovation, business development, and new forms of governance determine the future of the world economy. In the comparison between the practical appliance of the strategic innovation in the West and China, it will appear that only those leaders who understand the fundamentals are able to prepare their organizations for the future. These fundamentals are changing the way of working in both the West and China. All have to adapt to a new emerging business world in which strengths and weaknesses create huge challenges for China, the USA, and the EU. Now it is the time for real global business leaders understanding each other's world.

5.1 Growth Curves and Challenger China

Chinese strategic innovations including Chinese business models will be part of our future world. It depends on the countervailing innovation power of the USA and the EU on how successful Chinese companies will be. The core question is to which extent Western and Chinese organizations are capable of pushing the strategic innovation envelop forward. In the previous chapters, it became clear that governmental policies in China, the USA, and the EU differed depending on history, context, starting position, and ambition. But all need innovative entrepreneurs and organizations.

Growth and development are the core purpose of innovation and taken together they form (S-shaped) growth curves. As Fig. 5.1 indicates the perspective on growth and development can differ greatly between countries, organizations, and individuals.

In this chapter some cases mainly based on our practice are presented which highlight the appliance of the strategic innovation theory. The main purpose is to show some relevant different features of strategic innovation in the West and China.

T.C.R. van Someren and S. van Someren-Wang, *Innovative China*,
Management for Professionals, DOI 10.1007/978-3-642-36237-8_5,
© Springer-Verlag Berlin Heidelberg 2013

Fig. 5.1 Growth and development curves

Challenger China is not the winner of the strategic innovation race yet. But may be at the end, the USA or the EU will be the winner. It all depends on the ability to create and implement strategic innovations. The business cases show that strategic innovations are necessary in both private and public sector.

5.2   Western Strategic Innovation Cases

In this section we present some hands-on experience from our own practice dealing with strategic innovation and applying the SIT. As will become clear, strategic innovation is not daily business even not for the most experienced top manager. Moreover, it is without exception a very bumpy process of new insights and new directions with huge opportunities intermingled with doubts and great uncertainty about possible future options. But in the end, all the pieces of the new puzzle fit together and represent a new future for everybody involved. The renewal process goes beyond the regular improvement strategy based on old concepts requiring regular and never-ending new cost-cutting programs. In the West this is a common practice based on short-term balance sheet and profit and loss management.

In the next sections, the case of Shell demonstrates the struggle of a private multinational to deal with sustainability and strategic innovation, the fire department case demonstrates that strategic innovation is not limited to private- and market-based organizations but also is a necessity for public organizations, and the TTR-ELAt case shows the potential of cross-border innovation in which both private and public organization have to play their part.

5.2.1 Shell

A lecture in 1998 about new strategic innovation options based on the central idea that ecology and economy are not opposites but reinforce each other and represent a new big growth curve driven by strategic innovations attracted the attention of a senior Shell manager (van Someren, 1998a). Especially the notion that ecology was presented as business opportunities and a business case to earn sustainable profits was at that time revolutionary. In a series of workshops, this idea had been worked out with managers from different positions working at worldwide locations to strategically renew their company from an oil company into a sustainable energy company (van Someren, 1998c). At the end of short-term pressures, a focus on exploiting existing infrastructure of the current business model (e.g., exploration and selling) and different calculations by top management about the dynamic value conversion, the more conservative option of transforming Shell into an oil and gas company was preferred.

The core business of Shell is both downstream and upstream oil and gas activities and chemicals. Together with ExxonMobil, ConocoPhillips, BP, and others, Shell belongs to the biggest in industry. At the end of the twentieth century, new contenders like Russian Lukoil, Brazilian Petrobras, and state-owned Chinese CNPC, CNOOC, and Sinopec stood up. Since the 1990s, the issue of the amount of oil reserves has come up. In this respect, exploration and exploitation become increasingly relevant. Simultaneously, due to the Brent Spar disaster, sustainability translated into transparency became agenda top priority at the oil multinationals. But the oil and gas reserves dominated the industry and stock prices. Simply put, exploitation provides the money to do exploration. In the search for new oil wells, exploration is a very technical-oriented business, and the amount of proven reserves determines the future of an oil company.

In Fig. 5.2, the strategic outlook for Shell is demonstrated by the simple illustration of the old growth curve based on fossils and the new growth curve of renewables.

The bottlenecks of the existing growth curve combined with the emerging (mega)trends indicate the end of at least the oil growth curve. The fossil fuel growth curve can be extended by new oil reserves or discovery of other reserves such as shale gas. A new growth curve based on renewables has a chance to grow when, for example, grid parity between gas and solar panel based supply is reached.

Analysts say that for the whole industry, the time when the reserves together with proven new reserves cannot keep up with demand and use of oil—Peak Oil—has been reached around 2010. Therefore, the bottlenecks of the existing growth curve are related to Peak Oil, the increasing investments, and costs levels of exploration and exploitation; the political dangers and the climate issues slow down the endless growth perspectives of oil and gas.

The megatrends of sustainability and the increasing competitiveness of renewable forms of energy and decentralized energy supply systems threaten Big Oil. A new growth curve of renewable is thought to be the winner of the energy game by at least the second half of the twenty-first century.

In the 1990s, as one of the first oil companies, Shell started in the Netherlands a solar panel plant. However, this small-scale project was more a tryout to gather

Development

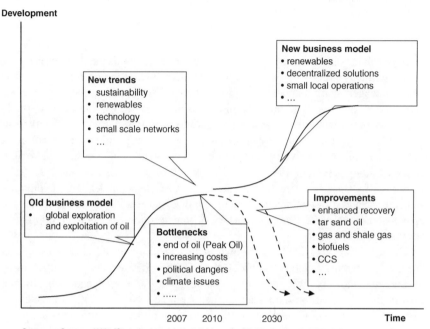

Source: van Someren, 1998c, "Strategies for Sustainable Profits", International Shell Seminar Managing HSE in the Business, 7th December 1998c, Noordwijkerhout, The Netherlands

Fig. 5.2 Old fossil fuel growth curve versus new renewables growth curve

knowledge about the potential threat of a new technology than a strategic redirection towards renewables instead of oil and gas. Later on it was sold to other parties. The most early start with solar panels can be interpreted as a think forward project beyond scenarios.

At the end of the 1990s, we had some relevant discussions with senior management about the necessity to think about strategic innovation towards a world beyond oil and gas. The core idea for renewables was not to transform Shell because of ecological or social motives but because renewables represent excellent new business opportunities and potential of the Energy Company of the Future (van Someren, 1998a, 1998b, 1998c). Simultaneously, a radical improvement of social and ecological dimension would be possible. Despite interest, top management decided to stick to the core business of oil and gas due to strategic short-term problems and opportunities. The proven oil reserves represented the acute problem of Shell. The proven reserves were lower than communicated, and it leads to another much publicly discussed issue of Shell's future. The strategic answer was to invest in large-scale projects such as the search for very large new oil and gas fields and Carbon Capture and Storage (CCS). The opportunity boiled down to the belief that gas would be the biggest future market which renewables could not match.

With regard to renewable energy, a former CEO of Shell, Jeroen van der Veer, made a statement that to his opinion the world would be for decades dependent on oil because the alternatives could not be build up so fast in the scale as needed. It is the same reasoning as the in the automotive industry about electrical cars. Moreover, the price of renewable energy forms would be much higher. Around 2010, the other focus was on biofuels and CO_2 storage. The reason is that biofuels were supported by European government and countries like Brazil showed the potential of this form of energy. More important is the fact that biofuels perfectly fit into the existing business model of the pipelines and distribution to end consumers. CO_2 storage offers an opportunity to extend the lifetime of the existent growth curve based on fossil fuels. Therefore, both priorities, biofuels and CO_2 storage, are improvements of the existing business model. Solar energy is apparently a step too far.

The extension of the existing business model combines several (technical) improvements. Some examples are oil sands, shift to gas and shale gas exploration and exploitation, gas to liquid (GTL), enhanced recovery (higher productivity of oil wells), CCS, and biofuels. All these cases fit into the large-scale centralized energy production and distribution. They all contribute to an extension of existing growth cycle. These fossil oil-based alternatives together make the Peak Oil theory not obsolete but postpone considerably the moment in time when oil consumption is higher than supply. Moreover, the output of OPEC measured in its reserves-to-production ratio is more than 85 years. Therefore, the constraint is probably not the amount of oil but climate discussion and the public opinion influenced by interest groups promoting renewables. It is again the trap of facts and public opinion—technology against non-technology.

Brent Spar and Nigeria show the technology bias for innovation instead of the soft side of communication or non-technological innovation areas. In 2011 Shell opened the large-scale GTL installation in Qatar. These upscaling activities, geophysical search, and exploration belong to the core competences of Shell. The myopic view on technology is confirmed by the recent newly created function of technology officer instead of something like a strategic innovation officer.

The improvement of the existing growth cycle is characterized by exploitation of existing knowledge, existing infrastructure, current procedures, current organization, and current project criteria and doing business as usual with highest governmental leaders. From the perspective of Shell within the context of stock markets, investments in knowledge, competences, and infrastructure and abundance of fossil fuel like shale gas, the attempts to improve the existing growth cycle can be understood. But one must not be surprised when others or even newcomers grasp the opportunity to become the dominant players in the renewable industry.

Strategic innovations like decentralized energy production and consumption are exactly the opposite of their existing business model and current features strategic innovation. Decentralized concepts are based on simple projects, local municipal political leaders, small-scale projects, competition from local companies, and electricity grid problems instead of geophysical issues. Also blurring industry borders with water industry is relevant here. Classical large-scale operating water companies have to think about decentralized drinking and sanitation water concepts. In this respects, subtracting energy (heat) from warm waste tube water is an application on the household level. Companies like Shell do not have experience in these fields; they do not have the competences, knowledge, and culture to work on such a microscale

Table 5.1   Renewable energy requires inversion of fossil-based business practices

	Fossil Goliath Current business of oil and gas	Renewable David Decentralized renewable energy
Level	Doing business on macro level with highest governmental representatives	Doing business on micro level with municipalities
Business model	Large scale exploration and exploitation of fossil fuels based on 'drilling and pipelines'	Multiple small scale decentralized energy operations based on 'grids'
Core knowledge	Geo-physical exploration, large scale operation, complex projects, global business	Creating profitable local energy concepts, small scale operation, simple projects, local business
Competition	Largest world leading energy companies	Small local companies
Key innovation area	Exploration and exploitation technology of fossil fuels	Non-technical aspects of exploiting local energy markets such as administration, reversed financial streams and grid management
Culture	Technology driven	Flexibility network

level. The deep pockets would still loose from local operating fast-moving newcomers accumulating knowledge in a new energy subindustry. A complete inversion of all relevant aspects of doing business is shown in Table 5.1.

The criteria of Goliath players boil down to the following: if it is not possible to create large-scale profitable business, it will be rejected.

The large investments in existing pipelines, core competences reflected by, e.g., knowledge databases and human resources capabilities, will be naturally defended. These defense mechanisms are sometimes playing hard ball like attacking newcomers, lobbying at ministries and governmental leaders, and influencing national innovation and economic programs. The newcomer in the renewable sector has no time for these MNE practices since these SMEs are focused on realizing their new business model. The more the incumbent defends its old industry, the more chance the newcomer has.

With the classical profit criterion, the strategic course can be understood. Therefore, it is useless to complain about the power of the large multinationals but instead build up and accumulate experiences in the renewables. They will then be unbeatable, and their business culture will not fit to the culture of the old giant. How does the nightmare of the oil companies look like? Exactly, Renewable David beats Fossil Goliath.

The focus on improvement and life extension of the existing opens the opportunity for growth and development of new entrants based on comprehensive strategic innovations. The new small-scale technology is too small to be economic viable for the Big Oil companies. Therefore, three options are left for Big Oil. First, destroy the newcomer by creating entry barriers. Second, buy the newcomer and use its technology or neglect it by letting it die within Big Oil project criteria. Thirdly, create new growth curve by strategic innovations. The latter option is not chosen very often because it is the most difficult one but the only one to survive.

Based on the dynamic value conversion principle, the alternative fossil oil techniques on short and long term make an extension of the current growth cycle profitable.

For the Big Oil companies, the dynamic value conversion principle will reject the small-scale renewable alternatives due to small-scale and long learning curve and accumulation combined with timing and slow implementation of available smart grids. Moreover, the small-scale projects at the start of the renewable growth cycle do not fit into the organization of Big Oil trimmed on large-scale projects. The implementation of decentralized concepts can be done by local organizations. A soon as it becomes a worldwide business, international mergers and acquisition will be used to stay in business and expand market share. However, the smart grid as a complex long-term project would fit to Big Oil, but here other organizations in the network business are good positioned as well.

For SMEs, the dynamic value conversion gives another calculation. Because of the small scale with regard to, for example, solar panel installation, small profits are possible, but the long-term investment and time-consuming process in the smart grid hamper economies of scale. This is the reason that both fossil and renewables can coexist in the beginning for many years, but later on, a breakthrough or dominance of renewable is to be expected. The argument that renewables can only survive because of the subsidies does not hold. Even nowadays fossil fuel is still directly and indirectly subsidized. The core issues of the success of renewable energy boils down to expanding and transforming the grid suitable for feed in, energy storage capabilities, and cross-regional supply and demand coordination including financing.

The defensive reaction of Shell is based on dynamic value conversion calculations revealing that current growth curve based on improvements will be very profitable for the next years. The defensive reaction is also based on the knowledge that the strategic innovations necessary to make renewables a success do not fit to their heritage, knowledge base, management capabilities, organization structure, innovation competence, and corporate culture. The more the existing growth cycle will be followed, the more chances the new founded companies in the renewable subindustry have to survive and become the dominant energy supplier.

In these situations it is insufficient to use proven management technique of scenario analysis or to renew your business model. The reason is that the required new business model does not fit into existing leadership styles, institutional innovation programs focus on complete other areas, business development is different, and governance of, e.g., project criteria is different. Furthermore, scenario analyses leads to interesting views on the world but not to the necessary change. Hence, strategic innovation is the only way out to survive and adapt to new industry structure and behavior.

5.2.2 Dutch Fire Department

Over more than a decade, the Dutch Fire Department, often with support of numerous consulting bureaus, was trying to reorganize their organization. They had to find answers on several issues that popped up such as increasing costs, lower availability of volunteers, and increasing complexity of tunnel systems. New strategies, new HR policies, and new internal organization and governance structures were proposed without the desired bottom-line results. They felt like fighting with a dragon, and each time the head was chopped off, two new heads appeared. In 2008, the new "CEO" of the fire department, Caroline van de Wiel, knew about the SIT, and we were assigned to strategically innovate the fire department. Due to the fact that the SIT questions every aspect of doing business as usual in the beginning, a lot of scepsis about the usefulness and applicability of the SIT approach spreads among all levels of the fire department. Even in the special task force assigned to take care of the strategic renewal process, a lot of uncertainty and disbelief in the approach and its preliminary results came up. However, this is a normal reaction which appears every time and is based on the fact that strongly held beliefs and normal practices are being questioned and radical new ideas are being proposed. Enthusiasm, radically new insights, a total solution, and members of the task force who became true believers of the new future replaced scepsis and single-issue solutions in functional areas focused on improvement.

The case of the fire department demonstrates that strategic innovation is also relevant and applicable for public organizations and in this case a societal service organization. In this respect, for centuries, fire departments bring water to the fire and that is it. With regard to innovation, fire departments are more characterized by uncoordinated ad hoc bottom-up improvements instead of market-driven innovations. Each fire department or every team creates new minor often technical solutions for solving any problem during call of duty.

Due to new safety notions by the public in the western part of the world, increasing costs of fire and disaster fighting, decreasing availability of volunteers, new technologies, and urbanization required the development of new business models. The Dutch fire service is highly decentralized. There are 25 regional fire chiefs ("top managers") and 435 municipal fire chiefs. Each fire department is governed by a local mayor. In addition to mayors and fire chiefs, there are approximately 30,000 firemen and women, of which 4,000 are permanent employees and 26,000 are volunteers.

There was an increasing gap between required skills and availability of firefighters and requirements in practical emergency situations. Why did this happen?

New trends lead to new situations requiring adaptive and flexible changes in existing organizations and offering opportunities for the founding of new organizations. For the fire and rescue service, the availability of new technologies like anticollision systems for cars reduces the risk of traffic accidents. Secondly, bottlenecks like payment agreements with unions and increased complexity such as in tunnel systems in existing firefighting organizations are predominantly solved by a reactive approach, continuously improving the existing situation.

Taken together, the new trends and bottlenecks lead to the conclusion that the existing business model cannot cope anymore with these developments and a new business model has to be created which address future societal requirements and removes current bottlenecks. Deputy Chief Ricardo Weewer states that "In recent years, it has become nearly impossible to respond to all service demands of the society due to the complexity and risk of fire service tasks, as well as a general lack of funding. Currently all financing goes through municipalities, which makes it almost impossible to coordinate activities at a national level." In the face of these challenges, we have carried out the assignment to create a new service business model for the fire department. The aim was to create a new sustainable fire department (van Someren & van Someren-Wang, 2009). In the global fire department world, this was the first time such a fundamental rethinking was launched (Weewer, 2009).

Apart from the political leaders, the board of regional fire chiefs empowered the project group to create and elaborate a completely new future business model. In order to avoid a growing discrepancy during the process, it is important to keep the stakeholders involved and committed to the process and preliminary outcomes. Several moments to reflect with them and to collect directions were part of the process. Some large-scale events were organized to obtain opinions of employees of the Dutch fire service. But also external partners of the fire service, such as police and insurance companies, have been occasionally involved and informed about progress and possible new directions. In this manner, the complex field of stakeholders has been part of the whole process of strategic innovation.

The analysis showed that the existing business model based on repression as core activity (fighting fire) accompanied by increasing costs and low results was out-dated. Figure 5.3 demonstrates a few relevant arguments.

In the strategic innovation process, five different options including corresponding business models have been worked out, of which one has been chosen as the Fire Department of the Future.

This path the future called the *continuity concept* aims at avoiding discontinuities disrupting society. Eight strategic innovations have to be implemented to obtain the overall goal of societal continuity. Note that the business model is only used to point out the direction of the development of the fire service to 2040.

1. New strategic fire safety doctrine. In the new doctrine, the focus will be more on prevention and control of risks than on reducing the effects, such as suppression.

2. Risk differentiation. The fire service of the future will replace standard and uniform norms, which were required by regulation, by the risk differentiation principle. Risk differentiation means that regions will be differentiated on basis of their risk profiles.

3. Crisis management. The new vision here boils down to the enhancement of the role of resilience, an extended cooperation with other organizations active in the field of safety and crises, and better knowledge of the processes within fire service enabling to cooperate more intensively with other organizations.

4. New technologies. From the perspective of firefighting, the emergence of new technologies means new risks and sometimes increasing complexity. Examples are

Development

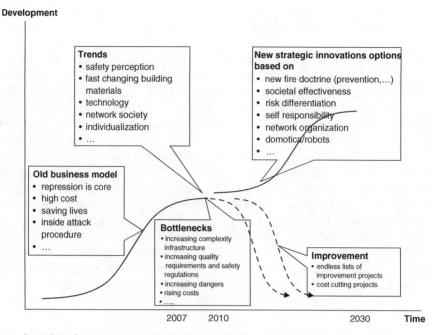

Trends
- safety perception
- fast changing building materials
- technology
- network society
- individualization
- ...

New strategic innovations options based on
- new fire doctrine (prevention,...)
- societal effectiveness
- risk differentiation
- self responsibility
- network organization
- domotica/robots
- ...

Old business model
- repression is core
- high cost
- saving lives
- inside attack procedure
- ...

Bottlenecks
- increasing complexity infrastructure
- increasing quality requirements and safety regulations
- increasing dangers
- rising costs
- .....

Improvement
- endless lists of improvement projects
- cost cutting projects

2007   2010   2030   **Time**

Source: Project Group based upon Van Someren, 2005, Strategische Innovationen, Gabler Verlag

Fig. 5.3 Elements of the fire department of the future

domestic sprinklers, domotica, anticollision technologies in transport sector, building automation, and robots for firefighting.

5. New volunteers and retained firefighters. Actually, in the Netherlands, the majority (22,000 of 28,000) of the fire service personnel are retained firefighters or volunteers. New types of volunteers will be employed. Examples are volunteers already working for communities to carry out community safety activities and specialist volunteers who are not trained and educated to do the whole job, maybe even working for companies which have experience in this field.

6. Societal outcome. For performance measurement, "societal outcome" as a new performance indicator has been formulated. Societal outcome means that result of any action of the fire service should be related to the investments and operational costs.

7. Organization and cooperation at the national level. Both centralization and networks are the key notions for the new organization. In order to cope with the adequate level of competence and cost-effectiveness of specialisms, like diving and industrial and ship firefighting, it is necessary to centralize these activities in a few interregional places. Another efficiency measure is the introduction of a shared service center.

8. Systemic knowledge and research. The implication for knowledge and IT systems is evident. Fire services have largely neglected data and information collection on a systematic way. This was caused by the fact that the current organization is incident driven and is preliminary focused on finding solutions for an incidental case on spot.

The result is a bearing point in the future—i.e., the continuity concept—and the eight strategic lines creating a new business model to be followed to realize the fire service of the future. Equally important, commitment of all stakeholders including politicians has been achieved during the process of creating the Fire Department of the Future.

5.2.3 Creation of a Supranational Technological Top Region (TTR-ELAt)

In Europe, one of the biggest governmental challenges is to make policies work and realize bottom-line results. Chapter 3 has demonstrated that European innovation policies need improvement. A special case occurs when cross-cultural borders have to be bridged between member states. The case of TTR-ELAt is a cross-border cooperation between regions in the Netherlands, Germany, and Belgium. The assignment was to create an innovative business plan to realize the policy to foster innovation in and between the regions involved. In this project, it was our role and task to set up a strategic innovation agenda, a business plan, and a road map to realize the supranational ambition. A cross-border governmental working group including the connected regions of the Netherlands, Belgium, and Germany under technical presidency of Ynnovate had the task to work out the strategic issues. The appliance of the SIT boiled down to fostering innovative entrepreneurship and the need for business developers supported by creating favorable conditions for cross-border initiatives. For the process, most relevant were the cross-cultural differences. Most interestingly, not the differences between the member states appeared to be crucial but the inner rivalry between the involved provinces of the Netherlands.

Since several decades, the southern part of the Netherlands, the Province of Limburg on the border with Germany and Belgium, is being economically renewed. The original coal mines were the traditional economic basis of Limburg, but in the 1970s, these mines were successively closed and unemployment rate increased. Since then the region has been active to turn these trends. For example, the creation of a chemical company DSM emerged as Phoenix from the previous corporation exploiting the former coal mines. DSM successfully implemented several turnarounds from coal mine to chemical company followed by the transformation to a biotech firm. Between these regions and cities in these three countries, clear borders exist. Despite the relatively very short distances between the main cities and their regions, economic activity is largely separated from each other. A good example is the region around Eindhoven, Maastricht (Province of Limburg, the Netherlands), Leuven (Flemish Brabant, Belgium), and Aachen (North Rhine-Westphalia, Germany). This is the so-called TTR-ELAt region. TTR-ELAt stands for Technological Top Region Eindhoven, Leuven, Aachen triangle. All these cities and regions have their own national and regional innovation policies and private firms that mainly work in their own region.

Each separate region has some potential for development. But when we remove the psychological and physical borders of belonging to different nation states and different cultures, the potential of the whole region changes. The region as a whole has a much bigger innovation potential than the separate regions alone.

According to a study carried out by Province of Limburg, measured along the number of patents, the TTR-ELAt region ranks number three after Stuttgart and Munich. Together, the cities in the TTR-ELAt region offer a lot of research and knowledge carried out in their universities, institutes, and new business areas. However, cross-border cooperation between the regions in the Netherlands, Belgium, and Germany was on a rather low level. The region TTR-ELAt as a whole takes the third place measured along the number of patents. Each of the cities separately would not attain this high ranking.

But counting patents is something different than earning money with it. The technical competitiveness of the TTR-ELAt region is lower than the number of patents would suggest. According to the technical competitiveness index, the regions Oberrhein, Munich, and Stockholm rank number one to three, whereas TTR-ELAt is found on number six. This implies that the commercialization and entrepreneurial activity in the TTR-ELAt region are on a lower level than in Oberrhein, Munich, Stockholm, Stuttgart, and Lyon.

Given this context, research revealed that compared to other regions, the TTR-ELAt region has a high-technology potential in some industries, but this potential is not commercially exploited in the form of added value creation. Compared to other European regions, three industries in the TTR-ELAt region scored above average: chemicals and advanced materials, high-tech systems (engineering), and health sciences. Moreover, complementarities between the regions are existent.

In reaction on this investigation, the local governments took the initiative to set up a crossover cooperation between the regions. This TTR-ELAt region is an attempt to break up national borders and to work as an integrated European region.[1]

The business plan had to show existing but not connected initiatives, new opportunities, organization, financing, and legal and institutional bottlenecks as shown in Fig. 5.4.

During the project, it appeared that a large number of obstacles had to overcome to realize this idea. They appeared on all levels. Private firms were unaware of knowledge available at universities in other countries, international financing of combined projects was very difficult due to European rules, other institutional bottlenecks were the difficulties of labor to work across borders due to fiscal regimes, and cooperation on governmental level had to be set up from scratch. Triple Helix was not present at all; not even Double Helix existed except a few cases. Willingness to invest cross border by the local governments in this region existed only on a very low level. Quadruple Helix is a dream.

---

[1] Communiqué van Luik, Province of Limburg, 3 November 2008.

Development

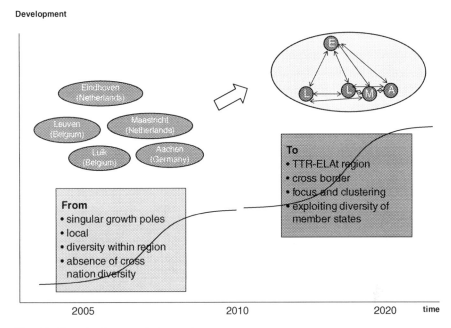

Fig. 5.4 Cross-border strategic innovation

These high-potential crossover economies are largely untapped and offer opportunities for innovation and a truly European integration. Hence, the top-down approach to realize political ambitions appeared to be a bridge too far, and now the bottom-up approach of creating cross-border projects is the short-term road map. The new strategic vision for the TTR-ELAt region is presented in Fig. 5.5.

These activities were divided into three linked core strategic lines consisting of networks, business development, and institutional development

For each industry such as health, life sciences, and new material, already several network groups have been established. However, these networks differed in their generation of output and results. These networks more or less boiled down to exchanging information but not necessarily the next steps of new business ventures. Therefore, business development appeared to be the most relevant issue.

A crucial issue is what the opinion is of the role of government in creating new business. Extremely said, should it be top-down or bottom-up. In a Western context, normally a bottom-up approach requiring entrepreneurial activity is favored. But when results are behind expectations, national governments and, e.g., the European Union start to formulate innovation policies. Then a mix between bottom-up and top-down exists. But in the case of the European Union, no difference is made between national history and cultures ending in a very ineffective approach.

It shows the difficulty in the Northern European context of mixing top-down and bottom-up together with government and private business. Only tailor-made solutions for individual organizations and/or regions and clusters work. This brings

Development

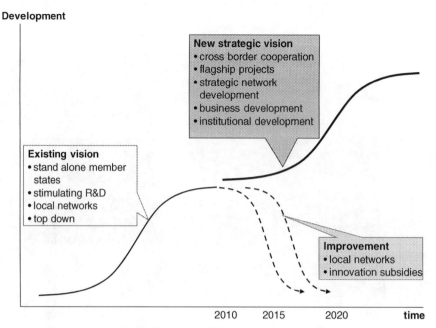

Source: based upon T.C.R. van Someren, 2005, Strategische Innovationen, Gabler Verlag

Fig. 5.5 New strategic vision TTR-ELAt

us to the third strategic line of institutional development. Here, some examples illustrate institutional development. One is the opening of a political debate to allow national funding for cross-border projects and flagship projects. Another refers to foster an international labor market mobility requiring aligning of regulations and laws. A last example is a joint cross-border IPR framework. This case shows the difference between the European project on a macroscale as a political idea without practical experience and its slow and difficult implementation and realization on a microscale. If Europe would be an island, it can take thousands of years for implementing the great idea. But with the rise of China, such a time line is deadly and devastating for its future.

The business cases of strategic innovation show the potential of business renewal in both private and public organizations. The next issue is how the relation with China has been developed.

5.3   Increasing Dependency on Chinese Market

In general, there is a tendency towards a rising dependency of Western firms on Chinese market. In times of financial crisis, these growing markets and additional revenues are of course manna from heaven. This development holds for industry

Table 5.2 Growing dependency on China

Company	Emerging markets incl. China (% of revenues)	Asiatic countries incl. China (% of revenues)	China (% of revenues)
BMW			14.9 % (2010)
VW			33 % (2010)
GM			33 % (2010)
Bosch		23 % (2010) 30 % (2015)	
Alstom		26 % (2010/2011)	
AKZONobel		11 % (2002) 21 % (2010)	
DSM	20 % (2005) 36 % (2010) >50 % (2015)		
Procter & Gamble	31 % (2009)		
Dow Chemical		18 % (2010)	7,5 % (2010)
Danone	>50 % (2010)		
Nestlé	33 % (2010) >45 % (2020)		
Unilever	53 % (2010)		
Siemens	20 % (2005) 30 % (2010)		
Nokia			19 % (IV 2010)

Sources: Brookings, Het Financieele Dagblad, Siemens, ManagerMagazine, Sueddeutsche, Der Spiegel, Gazet van Antwerpen, Business China, Alstom Clean Power day, 03.11.11, p. 14

leaders like BMW and also for their suppliers. New markets mean new opportunities, but there is a downside. The Chinese trick of trading market share for technology is applied in almost every industry.

Three risks have to be dealt with. First, will the market share lead to profits? Second, by trading technology for market share, potential future competitors are created. Third, when successful, the market share will initially rise but that represents a risk as soon as alliances are being ended or continued against less favorable conditions or even worse Chinese competitors take over the business.

The latter risk is increasingly becoming a strategic issue. What if indeed revenues and profits from China drop within a short period of time? Would your company survive? And what kind of company do you get when your revenues and earnings are dependent on emerging markets? A few cases and Table 5.2 illustrate this development.

For several car manufacturers, China has become one of the most relevant markets.[2] Total sales in 2010 in the Chinese market are 13,757,800 cars. In January

---

[2] Los Angeles Times, 25.01.11, GM's China sales top U.S. total, a first for the automaker; China Daily, 09.05.11, Time for GM to shift in top gear (FAZ 18.10.11 "Wir bleiben die Nummer eins"; FT 02.08.11: China demand boosts profits at BMW).

2011, GM sold 268,071 cars, a record sale. GM's total sales in 2010 are 2.35 million cars, and its market share is now about 9.4 %. GM is the Western market leader. Although China is now GM's biggest market, sales are not as profitable as the automaker's business in North America. One of the reasons is because it splits the proceeds with three joint venture partners. Volkswagen sold about 1,500,000, Toyota around 900,000, and Volvo 30,000. Since Geely acquired Volvo from Ford, it is expected that sales will rise sharply. VW was the first Western manufacturer to set up ventures in China, and as a consequence, it had been the market leader for over two decades. GM could have emulated VW around 2005, but because of its aging fleet (Regal, Sail, and Excelle), it missed sales. GM's market share in 2008 fell to 8.4 %. New models rose market share, and China is now the most important market for GM. BMW's China sales are 14.9 % of its total car sales. Demand for the carmaker's vehicles is growing three times faster than the overall Chinese car market. BMW's sales in India doubled. But as we will see below, the real battle for the Chinese is not in the segment with traditional fossil fuel-based technology but renewable energy-driven automotive industry. What happens to the success of companies like BMW when Chinese government decides to abandon fossil fuel-based cars and allows only electrical or hydrogen cars?

Dependency on Chinese markets is not only existent in the hot desired Western car industry. Siemens AG announced a strategic plan in which all divisions grow faster than their markets in emerging countries. The share of Siemens' total revenue generated in the emerging markets rose from about 20 % in fiscal 2005 to more than 30 % in fiscal 2010.

Local value creation—encompassing not only sales and production but also research and development (R&D) activities and engineering—is a key success factor for business in emerging markets. In 2005, Siemens had about 46,000 employees in the emerging markets. By 2010, the figure had risen to 85,000. During the same period, the number of Siemens main production facilities increased from 64 to 117.[3] In this respect, on Monday, 17 October 2011, Siemens announced to set up an industrial automation manufacturing and R&D base in Chengdu. This location will be the largest digital factory in China and the third largest R&D center for industrial automation business in the world. According to Siemens, "The idea behind the digital factory is to cover the whole production chain—covering design, manufacturing, logistics, marketing and sales—digitally and integrate the use of IT systems throughout, which is expected to shorten the time it takes products to reach the market by 50 percent".[4]

In 100 years' time, DSM reinvented itself twice. It started as a state held coal mine company and during the 1980s transformed to a bulk and later on specialty chemical company. In the last decade, the focus changed from chemicals towards food and biotechnology such as vitamins. Its total revenues in 2009 were 8 milliard €. From 2005 till 2009, the revenue share of upcoming economies (Central–East

---

[3] Siemens Press release, 280611, Siemens to expand market share in emerging markets.

[4] China Daily, 18.10.11, Siemens to build Chengdu plant, R&D base.

Europe, Latin America, and Asia) rose from 20 % (2005) and 32 % (2009) to 36 % (2010), respectively. In 2015, this share should exceed 50 %. Furthermore, DSM also focused on creating sustainable products. The share of innovative so-called ECO+ solutions, products which have a better Triple P performance than existing products, rose from 78 % in 2009 to 89 % in 2010. In 2015, DSM wants to have doubled its revenues to $3 billion in China.[5] DSM cooperates with Sinochem, and based on an EBITDA margin of 15 %, the alliance has to reach 600 million revenues in 2015. As the world's leading paint manufacturer, AKZONobel's Asiatic share of revenues have risen from 11 % in 2002 to 21 % in 2010.

The share of developing countries in the total revenues of Danone exceeded 50 % in 2010 and outperforms its rivals Nestlé and Unilever.[6] "Nestlé currently gets 33 % of its total sales from emerging markets and said it hopes to boost that proportion to 45 % by 2020."[7] Moreover, in Europe, Nestlé grows based on a series of innovations and outperforms Unilever in that respect.[8]

Another form of dependency can be seen at some early adopters of becoming a true global integrated firm like IBM. These global players try to make China part of their global business. They do so by transferring some key activities to China. For example, the center of IBM's procurement is in China. For Nokia, China is their core production center. Of course, Chinese staff is employed. From a Western perspective, this is a classical labor division and a next step of outsourcing. From a Chinese perspective, it is an opportunity to learn from their peers how these excellence centers have to be managed and developed. It is another step in the emulation process to learn how to deal with nontechnical innovation issues.

However, these cases only tell half the story. The other side is that Chinese firms also gain market share in their own markets. Sometimes, Chinese firms grow faster and have larger market shares than their Western rivals. China's homegrown private companies steadily increased their stake in total output from 3 % in 1998 to 23 % in 2007. Foreign multinationals and joint ventures in the same period first slightly increased their share from 25 % to nearly 35 % in 2004 but then decreased to 31 % in 2007.[9] But the spectacular growth of the private sector should not be interpreted as the disappearance of state-owned enterprises (SOE). Here also, since 2008, the pendulum is swinging back to a more relevant role for SOE as a consequence of central governmental policies as discussed in Chap. 3 related to the selected key industries.

With regard to value conversion, research indicates that private companies are much more profitable than SOEs. SOEs have a return on equity of 4 %, whereas private companies return is 10 % higher.[10] Private companies increasingly got

---

[5] FD, 30.09.2011, DSM optimistisch over 2011; NRC 23.02.11 DSM na transformatie klaar voor nieuwe groei.

[6] Gazet van Antwerpen, 15.02.11.

[7] Business China, 12.07.11.

[8] FD, 21.10.11, Nestlé weet met innovaties wel te groeien in Europa.

[9] China Daily, 30.03.09, Multinationals battling locals for market share.

[10] The Economist, 10.03.2011, Entrepreneurship in China.

involved in Western markets on top of their traditional developing countries like Africa and Latin America. Moreover, in their home markets, private companies shifted their interest to third- and fourth-tier cities, thereby moving in westward direction away from well-known east coast megacities. But another very relevant aspect of the other side is that many Chinese firms are largely dependent on export. For example, 80 % of telecom infrastructure equipment ZTE's total sales come from overseas markets.[11]

But with rising labor costs, inflation, and possible protection measures from foreign countries, private companies might get into stormy weather. This is the case for Unilever and Procter & Gamble. Unilever invests in upcoming markets like Russia and China. The business model of Unilever is vulnerable for rising food stock prices for its ice cream and margarine. Although Unilever compared to its rivals has a good penetration in emerging markets, the current but especially future share of Chinese Dragons is a threat. The developing countries now count for 53 % of the total revenues of Unilever. In order to supply the rising demand in these countries, the food production has to be increased by 70 %. But in the Chinese detergent market, a different picture emerges. But both Unilever and P&G have a market share of 8.5 %, and formerly state-owned Chinese companies like Nice Group and Guangzhou Liby Enterprise have a combined share of 35 %.

Rising market shares have an impact not only on country risks but also on corporate governance. Top management positions will be taken by managers from the emerging countries. For many Western multinationals, a board with a diversity of national backgrounds is already a normal business. In the case of China, it depends who including his or her informal network will occupy the seats in the board. More specifically, are there any hidden agendas from the network to favor Chinese Dragon rivals in future? For less-known small- and medium-sized companies, this trend towards Chinese management instead of expats can be a future bottleneck. It often happens that Chinese business partners start for themselves and take away the Chinese business. In multinational companies, this risk is lower, but they are still vulnerable for the dependency on Chinese markets and Chinese decision makers inside and outside the firm.

The increasing market share of China in revenues of Western companies is accompanied with outsourced production facilities and in future increasingly design and innovation functions. The dependency on China for Western firms is becoming larger and larger. The key question is whether it will reach dangerous or unacceptable levels. What about China's aims to be independent? Can you maintain your market position? The answers depend on your world view and ability to adapt to this future fact of life. Moreover, Chinese firms want to try to create their own firms and grasp the market share. You remember the aim formulated in the central government policy to be being independent of the West as of 2020? This is the flip side of growing dependency on Chinese markets.

---

[11] China Daily, 29.10.11, ZTE eyes 80 % sales from overseas.

Fig. 5.6 Newly installed capacity market share between Chinese domestic and foreign suppliers of wind energy

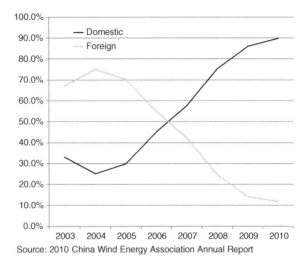

Source: 2010 China Wind Energy Association Annual Report

5.4   Growing Market Share of Chinese Enterprises

The growing market share of Chinese enterprises is the opposite development of the dependency on Chinese markets. In several industries, Western firms are confronted with rising market shares and market power of Chinese enterprises. Frequently, the symbiotic relation between Chinese firms and government is playing industrial power politics. Through Western eyes, the Chinese are creating unequal playing fields by deliberately discriminatory measures such as certification rulings. This power play fits into the aim of being independent of Western technology and creating Chinese powerhouses.

In particular, in industries like banking, insurance, automotive, wind power, IT and telecom equipment, petrochemicals, construction, health-care equipment, and power transmission, Western companies experience the excluding policies. In Fig. 5.6, the fast replacement of Western suppliers by Chinese suppliers is clearly demonstrated.

Chinese enterprises in the wind industry like Sinovel and Goldwind apply different strategies simultaneously: fast follower, fast learning, and quick improvements to products and processes and using the umbrella of governmental protection of buy local policies—an almost perfect illustration of exploiting economies of time leading to economies of scale and scope. These Chinese firms apply the emulation principle: learning from the West and surpassing in the East. Prominent victims of the Chinese industrial strategy are Vestas, GE, and Siemens.

Being a fast follower fits to the Chinese saying "The early bird gets the worm, but the second mouse gets the cheese." Within a time period of 5 years, the Western suppliers of wind energy have lost the Chinese market. The typical Chinese strategy of signing MOUs and LOIs followed by pilot projects and prospects for large market shares attracted many Western firms. But the Chinese strategy boiled down to transferring knowledge and creating Chinese powerhouses. Is it naivety of lack of strategy? The latter is in most cases the main cause of not achieving the ambitions in Chinese markets.

Meanwhile Western firms, particularly SMEs, are aware of these Chinese tactics, and their reaction is to retreat and to find other markets such as India. Western firms have still a lot of opportunities in Chinese market, but it requires a smart tailor-made strategy. In fact, Chinese central plans openly reveal what the ambitions are in several industries enabling Western firms to choose their battles.

5.5   Obstacles for Strategic Innovation in the West

The two simultaneous developments of increasing dependency on Chinese market as well as growing market share of Chinese enterprises require an adaptation of the Western business models in many respects. For the longer term an adequate China strategy is necessary to deal with the largest slice of the total revenue cake and the Chinese Dragons of the near future. But how the Chinese competitors and their business models will look like is still a mystery to many boards. Instead they all follow more or less the same strategy of getting access to and expand market presence. However, Western firms do it with incidental backup but without team up with governments. All Western MNEs from different industries like IBM, Apple, Procter & Gamble, VW, BMW, BASF, DSM, and PwC and many SMEs expand their China activities. The strategic background is the same: the Chinese market cannot be missed. The consequence is that an increasingly large portion of revenues and hopefully profits is coming from China.

What the examples show is that traditional strategy thinking does not give an answer to the challenges of the future. At least the perspective of rethinking existing business models is necessary but not sufficient. The risk that the required approach to renew business will be insufficient is substantial. More strategic innovations are needed to be ready for the twenty-first century. Figure 5.7 presents some highlights.

From these Western cases, we learned that Western strategic innovations in Western private and public organizations are necessary to conquer future markets and to earn a right to exist. However, the main focus is on improvement. A few are now discovering creating new business models but even less have a China strategy let alone a China business model beyond outsourcing. The sword has two sides. First, dependency on Chinese market increases: manufacturing activities as well as market. Second, future Chinese competition comes up.

5.6   Chinese Cases

The Sinochem case demonstrates classical strategic thinking in a Chinese way. Yingli shows the fast growth in a newly created solar panel industry in which cost-driven process management and proven technologies conquer the world. BYD is an

Leadership
- rise of new world order requires renewal of corporation beyond business model
- absence of China strategy at both private and public organization
- hype driven corporate strategies and policies

Institutionalized Innovation
- potential of strategic innovation underestimated
- weak link between corporate and governmental innovation system
- innovation in public organization necessary
- reliance on superior technology is dead end

Business model
- creating and defending superior brands and technology dominate

Business development
- China as an additional market and source of cheap labor
- defending existing growth curve preferred
- emulation by future Chinese rivals is underestimated
- dependency on Chinese market is increasing risk

Governance
- separation between corporate and political leaders
- ongoing concern dominates
- short term results dominates
- new governance rules leading to new world order disregarded

Fig. 5.7 Strategic innovation

illustration of flexibility and the difficult path of radical technical innovation and the attempt to emulate Western car manufacturers.

5.6.1 Sinochem

Sinochem is one of the largest chemical companies of China. Sinochem was founded in 1950 and still is a state-owned company under the supervision of State-owned Assets Supervision and Administration Commission of the State Council (SASAC). In 2011, Sinochem owns more than 200 subsidiaries; they employ more than 40,000 people (Sinochem). The total operating revenues in 2010 were \$49.5 billion and operating profit was \$0.798 billion. Therefore, the profits as a percentage of revenues are less than 2 % (Fortune, Global 500, 25 July 2011). In the ranking of China's top 100 enterprises, it slowly moved downward from rank 7 in 2002 to rank 17 in 2010. In the Global Fortune 500, Sinochem as a whole could be found on rank 209 in 1995 and moved to rank 168 in 2011. But when measured as a trading company, in the Global Fortune 500, it moved upward from rank 15 in 1995 to rank 3 in 2009. However, one should be very careful with the numbers and statistics with regard to their reflection of the exact book value. Therefore, it is more interesting to have a closer look to their development and nature of business. This gives insight into their strategic behavior.

The history and development path of most state-owned companies are the mirror of the history of its only "shareholder" the People's Republic of China and their

Development
phases

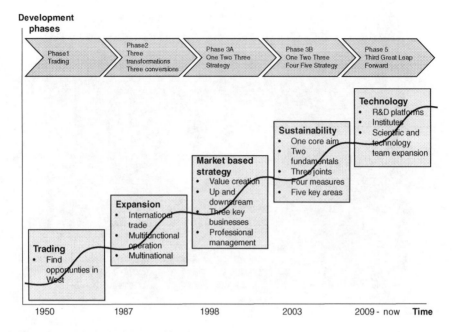

Fig. 5.8 Development stages of Sinochem

policies. To understand its current position and its role in Innovative China, one has to understand its history and in particular its strategic development path.

The policies on state-owned activities and private companies, as mentioned in the previous section, are reflected in this case. Moreover, all the policies on internationalization, increasing scope by becoming active in the whole value chain, becoming a global player, and creating sustainable business and technology development, are almost immediately copy–pasted in the strategy of the state-owned company Sinochem. Figure 5.8 shows the various stages of development.

In the West a well known manager mantra is 'structure follows strategy' or sometimes in reverse order 'strategy follows structure'. In China with regard to at least state-owned enterprises it has to be reframed as: 'Strategy follows policies.' Figure 5.8 clearly reveals the successive stages being identical to implementing the policies of the central government and the relevant plans such as the five-year plans and the technology policies. The several stages of renewal are more reflections of new ideas of the central government than market-based-driven change. For Sinochem, the movement from one phase to the next was often caused by any sort of crisis like Asian crisis and the recent financial crisis. Every time, the company had to be redefined based on leading governmental new policies or aims lacking a sound connection with markets.

In the first phase, it was established as an import–export company providing China with the necessary goods such as rubber, fertilizer, and agricultural membrane. In the 1960s and 1970s, it specialized in petrochemical trade.

In the second phase, the leading strategy named "Three Transformations, Three Conversions" covers the changes from import and export to international trade, from commodity trade to multifunctional operation, and from nationwide foreign trade company to a multinational company, creating a socialist company with modern management, international operation, and group-like organizational structure.

The third phase is featured by the introduction of market based strategic outlines thereby acknowledging the obsolete traditional central planning management methods. The "One Two Three Strategy" is cultivating one's ability, conducting two expansions, and building three key businesses. It aims at a threefold market-based philosophy containing the creation of value for customers; the expansion in activities of the whole value chain, upstream and downstream; and the focus on three key business, being oil, fertilizer, and chemical.

In the fourth phase, the "One Two Three Four Five Strategy" is being regarded to be an "extension and deepening" of the previous One Two Three Strategy. The vision of Sinochem is to become a great respectable company with global presence. The strategy consists of five elements: "one ability" (sustainability), "two fundamentals" (internal management and external expansion), "three joints" (resources, technology, and market), "four measures" (innovation, integration, M&A, and collaboration), and "five key areas" (energy, agriculture, chemicals, finance, and real estate). The hierarchical relation is presented in Fig. 5.9.

In the fourth phase, Sinochem further expanded its product portfolio. The portfolio of Sinochem comprises various products and services such as oil, chemicals, energy, fertilizers, real estate, logistics, and finance. The collaboration with foreign companies, sometimes mergers and acquisitions, should contribute to an integrated company. The goal is to become a lean company in which the integration of activities is key.

In the fifth phase, technology plays the main role. In the guideline, the focus on technology is called "the third great leap forward." The aim is to foster innovation—in fact technical innovations—by means of R&D investments, the foundation of all kind of institutes and R&D platforms and hiring of technical engineers. Cooperation is sought with Western companies like DSM and Monsanto.

When using the evaluation matrix as presented in Fig. 5.10, some profound characteristics of the Sinochem case appear.

The Sinochem case is a clear example of classical strategy formulation based on slogans instead of Western analytical building blocks like trends and competences. Sinochem is an operational vehicle for executing governmental aims.

5.6.2 Yingli Solar

Yingli Solar is a private-owned company and is almost the opposite case of Sinochem. It has made use of the privatization wave mentioned earlier in this chapter. But before we zoom in on Yingli, it is necessary to understand the growth and development of the whole industry.

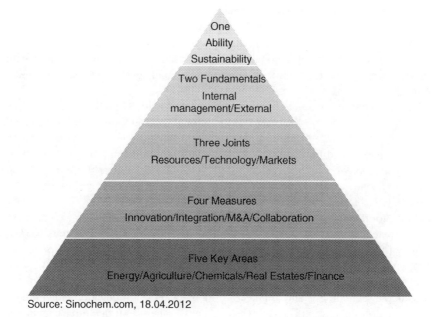

Source: Sinochem.com, 18.04.2012

Fig. 5.9 The strategy pyramid of Sinochem

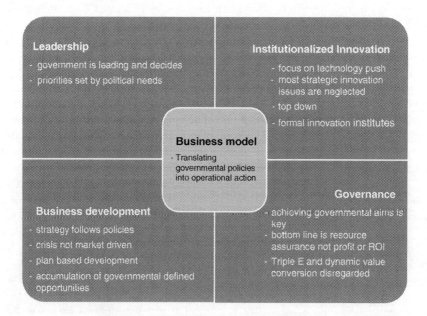

Fig. 5.10 Characteristics strategic innovation areas of Sinochem

The global PV market, as measured by annual PV system installation at end-user locations, increased from 1.6 GW in 2005 to 18.4 GW in 2010. In addition, as of 3 May 2011, PHOTON Consulting forecasted global PV industry revenues and PV system installations to be US$159 billion (total solar power installations revenue pool) and 51 GW in 2015, respectively.

Although Yingli is a private company, it cannot unfold its strategies and path of development independent of the central and local government. A few examples are as follows. In June 2005, the Chinese Ministry of Construction issued a directive, which seeks to expand the use of solar energy in residential and commercial buildings and encourages the increased application of solar energy in townships. Also in June 2005, the State Council of China issued a directive to conserve resource and to promote renewable energy especially the use of solar energy in the western parts of China. On 1 September 2007, the Chinese State Electricity Regulatory Commission issued the Supervision Regulations on the Purchase of All Renewable Energy by Power Grid Enterprises. This regulation promoted the use of renewable energy for power generation including the purchase of all the electricity generated by renewable power companies. Moreover, it also required the timely connection between grids by the electricity grid enterprises.

The birth of Yingli could not have happened without the policy to give entrepreneurs the chance to establish new private-owned firms. In the beginning of the growth cycle, the government supported the start-up of solar wafer appliances by very low rates for capital loans and by creating demand market. The purpose was to bridge the initial losses of low volume markets. The Chinese are masters in applying and commercializing existing and proven technology. The availability of solar wafers launched a bunch of entrepreneurs to apply them in all kind of products. Of course, the solar panel was one of them. Soon Chinese entrepreneurs applied the solar wafer in all kinds of newly created products such as flashlights, streetlights, and traffic lights, another example of fast adapting to new circumstances and grasping opportunities.

Together with early timing and the increasing scale and scope attracted more entrepreneurs. Overcapacity was the result. In order to avoid a pig cycle, or at least dampen the consequences, the Chinese government took measures which are unthinkable in Western markets. Existing solar manufacturers were forced to merge in order to create viable companies with economies of scale advantages. Furthermore, both end and parts of markets were divided among suppliers. The Chinese were lucky because of German legislation favoring renewable energy.

In 2000, the German government introduced the German Act (in German: Erneuerbare-Energien-Gesetz, EEG) to stimulate renewable energy. In short, this law is based on a feed-in tariff paid by the German consumers. This tax revenue is then spent to stimulate solar panel industry and make affordable for consumers to buy PV solar panels. Soon new firms were founded with great prospects. However, Chinese overcapacity was exported to worldwide markets and in particular the German market. Chinese manufacturers started a price competition which many German manufacturer could not equal. As of 2010, several German manufacturer went banktrupt.

The German perspective, in conformity with other Western countries, is that the Chinese intruders violate WTO rules due to dumping. According to German manufacturers, the low end price is below cost price. Some of the German manufacturers who have outsourced their manufacturing to China could not equal Chinese prices. The reality might be a little bit different. First, German manufacturers also get subsidies besides the feed-in tariff and often by local governments when setting up a new factory. It is estimated that in 2011 the solar PV contributes 5 % of total energy supply in Germany, but the system costs 100 billion € of tax money. Of course, Chinese manufacturers are indeed supported by their government. Second, the Chinese manufacturers had the strategy of high quality combined with economies of scale to keep costs low. Chinese government forced Chinese suppliers to merge in order to become a global low-cost player.

The structure of the supply side in Germany is totally different. Apart from some big players, there are many small-scale manufacturers with sometimes only 50 employees. Some of them tried to become a premium brand player that failed because the machines to make high-quality solar panels are also present in Chinese factories and delivered by the same supplier. The result is that Chinese quality equals German quality. Another economies of scale effect is that many German manufacturers are listed on local stock exchanges like SDax or TecDax, whereas Chinese rivals get their capital from Nasdaq or even NYSE. Some German manufacturers choose a way out by outsourcing to China.

But producing in China has its risks and increases economies of scale of Chinese producer. Moreover, local German governments see their support vaporize. The economies of scale effect dropped prices. Moreover, in China, other appliances of PV cells were exploited leading to economies of scope advantages. On top of that, because of high feed-in subsidies, it became profitable to sell high volumes instead of investing the money in technological development. The strategy adopted by, for example, SolarWorld to integrate the whole value chain under their roof did not work. In the first instance, it was an advantage to control the whole chain, but situations like a recession make it a heavy burden and lead to low flexibility. With support of the Chinese government, decisions to close parts of the activities in the value chain can be taken from one day to the other.

At the end of 2011 and beginning of 2012, five German manufacturers, most of them located in Solar Valley and in former East German chemical complex Bitterfeld, went bankrupt. These milestones in the young PV market show that the current dominance of the Chinese manufacturers is not only based on governmental support and cheap capital. Western and German manufacturers also got substantial subsidies. The main problem of Western PV manufactures is the lower dynamic value conversion compared to the Chinese dynamic value conversion. Dynamic value conversion beats subsidies.

But there is more. The production of panels is only a part of the whole value chain. The other activities in the value chain generate a higher added value than the manufacturing of panels. The Chinese brought down the panel manufacturing costs, but the pre-panel and post-panel activities (R&D, silicon production, panel manufacturing equipment, installation structure, inverter, services) remain for the moment stable with regard to added value potential. Moreover, installation is often a local activity within a country or region, whereas the manufacturing of panel machines requires knowledge and capabilities in machine tooling which can be globally based. It can be compared with chip machine maker ASML making high-tech machines for making chips. The downward pressure on manufacturing leads to a lower portion of manufacturing costs in the total cost of solar energy. In the beginning of the value chain, the research institutions, silicon production, and machinery for panel manufacturing are far more complex than panel manufacturing itself. A system integrator can earn good money if the right choices have been made and technology does not change rapidly.

But is it all gold what shines? Are the golden mountains of PV industry Chinese pure gold or is it only a shiny surface which can be scratched away quite easily?

Now is Yingli an undefeatable dominator or a weak Green Dragon? Chinese manufacturers may have won some battles but not yet the solar war. But the rise and dominance of Chinese manufacturers is not without risks. The case of Yingli gives insight into the success and risks of its way of doing business.

Yingli is originally Baoding based where a high-tech zone has been established since late 1990s in which solar energy besides wind power has a pivotal role. In 1998, the State Planning Commission initiated a polysilicon battery and application demonstration project. It has now grown towards a China Power Valley. The Baoding High-Tech Zone not only has Yingli as MNE, but also SMEs are present in the cluster. Yingli Green Energy Holding Company Limited is owner of the brand Yingli Solar. Yingli Solar was founded in 1998 by Mr. Liansheng Miao which makes it a relatively young enterprise. It started selling PV cells in January 2003. Yingli has a capacity of over 1,000 MW per year (2011) and has a vertical integrated manufacturing structure covering the entire PV value chain. The value chain includes the production of crystalline polysilicon, ingot casting, wafering, PV cells production, and PV module assembly. In 2010, Yingli established the first solar research center.

In its business culture, Yingli integrates social and ecological aspects in decision making all contributing to low-cost production. Based on its vertical integrated business model, Yingli is outcompeting its European and American competitors. Moreover, in Germany, Yingli is making use of the feed-in tariff paid for by German citizens. In the USA, together with other Chinese manufacturers, like Suntech, it is supplying 40 % of Californian market in 2010. American competitors like SunPower, founded in 1985, are competing on costs but not on being a low-cost manufacturer. Instead, SunPower wants to provide best technologies with Apple as their peers.

For Yingli, technical innovation is the main driver to reduce costs of PV power. The primary focus of research and development efforts of Yingli is on improving the manufacturing processes at every stage of the production in order to improve the output quality at each stage and deliver more energy-efficient and aesthetically improved PV products at a lower cost. Yingli believes that crystalline silicon will dominate the PV industry in the future.

In December 2010, Yingli has been selected as a PV module supplier of the central government's Golden Sun Program, asking for 272 MW, supported by Ministry of Finance. Yingli is expected to supply 70 % of the total volume.

So far the up-side of the rise and great success story of Green Dragon Yingli. There is a down-side as well. When looking in depth, there are numerous market developments and business risks which demonstrate that the golden mountains do not exist. Other than the Chinese, manufacturers still have opportunities to enter market and become tough rivals of Chinese manufacturers.

The success story of incredible fast growth and development to one of the largest PV cells manufacturers of the world hides the risk of the industry and the specific business risk of Yingli itself. To the industrial risks belong the defensive strategies of incumbent firms like Shell as seen before, the various alternative options of other renewable energy options, shortage of basic input material, the failing infrastructure such as grids, and the lack of bank credits for growth.

The high expectations by stock market are reflected by the increase of Yingli's stock price till 2009.

After 2008, the stock market price plummeted and stabilized on a relatively low level compared to the high of end of 2008. Are the several crises responsible or is there more behind the scenes? The Dow Jones Industrial average suggests the latter. In Table 5.3 the net revenues and profits for the period 2007–2010 are presented.

From Table 5.3, we can derive that there has been a steep growth of both net revenues and net profits except for the year 2009. Also the profit margins as a percentage of net revenues show an upward trend except for 2009 as Table 5.4 reveals.

In 2010, Yingli was able to increase revenues and profit levels to all-time highs, and still stock market price did not follow. Most interesting is of course the loss situation of 2009. It is not only the financial crisis starting in 2008 which explains the sudden downfall of stock price and the operating results. The expectations for the whole industry and the reaction of the individual firm Yingli have to be the explanation. The nature of the young PV subindustry is very volatile and uncertain. Winners of today can be losers of tomorrow.

A closer look to the strategic issues and the business risks demonstrates the numerous issues to be tackled to survive as a major player. The core of the business model of Yingli is vertical integration throughout the whole value chain. This business model offers four advantages. First, it enables Yingli to grasp the profit margins at each stage of the value chain. Second, striving for an efficient manufacturing process lowers cost levels of production, storage, and transport. Third, due to the control of the whole value chain, quality levels can be managed better. Fourth, many competitors are dependent on third parties for component sourcing. But as we will see below, in this respect, Yingli is not self-supporting.

Although the business model appears to possess a few USPs, the danger and risks come from the issues linked to strategic innovation. In Table 5.5, a few relevant risks and strategic issues are listed. With help of Table 5.5, the downturn in stock price and lower expectations for Yingli can be explained.

Table 5.3 Yingli Green Energy net revenues and net profits

	2007 (31.12) (In thousands RMB)	2008 (31.12) (In thousands RMB)	2009 (31.12) (In thousands RMB)	2010 (31.12) (In thousands RMB)	2010 (31.12) (In thousands $)
Net revenues	4,059,323	7,553,015	7,254,869	12,499,987	1,893,937
Gross profit	1,040,604	1,767,216	1,714,373	4,152,785	629,210
Net income (loss)	387,909	653,826	(531,595)	1,386,776	210,119

Source: Yingli Green Energy Holding Co LTD(YGE), Annual and transition report of foreign private issuers pursuant to sections 13 or 15(d) Filed on 05/11/2011, Thomson Reuters Westlaw. Business, US SEC filings

Table 5.4 Profit margins as percentage of revenues

	2008 (per 31.12) %	2009 (per 31.12) %	2010 (per 31.12) %
Germany	41.3	63.1	56.6
Spain	40.3	5.9	5.7
Italy	1.3	6.1	6.8
PRC	2.5	4.5	6.0
United States of America	1.7	2.0	9.7

Source: Yingli Green Energy Holding Co LTD (YGE), Annual and transition report of foreign private issuers pursuant to sections 13 or 15(d) filed on 05/11/2011, Thomson Reuters Westlaw. Business, US SEC filings

The case of Yingli proves that not the business model is key for future success but the required strategic innovations issues to be solved. Below we will highlight some of them.

On the supply side, till the end of 2008, the availability of the main material, polysilicon, was limited. Moreover, there were and are only a limited number of suppliers in the market. Shortage of polysilicon leads to a disruption of customer deliveries. On top of that, contrary to some of its competitors, Yingli has no long-term relationship with most of the suppliers. In the eyes of Chinese, this leads to disadvantages in procurement conditions and especially procurement pricing. To reduce these risks, in January 2009, Yingli bought Cyber Power Group Limited, a development stage enterprise designed to produce polysilicon. Nevertheless, the capacity of Cyber is not enough to meet the total needs of Yingli, and therefore, it remains dependent on third-party suppliers. Apart from volume, the price of the basic material polysilicon was very volatile, and it remains to be seen whether the in-house supplier can deliver as efficient as third parties.

Yingli's dependence on third-party suppliers is shown by the following figures: in 2008, 2009, and 2010, the five largest suppliers supplied in the aggregate approximately 55.0 %, 84.5 %, and 93.1 %, respectively, of total polysilicon purchases. For this reason, excellent relationships on the long term are crucial.

Table 5.5 Overview of some relevant strategic issues and business risks of Yingli

Supply side	Demand side
Availability, supply, and price volatility of basic materials	Home market largely absent
Limited number of suppliers	Extreme dependency on non-Chinese markets
New regulations and governmental policies	Limited number of clients
Governmental regulations with regard to, e.g., renewable sector, labor laws, merges and acquisitions, resource allocation	High volatility in client base
Absence of long-term relationship with suppliers	Absence of long-term relationship with client base
Competition from alternative renewable energy options	Uncertainty and adverse economic situation in target markets
Intensive competition from incumbent firms and new entrants	Changing subsidy and economic incentives regimes
Deep pockets and scale from rivals	Plummeting market prices
Potential rivalry from own Chinese alliance partner	Changing regulations in electricity industry
Failing grid structure	Insufficient brand name, recognition, distribution network
New technologies	Due to uncertainties in supply chain risk of not meeting on time delivery
Absence of institutionalized innovation	Insufficient credit facilities for customer, less advance payments, and warranties risk lowers market expectation
Limited IP protection in non-Chinese markets	Exchange rates
Sufficient internal resources and capabilities such as capital, human resources, and manufacturing capacity	
Majority of production, storage, administration, R&D are clustered in one region in China (Baoding)	
Limited operating history	

Source: based on Yingli Green Energy Holding Co LTD(YGE), Annual and transition report of foreign private issuers pursuant to sections 13 or 15(d) Filed on 05/11/2011, Thomson Reuters Westlaw.Business, US SEC filings

Rivalry from competitors, both incumbents and newcomers and also outside the PV industry, is a high risk or even threat for survival. Some of the rivals are bigger and have higher economies of scale advantages, deeper pockets, more technical knowledge, and in-depth knowledge of target markets. The deep-pocket advantage can be crucial for expanding capital-intensive production capacity. The competition comes from domestic Chinese rivals and from international conglomerates such as BP Solar and Sharp, PV module manufacturers like SunPower, thin film solar module manufacturers such as First Solar, and integrated PV product manufacturers like SolarWorld, Suntech Power Holdings, and Trina Solar.

As a demonstration of cutthroat Chinese competition, the biggest rival, however, may come from within. Yingli has a joint venture with Tianwei Baobian. The original business of Tianwei Baobian is the production of electricity transformers. Tianwei Baobian has only recently entered the PV market through investments in various companies that engaged in the manufacture of polysilicon, ingots, wafers, PV cells or PV modules, and thin film modules. There is a chance that in the near future, these companies of Tianwei Baobian start to compete with Yingli. At the moment of writing, Tianwei Baobian owns 25.99 % equity interest in one of the principal operating entities, Tianwei Yingli. The joint venture contract has no noncompetitive clauses with regard to Tianwei Baobian. Furthermore, with respect to the governance structure, the board of Tianwei Yingli has nine directors, of which six are appointed by Yingli and three by Tianwei Baobian. The supervisionary board has two members of which Yingli and Tianwei Baobian each appoint one member. In the end, Tianwei Baobian has a significant influence on Yingli.

The changing ownership relations include a reputation risk as well. The SEC report mentions the following issue (Thomson Reuters & Westlaw.Business, 2011, p. 28): "Tianwei Yingli, was acquired by China South in March 2008. There have been news reports that China South, Tianwei Group and Tianwei Baobian conducted construction activities in or exported transformers to some sanctioned countries, including Iran and Sudan, in recent years. China North Industries Corporation, or Norinco, an affiliate of China South. We have no control over Tianwei Baobian, Tianwei Group, China South, Norinco or other affiliated entities resulted from China South's acquisition of Tianwei Group, nor has any of such entities requested Tianwei Yingli or us to have contacts with or otherwise conduct any sanctioned activity . . .." It shows the troubles and challenges of a private company working in the Chinese context.

On the demand side, Yingli has to cope with some very relevant issues. Again only a few aspects of Table 5.5 are highlighted.

Most interesting is the absence of a home market. Although the Chinese central and local government of Hebei created favorable conditions for companies like Yingli, by capital support, clustering activities, and capital support and acting as launching customer, the home market is very small. The overcapacity of Chinese market is exported to other world markets. Table 5.6 shows the main markets on the years from 2008 to 2010.

The home market China contributes in 2008 only for 2.5 % of total volume sold and has slowly risen to 6.0 %. The main market is Germany based of course on the renewable energy act stimulating PV and other technologies. Due to changing regulations and subsidies, the market in Spain suddenly disappeared almost completely. Yingli has desperately sought new markets, and one of the promising ones besides many others is the USA. Extreme flexibility is required to follow these large fluctuations in market conditions.

In this respect, Yingli's number of customers is limited. The SEC filings (p. 8) reveal that "In 2008, 2009 and 2010, sales to our customers that individually exceeded 10 % of our net revenues accounted for approximately 11.6 %, 16.9 %

Table 5.6 Main world markets of Yingli

	2008 (per 31.12) %	2009 (per 31.12) %	2010 (per 31.12) %
Germany	41.3	63.1	56.6
Spain	40.3	5.9	5.7
Italy	1.3	6.1	6.8
PRC	2.5	4.5	6.0
United States of America	1.7	2.0	9.7

Source: Yingli Green Energy Holding Co LTD (YGE), Annual and transition report of foreign private issuers pursuant to sections 13 or 15(d) filed on 05/11/2011, Thomson Reuters Westlaw. Business, US SEC filings

and 12.0 %, respectively, of our net revenues. Our relationships with such key customers have been developed over a short period of time and are generally in their early stages. As of December 31, 2008, 2009 and 2010, our five largest outstanding accounts receivable balance (net of provisions) accounted for approximately 81.2 %, 38.9 % and 33.3 %, respectively, of our total outstanding accounts receivable. We are exposed to the credit risk of these customers, ..."

On the demand side of the value chain, also the branding, sales, and distribution of the products of Yingli are still in the early stages of development. A large potential for improvement is present and should be addressed soon.

The demand side is very unstable and highly dependent on foreign markets and customers. On the one hand, the absence of long-term relationships is almost a nightmare for Chinese managers, but on the other hand, they showed extreme flexibility to cope with these fast changing conditions.

The vertically integrated value chain is at risk as soon as the above-mentioned issues and risks turn against the current organizational setup. Options for strategic renewal should be kept open to prepare for the future. In this respect, strategic innovation themes like leadership, institutional innovation, business development, and governance become more relevant than the business model itself in order to be able to create the Yingli of the Future.

Contrary to Sinochem, Yingli is a private-owned company, but as Fig. 5.11 reveals, the differences are smaller than one would expect. Chinese culture together with the greater context of the role of the government and Chinese business behavior as discussed in Chaps. 2 and 3 form the background of this outcome.

The case of Yingli demonstrates the aim of Chinese entrepreneurs to dominate their industry. It also shows the cutthroat competition from Chinese rivals and the urge to expand globally and grasping every opportunity by being flexible and fast moving. But dynamic value conversion requires to renew their business by means of strategic innovation to be ready for future growth of the industry. Yingli is in the midst of jumping from the imitation–improvement to innovation–internationalization phase.

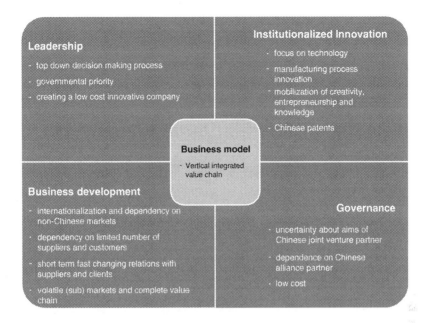

Fig. 5.11 Characteristics strategic innovation areas of Yingli

5.6.3 BYD

A very short history of Chinese automotive industry demonstrates the fast development as a strategic industry sector and sets the scene for BYD.

Since the opening of China, also restrictions in the automotive sector were increasingly removed. The main focus of the central government was more on commercial trucks segment than on passenger cars. In 1994 the Automobile Industry Policy gave way for Western automotive companies to enter Chinese market. The aim was to attract foreign, Western manufacturers. However, foreign companies were obliged to set up a joint venture with a Chinese counterpart and were not allowed to own more than 50 % of the venture. Parallel to these developments, the Chinese government consolidated the Chinese supply side of manufacturers. State-owned car manufacturers were merged into new big players such as First Automobile Works (FAW), Shanghai Automotive Industry Corporation (SAIC), and Dongfeng Motors. Together they are known as the Big Three. The Chinese motor vehicle production increased from below 1 million per year in 1980 to over 16 million per year in 2010. China's worldwide share increased from near 4 % in 1999 to 22 % in 2009, whereas the USA dropped from over 20 % to below 10 %. German production stayed stable around 10 %, and South Korea slightly increased above 5 %.

In 2004, the Automobile Industry Policy has been updated, and focus was redirected towards R&D and technology. The steep increase of Chinese production as of 2008 and 2009 is due to a stimulation program of the central government to

Table 5.7 Market share of top ten car sellers in China

Manufacturer	Sales units (2010)	Market share (%)
SAIC-GM-Wuling	1,135,600	8.3
Shanghai GM	1,012,100	7.4
Shanghai Volkswagen	1,001,400	7.3
FAW Volkswagen	870,000	6.3
Chongqing Changan	710,000	5.2
Beijing Hyundai	703,000	5.1
Chery	674,800	4.9
Dongfeng Nissan	661,000	4.8
BYD	519,800	3.8
Toyota	505,900	3.7

Source: Reserve Bank of Australia Bulletin, March Quarter 2011, China Association of Automobile Manufacturers

fight against financial crisis. Measures were a car scrap scheme and a reduction of the sales tax on cars with an engine size less than 1.6 L from 10 % to 5 % and a subsidy on rural purchases of light trucks and minivans. Both programs ended in 2010.

The estimated total Chinese market is estimated at 30–40 million cars in 2020. However, in 2011, the domestic share of Chinese automakers has dropped to 42.9 % (ChinaDaily, 26.04.2012). The background is that domestic manufacturers traditionally focused on the lower-end market and the foreign companies on the luxury segment. For BMW, Audi, and Daimler, China is becoming a very relevant market. For some, such as BMW, it is already the most important market for selling the most luxury cars such as the 7 Series. Despite recent profitable business for Western luxury manufacturers, this top market segment also represents future risks in form of governmental regulation and Chinese rivals with new energy cars.

Based on the total size of the market and the number of vehicles per 1,000 people, the potential for selling cars is huge. In the USA, the number of motor vehicles per 1,000 people is approximately 800, in Japan 600, and in China below 50 in 2009. Consequently, foreign companies are entering lower segments as well, thereby intensifying competition. The demand of Chinese car buyers has changed to higher-quality preferences. A battle between foreign companies together with their Chinese alliances can be foreseen. The division of market shares is presented in Table 5.7.

In China, there are over 100 car manufacturers, each developing its own car portfolio. Foreign car manufacturers challenge their Chinese rivals by entering lower-end markets with relatively high-quality cars and good brand image against reasonable competitive prices. Chinese car dealers of luxury car manufacturers grow very fast and entry barriers are low. As a result, profit margins come under pressure. Therefore, in the traditional petrol- and diesel-based car market, despite huge market potential, Chinese car manufacturers have an enormous challenge to keep up with famous other brands. Chinese manufacturers try to take over weak rivals such as Volvo in order to get knowledge to be able to compete. But it is very difficult or even impossible, time consuming, and capital intensive to lift the Chinese car manufacturing industry on the same level as the Western OEMs. The only way out is emulation.

The Chinese government tries to emulate the global players by opening and creating a new subindustry based on sustainability. For example, the Chinese government formulated a New Vehicle Program in the 12th Five-Year Plan. The new vehicles focus on the electrical car. The Chinese central government allocated RMB 100 billion (11 billion €) to stimulate the electrical car industry. The aim is to increase the market for electrical cars to 500,000 sold in 2015 and 5 million in 2020. The overview of the Chinese car industry and the ambitious governmental plans set the scene for BYD.

Within this history of Chinese car manufacturing, BYD was founded by Wang Chuan Fu in 1995 in Shenzhen.[12] The 11th and 12th Five-Year Plans put forward the idea of renewables; circular economy, indigenous innovation, independency of Western technology, and automotive policies create the favorable circumstances for setting up a new value chain and create a new subindustry. In 1995, Wang Chuan Fu founded BYD in Shenzhen. He took his chances and initially started to manufacture components for the cell phone industry. The initial aim was to catch up with the Japanese producers of batteries and eventually to overtake them. Soon he became the largest producer of (rechargeable) batteries. In the next step, BYD broadened its scope in the value chain of IT by integrating design and manufacturing parts for Sony, Motorola, Nokia, Samsung, and Sony Ericsson. In Fig. 5.12, these activities are the first growth wave of IT.

The next bold move came in 2003 when BYD took over state-owned car company Tsinchuan Automobile Company Limited. With help of this company, the new brand BYD was introduced in the Chinese market. However, compared to other Chinese manufacturers, BYD was and is a small car company. In this respect, the classical measures such as cost reduction and building brand image were taken. BYD preferred vertical integration above outsourcing, and almost all parts except windshields and tires were manufactured in-house. As a result, almost 95 % of the total work is carried out in-house. Another inversion compared to Western manufacturers was to replace the expensive robot assembly line by cheap labor which contributed to lower cost levels. On the product side, the F3 car became a bestselling car in China.

But based on the megatrends of sustainability, the favorable conditions created by Chinese government, and the internal capability of rechargeable batteries, the main purpose was to build an electrical car. The strategic goals are not modest. On the contrary, BYD aims to be, first, the market share leader in China by 2015 and, second, to be the largest auto manufacturer in the world by 2025.

Furthermore, reversed engineering on competitor's cars was used to learn how they were made. It reduces costs by one-third and saves a lot of time. The founder

---

[12] History is based on http://www.gurufocus.com 13.07.10, Financial Times interview http://www.rationalwalk.com 11.05.09, http://www.ce.cn 25.11.10, http://www.chinaautoreview.com.

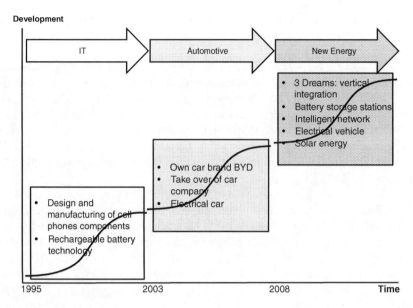

Fig. 5.12 BYD growth waves

Wang Chuan Fu is convinced that BYD will succeed and emulate the West based on two factors: the size of China and the quality of its Chinese workers. Chinese are working harder and the numbers of cheap engineers simply outnumber European capacity. Each year in China 5 million engineers come from universities, and BYD wants to expand from 10,000 engineers in 2010 to 30,000 in 2020.

Another move in controlling the value chain was the opening of factories near to the rare earth metal mining activities. Several cooperation and financial support agreements with local governments in different regions have been set up. But the electrical car is only a starter for getting involved in other industries as well especially energy-related activities.

The third growth wave was the involvement in solar energy. BYD contributed to making the solar panels more efficient but especially focused on energy storage systems and building intelligent networks. The aim of BYD is to become a large-scale solar manufacturer, and for this purpose huge investments in crystalline silicon (c-Si) solar cell manufacturing have been made. The goal is to build manufacturing facilities of 5 GW of annual capacity by 2015. BYD is investing well over US\$3.3 billion. The goal of BYD is to emulate the biggest Chinese solar panel manufacturer in a 5 years' time period. The new energy area will be the biggest growth area of BYD.

The three growth waves taken together represent three big Green Dreams of BYD: solar power including grid, energy storage and electrical transportation. By combining these three related activities, BYD wants to achieve first-mover advantage and to become a fully vertically integrated supplier of the electrical car.

Table 5.8 The top tech list

Rank (2010)	Company	Country
1	BYD	China
2	Apple	USA
3	Tencent Holdings	China
4	Amazon.com	USA
5	Tata Consultancy	India
6	Priceline.com	USA
7	Centurylink	USA
8	Cognizant Tech.	USA
9	Infosys Tech	India
10	Softbank	Japan

Source: Business Week 12.05.2010

In the beginning, BYD aimed at surpassing Japanese battery technology, and for this purpose Sanyo and Sony patents were studied to learn how they were made. BYD is the only manufacturer who never had a recall illustrating the quality of its battery quality which will be decisive in the competition with Renault, Nissan, Mercedes-Benz, and GM. But appliance in a car is a different game. According to Wang Jianjun, deputy general manager of BYD Automotive Sales Co., Ltd., only large-scale production in combination with the vertical integrated value chain will bring down costs, and material science is essential to make progress. But it is not only imitate and improve; meanwhile, it has become the biggest applicant of patents after Huawei and ZTC. Compared to other Chinese competitors focused on manufacturing, BYD heavily invests in R&D, about 2 % of total revenues. Table 5.8 demonstrates the international standing of its R&D efforts.

Table 5.8 demonstrates the focus on technology and the international acknowledgement. BYD also proves that it is not only the creation of knowledge and inventions but appliance to realize a new sustainable world.

Realizing dreams is a great driver to be successful, but, as in real life, nightmares happen as well. In the future, BYD has to avoid some serious problems as shown in Fig. 5.13; the potential nightmares to avoid can have their origin in five areas.

The case of BYD demonstrates the high risk-taking and controlling the business behavior. Supported by governmental programs, the aim is to emulate Western car manufacturers, but the realization of the necessary innovations remains a huge challenge.

5.7   Western Versus Chinese Strategic Innovations

The previous sections of business cases give some insight into the differences in several aspects of strategic innovation. In Table 5.9, a few highlights are presented.

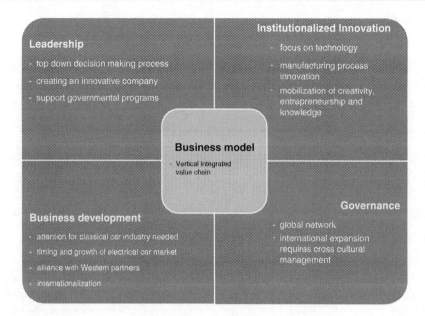

Fig. 5.13 Strategic innovation challenges

Table 5.9 gives a summary of several of the issues elaborated in this chapter. The previous sections have shown that the notion of strategic innovation has different backgrounds and meanings in the West and East. Furthermore, Chinese and Western business models differ in aim, content, time due to differences in context, and culture as the strategic innovation theory describes. Chinese business models are embedded in strategic innovations focused on total control, dominating industry powerhouses, globalization with governmental support, and enforced market supply structures.

Moreover, Chinese business models are based on both public support and private initiatives. Mostly, they lack internationalization, but the phase of global activities has started. This holds not only for securing natural resources but also for various industries. One of the drivers is intense competition on Chinese home market. Besides export, foreign direct investments are increasing.

Chinese firms, often supported by government due to strategic arguments, use vertical integration to secure supply of natural resources and to control the complete supply chain. Because of expected scarcity in rare earth metals but also to capture other strategic resources like iron ore, in the steel industry, mergers and acquisitions and vertical integration will be applied to increase control.

This is against the Western megatrend of network firms but already predicted by the strategic innovation theory. The reasons are that the concentration index in the steel industry is, despite well-known past mergers like ArcelorMittal, still very low. Second, the largest demand for steel is coming from China but also India and Brazil. More than 70 % of steel demand comes from these countries. The scarcity of natural resources increases the need for securing supplies, and vertical integration is the

Table 5.9 Some highlights in comparing strategic innovations in China and the West

	The West	China
Industry power	Some multinational companies have large influence on policy Industry structure, uniqueness, and brand determine market power	Central and local government have large influence on firms Guanxi and inner circle information
Entrepreneurship	Individual entrepreneurship Manager more present than entrepreneur Analytical professional management	Entrepreneurship within network Entrepreneurship dominant over managerialism Fast, experimental, and pragmatical
Strategy	Focus and customer orientation Trading technology for markets	Emulation and striving for industry dominance Becoming independent of The West
Governance	One-tier or two-tier Boards Triple P and increasing transparency Focus on individual firm Functional specialization Human interaction within company and business network	Governmental related Family and private business within network Holistic management Human interaction within business and government network
Leadership	Top-down and bottom-up decision making Following leadership hypes	Top-down decision making Becoming No 1
Innovation	Technology and R&D oriented Functional innovations, product innovation, new business models still rareHype of sharing knowledge, cooperation and open innovation Difficulty with commercialization of R&D Absence of EU wide innovation system, US believes in market-based innovation system	Emulation of technology and R&D Creating new industries, global powerhouses, Chinese business models From China Manufacturing System to China Innovation System Knowledge sharing only between inner circle network members Open innovation followed by closed innovation Difficulty with bottom-up innovation
Process	Growth by profit re-investment Internal and external growth (merger and alliances) Creative destruction Learn in the West, keep in the West	Efficient manufacturing Government supported growth, forced mergers Continuous accumulation Learn in the West, surpass in the East
Uniqueness	Technical patents, design, branding, and marketing Radical innovation	Industry dominance Fast emulation
Risk perception	Reward system favors risk avoiding behavior	Risk compartmentalization Grasping opportunities sometimes gambling behavior
Economic engine	Added value generation focused on shareholder value	Low cost manufacturing followed by dynamic value conversion

(continued)

Table 5.9 (continued)

	The West	China
Time	Predominantly short term Linear time concept	Combining short term and long term Speed and accumulation over time Flexibility and adaptability
Culture	American Dream no European Dream Confrontation Opportunistic cooperation	Chinese dream of becoming Number One Harmony and mutual interest with regard to inner circle Personal relations determines business development competition

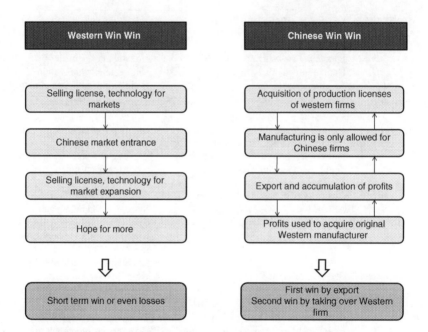

Fig. 5.14 Western versus Chinese win–win

favorite solution for Chinese players. Third, they want to form a countervailing power by gaining a market power position.

Chinese strategic innovations are focused on becoming the winner at the end of the game in the long term. Western managers prefer to speak about creating win–win situations. But the Chinese interpretation of win–win is different from Western win–win notions as Fig. 5.14 shows.

The Western win–win is often focused on the short term without having assurance on the long term. It is giving away without knowing what you get in the long term. Chinese win–win means the Chinese win all. Figure 5.14 shows a very common practice of building alliances, sharing knowledge in exchange of market entrance or development followed by emulation or even takeover by the Chinese partner. This power play of strategic advantages in the long run is part of Chinese dynamic value creation process.

Another relevant issue with regard to the application of the dynamic value conversion principle is the Triple E (economies of scale, scope, and time). The Western explanation of Chinese business success based on low cost and governmental support is too simple. Chinese enterprises gain their competitive advantage by applying the dynamic value conversion principle. Without this modus operandi, the governmental support would be ineffective. Yingli applied the dynamic value conversion, thereby gaining advantages on economies of scale, scope, and time including its multiplier effects. But next steps are necessary to become the dominant player.

Western firms have to replace the short-term shareholder value by the time-based dynamic value conversion principle. Otherwise, competition with Chinese firms will become very difficult. The prerequisite is a China strategy showing how to capture and secure dynamic value conversion in Chinese markets and in competition with Chinese powerhouses.

Tables 5.10, 5.11, and 5.12 summarize the strengths and weaknesses of American, European, and Chinese strategic innovations.

Tables 5.10, 5.11, and 5.12 reveal some striking differences between the three regions. They also show that a complete convergence of the elements of strategic innovation is impossible due to history, cultural heritage, and deep beliefs. But the opposite also holds that some elements have to be improved in order to be able to keep up with the strategic innovation frontier. A few highlights are shortly discussed below.

With regard to leadership and a clear visionary future, both the EU and the USA lag behind China. The EU leaders have no clue about a future world view and EU's future except a kind of European integration. The USA keeps believing in their technological ingenuity of their entrepreneurs. Both the EU and the USA have no answer on the worldwide expansion of China like control of resources and new strategic sectors. The Big Dream-driven societies of China and the USA focus on own prosperity in which prosperity of other regions can be helpful but is not an eternal necessity. But luckily, on the short term, the West depends on the ability of China to realize its future vision and ambitions. China needs time to become an innovative country. So the EU has some time left, but their leaders should act now. In several instances, China is also taking industrial steps forward by creating powerhouses and industrial standards. Industrial standards will be reinforced as soon as innovation is institutionalized.

The ability to create and implement institutional innovation systems within individual and network of enterprises will be crucial for the outcome of the ambitions. Here the USA still has a strong position and lies ahead on the EU and China. But part of the context and conditions are changing in favor of China. Sustainability is not an issue which can be solved by a single company but requires

Table 5.10 Strengths and weaknesses strategic innovation (USA)

Strengths strategic innovation USA	Weaknesses strategic innovation USA
Leadership • (Individualistic) entrepreneurialism • Economic history is strongly linked with innovation • Technology leadership in several industries	Leadership • Deliberate decoupled governmental policies and private business • US norms and values dominate • Lack of China strategy
Institutional innovation • Successful market-based innovation output • Bottom-up approach of entrepreneurship and innovation • Freedom of individual entrepreneurship	Institutional innovation • Nationwide strategic innovation issues like sustainability or rise of China relatively get low attention • National innovation systems of minor importance • Mobilization of entrepreneurship, knowledge, and creativity underdeveloped
Business development • Pragmatic short-term focus on bottom line result • Unlimited faith in progress and prosperity based on technology • Accumulated experience with high end, high profit margin value creation	Business development • Deliberate weak link between micro- and macro-level • Corporate competition not prepared for Chinese industrial competition • China strategy is limited to outsourcing or market entrance and development
Governance • Melting pot of human resources fosters entrepreneurship and innovation • Entrepreneurship is preferred over social security • High standard and integrity of research • Quadruple Helix is operational in many instances	Governance • Short-term view dominates • Focus on (short-term) financial results instead of (long-term) market and innovation orientation • Cross-cultural differences often disregarded

all business partners involved in the vlaue chain or the creatikon of a new value circle with old and new partners. Sustainability requires concerted actions of both private and governmental policies. Here China has already proven to be able to put into practice the required symbiosis. But China has to deal with their current bias for technology and underdeveloped bottom-up innovation process. Moreover, China's dependency on the direction and aims of national and local plans even hinders the bottom-up process.

Even Europe and USA have a large untapped potential for the bottom-up innovation process within enterprises or within society. Therefore, the stages of innovation and internationalization are for China, huge challenges for which they do not yet have the right structure, institutions, behavior, and culture. Within Europe, Germany is relatively close to the institutionalization of innovation. But even there, the system works for old industries like the automotive sector, but for the new energy or biotech industries, new challenges require new solutions. BASF has stopped gentech crop (GM) in Europe due to public resistance. Therefore, although the EU has a long tradition in innovation, it is not an assurance for future

Table 5.11 Strengths and weaknesses strategic innovation (EU)

Strengths strategic innovation EU	Weaknesses strategic innovation EU
Leadership • Long history in some EU member states and regions • Leadership in (moral) ideas	Leadership • Decoupled governmental policies and private business • Hypes and "me too" innovation policies with little impact • Context for innovation and institutional innovation within organizations largely missing • Risk of losing leadership over future industries • Lack of world vision and absence of China strategy
Institutional Innovation • Individual, corporate, and regional knowledge and innovation hot spots available but often distributed over many disconnected organizations and only partly commercialized • Bottom-up approach is regarded to be better than top-down approach • Large variety and diversity in Europe represents a high potential scope of innovation but still largely untapped • Freedom of individual entrepreneurship	Institutional Innovation • Potential of institutional innovation underdeveloped • Quadruple Helix underdeveloped. Academic research and policies dominate over commercial implementation. • Weak link between micro-, meso- and macro-level and national innovation systems insufficient and ineffective • EU national innovation system underdeveloped and divided and focused on R&D instead of commercialization • Mobilization of entrepreneurship, knowledge, and creativity underdeveloped • Cross border or pan-European innovation underdeveloped
Business development • Free market principles dominate • Competences in all functional areas like R&D, branding, marketing, logistics, and HR • Accumulated experience with high end, high profit margin value creation	Business development • China strategy is limited to outsourcing or market entrance and development • Corporate competition not prepared for Chinese industrial competition • Large potential for internationalization of business and pan-European market largely underdeveloped • Too less German like role of SMEs
Governance • High standard and integrity of research • Relations with stakeholders • Rise of Triple P as performance measure instead of profit	Governance • Member state policies and comitology dominate over EU level innovation strategy • Institutional barriers for pan-European markets • Rewards for innovation relatively low because of fiscal regime favoring employees and managers instead of entrepreneurs • National culture differences disregarded • Relatively slow decision making

new industries with new risks and opportunities. Being afraid of the future hampers innovation.

China has a long history in organizational and institutional innovation, but in the past decades, this heritage has been overshadowed by the admiration of technology.

Table 5.12 Strengths and weaknesses strategic innovation (China)

Strengths Chinese strategic innovation	Weaknesses Chinese strategic innovation
Leadership • Industrial instead of corporate competition policies based on future vision • Symbiosis private and public organizations • Big Dream-driven • Powerhouses / Chinese (Green) Dragons are in the make	Leadership • Short recent history with innovation • Dominance of government overshadows innovation leadership of individuals and individual organizations
Institutional innovation • New industry creation leading to new growth cycle • Focus on practical applicable innovation output • Fast adoption to new circumstances and new market demand • Substantial investments in R&D, technology, and education • Quadruple Helix for selected firms not for private and SMEs • Chinese forms of strategic innovation are being explored and implemented • Long history in organizational and institutional innovations but overshadowed by recent focus on technology	Institutional innovation • Institutional innovation is largely absent and slogan like strategies are not equal to strategic innovation • Technology bias and neglecting relevance of nontechnical innovation • Disconnection between central and local innovation policies • National innovation system in its infancy and high dependency on general governmental policies and plans • Innovation and internationalization phases of 4I scheme at their infancy but R&D, brands, trademarks, and business models are gaining momentum
Business development • Coherent long-term industrial policies and plans • Entrepreneurial culture • Recent acknowledgement of entrepreneurs besides governmental class • Fast moving and flexible • Scale and scope of home market	Business development • Copy cat behavior of both central and local policies lead to overcapacity and low profit margins • Current business models based on imitation and improvement is relatively easy money • Top-down and long-term approach in plans often lack implementation and lead to mal investments • Financial risks due to bonanza like past growth and economic short-term gain Issues like social security, health care, distribution of wealth will compete for resources • Focus on grasping opportunities and maximizing economies of scope and scale • Lack of international experience
Governance • Global sourcing and secured resources due to governmental policy • Strong link between micro-, meso- and macro-level • Exploitation of dynamic value conversion • Development of industry standards • Current preference for increasing scale, scope, and time instead of Western mantra of strategic focus	Governance • Rivalry between central and local government • National culture differences disregarded • Low standard and integrity of research and IP • Relation with stakeholders outside own informal network • Focus on economic profit in dynamic value conversion

But the key for future success is in the area of nontechnical innovation. The USA and the EU have a proven track record in this field, but still a huge potential is not exploited. China has to rediscover their heritage. The Total Innovation Management approach is a positive sign in this direction. The Chinese are moving towards one of the biggest strengths of the West. Therefore, the USA and EU have to be careful not to decide for a standstill but to renew their attention for nontechnical innovations.

The proven Chinese organizing capabilities should be applied on fostering creativity and strategic innovation without being afraid of released energy and unpredictable outcomes. It will be the biggest challenge for China and its leadership, but some may see the mobilization of creativity, knowledge, and entrepreneurship as opening the box of Pandora. It demonstrates the other big challenge of synthesizing the paradox of bottom-up/freedom and top-down/organized creativity.

The market structure of rivaling provinces, governmental governed organizations, and (informal) networks combined with copycat behavior of the majority of Chinese firms leads to overcapacity and a great vulnerability due to low profit margins in the near future. Moreover, rapid rising costs will force Chinese companies to renew their dominant imitation–improvement business model. World crises, overcapacity, and sometimes too high optimism demonstrated the limits of the Chinese business models based on imitation and improvement.

The entrepreneurial attitude to grasp any opportunity fits in a growing economy without resource limitations and a supportive government. Grasping opportunities leads to maximizing economies of scope in a short time period. Grasping every opportunity fits to a trading mentality but not to developing an innovative organization. Exploitation of the first growth curve consisting of imitation and improvement is relatively easy earned money. The first experiences of moving towards the second growth curve consisting of innovation and internationalization proved that more efforts are necessary and more time is needed.

In the area of business development, China has a world circumventing approach with regard to natural resources, knowledge, and market access. But they still lack the history and competences to deal with international deal making and handling an international client base. Buying technology and companies does not mean you can serve and satisfy non-Chinese clients. Western enterprises from the EU and the USA have to rethink their core strategy of outsourcing and market entrance by exchanging technology for markets. The dependency on Chinese markets measured in market share and profits is for many Western firms increasing. But rising Chinese competitors and protecting Chinese government represent an increasing risk.

The Chinese powerhouses pushing forward and Green Dragons driving sustainability are trying to conquer the value chains and create the value circles of tomorrow. However, with rising labor costs, increasing environmental regulations, and coping with social issues such as health and pension plans, the pressure on the Chinese enterprises will rise as soon as the gained profit margins have to be redistributed. The vertical integration will indeed lead to Chinese powerhouses and in some cases possibly reach the level of total control. But social inequality, the environmental issues, and the legitimacy of the government will depend on redistribution of wealth and prosperity and the ability to increase the level of creativity—read freedom—to fulfill the requirements of becoming an innovative society.

In Western countries, governance means corporate governance. But with the rise of China, also a governance on the meso-level, industrial governance, is gaining relevance. Western countries immediately complain about the absence of IP rights in China. But other industrial governance issues might become more relevant as soon as China enters the innovation stage of its 4I emulation process. One of these issues is standardization leading to Chinese standards to which the others have to adapt. The emergence of Chinese based standards can prove to be a huge hurdle for getting access or maintaining market positions. Europeans are far behind due to their failing integration of their home market.

The creation of a new growth cycle requires the application of dynamic value conversion instead of short-term profit-seeking linked with the downturn of the old growth cycle. The dynamic value conversion is linked with strategic maneuvering on various issues simultaneously aiming at winning the war not the battle.

Another one is the true coordinated global sourcing of natural resources and governmental backed globalization of all kind of enterprises in various sectors. But it requires to be able to cope with different cultures as well. Here, the USA and their famous heritage of being a melting pot have an advantage on their home turf. The EU and China each on their own way stick to their roots of cultural background of member states, respectively, Chinese mainland background. The governance of strategic innovation remains a challenge for all three main players: the EU, USA, and China. The EU governance lacks coordination, coherence, and impact. The USA lacks nationwide approaches for meso- and macro-issues like sustainability. China is dependent on traditional networks and dealing with internal rivalry between local governments.

5.8   Strategic Innovation Context: Hard Outside and Soft Inside

The differences between the strategic innovation areas can be traced back to the features of a hard outside and a soft inside as Tables 5.13 and 5.14 demonstrate.

Although the descriptions in the tables in reality will have much more nuances, both the hard and soft facts show some striking differences. In the end, business models are about the earning capacity bottom line, but the way Europeans and Chinese think about the background of business models is completely different. Together with the differences in the strategic innovation area discussed earlier, the outcome of the emulation process between the EU, USA, and China is dependent on many factors and not yet decided. Therefore, the future world will become a battlefield in the strategic innovation arena. The broad scope of strategic innovation comprises hard and soft aspects which can easily be summed up but will appear as a total picture in reality.

Table 5.13 Main features of hard outside current Western and Chinese context of strategic innovation

Hard outside business model	Current Western strategic innovation context	Current Chinese strategic innovations
Markets and customers	Global and local markets/niches	Export driven
Products	Brand driven	Copy cats
Process	Value chain management service	Manufacturing
Organization	Separation private business government Specialized	Symbiosis business and government Informal networks and conglomerates
People	Qualification driven	Network driven
Economic engine	Shareholder value Economies of scale and scope and market segment leader	Lead firm and network Economies of scale, scope and time and controlling value chain
Innovation	R&D and technology driven	Technology improvement driven
Time	Short term	Short term and flexibility Long term and stability

Table 5.14 Main features of soft inside current Western and Chinese context of strategic innovation

Soft inside	Current Western strategic innovation context	Current Chinese strategic innovation context
Philosophy	Truth, wrong or right	Contingent pragmatism
Strategy	Analysis driven and multiple targets	Action driven and becoming leading nation in technology
Knowledge	Ownership and sharing Create and keep in the West	Appliance of wisdom Learn in the West surpass in the East
Innovation	Creative destruction From closed to open innovation	Adaptation and accumulation From open to membrane innovation
Human relation	Competences Knowledge	Trust
Leadership	Head of ROI	Head of family/network/own business
Societal time	Birth-Life-Death (Christian religion)	Circular and stages (Taoism)
Business time	Linear and sequential Short term dominates	Circular and parallel Short and long term

Within the 4I scheme, the Chinese growth model till now was based on the hard facts of economies of scale low-cost production, easy and cheap imitation and improvement, and focus on manufacturing process based on reversed engineering. The approach of Total Innovation Management (TIM) is the first step to introduce a more holistic approach trying to grasp innovative engineering and also the soft facts. But the soft facts based on, for example, a balanced top-down–bottom-up approach, fostering individual creativity and cross-cultural innovation process require a tailor-made institutionalized innovation process far beyond TIM.

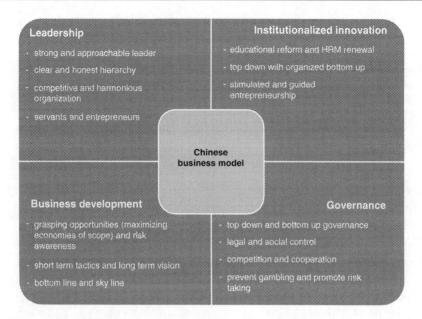

Fig. 5.15 Chinese culture and strategic innovation

The Chinese cultural influences and ideas as discussed in Chap. 2 on strategic innovations can be seen in Fig. 5.15.

New top management issues like sustainability and the rise of China clearly demonstrate that the renewing and adapting of the business model is not sufficient. The renewal of a business model is carried out on the micro-level. But issues like sustainability and innovative China require to set favorable conditions at meso-level and possibly macro-level including the role of government as well. At least the following four strategic innovation areas need to be addressed: leadership, institutional innovation, business development, and governance. Formulating the right action in these four arenas creates favorable conditions for a new growth curve. This is exactly what the Chinese are currently doing in many of their industries like solar panels, wind energy, and biotech.

The cases in this chapter have demonstrated that strategic innovations beyond business models are necessary to be prepared for the future. Especially in the phase of innovation and internationalization of the 4I process, Chinese enterprises need to apply the strategic innovation theory to realize their ambitions of becoming an innovation leader in 2050. The same holds for enterprises and public organizations from the USA and the EU.

References

China Wind Energy Association. (2010). *Annual Report*. Washington, DC: IEA Wind.

Thomson Reuters, & Westlaw.Business. (2011). *Yingli Green Energy Holding Co LTD (YGE)* (Annual and transition report of foreign private issuers pursuant to sections 13 or 15(d) filed on 05/11/2011). New York: Author.

van Someren, T. C. R. (1992, June). *Innovatie, Emulatie en Strategisch Milieumanagement Strategisch Milieu Management, MBA-course.* Amersfoort, Netherlands: Dept. Scientific Institute for Environmental Management, University of Amsterdam.

van Someren, T. C. R. (1995). *Strategies for sustainable profits.* Milieumanagement van Kosten naar Baten, Wetenschappelijk Instituut voor Milieumanagement, Universiteit van Amsterdam.

van Someren, T. C. R. (1998a, April). *Strategies for sustainable profits.* Milieumanagement van Kosten naar Baten, Wetenschappelijk Instituut voor Milieumanagement, Universiteit van Amsterdam, Amsterdam, The Netherlands.

van Someren, T. C. R. (1998b, September 17). *Strategies for sustainable profits.* International BMW Seminar, Dietramszell.

van Someren, T. C. R. (1998c, December 7). *Strategies for sustainable profits.* International Shell Seminar Managing HSE in the Business, Noordwijkerhout, The Netherlands.

van Someren, T. C. R., & van Someren-Wang, S. (2009, May). La pyramide inverse L'innovation stratégique par l'encadrement Intermédiaire. *Business Digest, 196.*

Weewer, R. (2009, May). A strategic journey for the Dutch Fire Service. *Business Digest.*

How to Win the Battle on Innovation?

6

To win the battle on strategic innovation will be the biggest challenge of the twenty-first century for China, the USA, and the EU. Although China is emulating itself towards an innovative economy, the innovation battle cannot be won by central planning and control. If we look at the strategic innovation issues of the twenty-first century, there are at least ten major issues each with their own dynamics and challenges. Although China, the USA, and the EU each have a head start on one or more of these issues, none of the contenders has a decisive advantage yet. The Global Strategic Innovation Index shows the different positions of China, the USA, and the EU. But foremost, this index demonstrates the huge untapped potential of strategic innovation each of the countries can still exploit. It will indeed become an eternal process of emulation on the level of countries, regions, industries, individual firms, and individuals and policies. Leaders from governments and industries will have to pick up the challenge of strategic innovation and create their own tailor-made solutions fitting to their history, culture, future world needs, and ambitions. The winner will be the one which knows its weakness and strength in a changing world with changing counterparts and be able to renew itself continuously.

6.1 Eternal Emulation

China's aim is to become prosperous and simultaneously emulate the USA and the EU. Although strategy is a strong point of the Chinese, innovation is not always appreciated in the Chinese history. To be successful China needs to turn their weakness into strength by strategic innovations. Particularly nontechnical innovations will be the biggest challenges and also provide the best chances. The USA and the EU have to adapt to the new world order and strategically renew themselves to have a chance to win. Strategic innovation can generate unique innovation outcomes which is difficult to predict and imitate. But a few common areas will give an indication of the innovation future of China, the USA, and the EU. Figure 6.1 gives a few examples of the strategic innovation directions.

T.C.R. van Someren and S. van Someren-Wang, *Innovative China*,
Management for Professionals, DOI 10.1007/978-3-642-36237-8_6,
© Springer-Verlag Berlin Heidelberg 2013

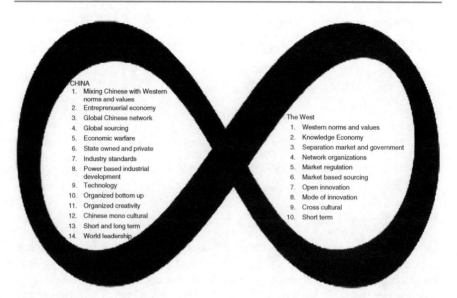

Fig. 6.1 Eternal emulation

If these countries choose the right directions, China has the chance to regain the position of one of the world's leading nations; the West will also have their chances to maintain and improve their position. It all depends on ourselves.

6.2   The Race for the New Welfare

A Chinese proverb "shang chang ru zhan chang (the market place is a battlefield)" expresses how serious the Chinese take economic interests. The future of economic development will be a battle between China, the USA, and the EU on strategic innovation. Western politicians believe that we live in an era of mutual dependency between the West and China. Another belief is that Asia and in particular China will be the dominant power of the future. In almost every aspect the current conditions, context, content, and creativity differ between China, the USA, and the EU. These four fields and more importantly the dynamic development in all four fields will decide about the ability to innovate.

"Innovative China" represents big opportunities but big threats as well. Extreme thoughts of either a future dominance of China or a creative incapable country are wrong. Within three decades, China was able to conquer a position from being a sleeping giant to a dynamic cat which caught the economic mouse. In the coming decades the Chinese devote their time, energy, man power, and eagerness to outgrow their image of a "copycat." China has great interest to become a giant in innovation, but knowing the Chinese innovation history, mutual dependence will be in Chinese interest too. But the EU and the USA need to notice this and reinvent themselves to stay in innovative strength. The competition on innovation will make each and all nations stronger.

To create strategic innovations in private and public sector can improve the chances to win. Luckily, the solutions will be different for China, the USA, and the EU, and one cannot copy the other. All involved parties have to find their own way through the potential gold mine called strategic innovation. The journey will not be easy, but the invested courage, energy, and effort will be rewarded by a new prosperous world. Before the battle is fought, it is important to know in which direction the field of innovation itself will develop.

6.3   The Future World of Strategic Innovation Is Beyond Business Models

The strategic innovation battle will reshape global industries. The battlefield is in fact completely open for new strategies, tactics, and resources used. And why? There are four main reasons.

First, both China and the West do not know how to win the innovation battle yet. The five-year plan, the White Paper, and the National Medium- and Long-Term Program for Science and Technology Development all show that China wants to set up a complete system of innovation, but it is still far from comprehensive. Nevertheless, the Western national innovation system is more or less in its infancy; many aspects of the Western innovation system can be improved considerably.

Second, the rise of a new world order generates more challenges and opportunities for innovations. To turn the challenges into opportunities requires more than only rethinking your business model. For example, the rise of China makes the Chinese norms and values more important in global economy. The Chinese ways of strategic innovation will make leadership, institutionalized innovation, business development, and governance even more important. Another example is the issue of sustainable development. It can only be realized with innovation in new leadership styles with eye for societal developments, institutional innovation, and business development with NGO's partly governments creating new regulations and industrial governance for dealing with natural resources.[1] In fact the whole concept of sustainable development is in its infancy as well. Of course, conceptual ideas like cradle to cradle exist, technologies have been developed, and institutional worldwide supporting systems like ISO 14000 have been created. But still many opportunities to generate economic growth and at the same time benefit the planet and the people are open.

Third, it depends on the other strategic innovation fields whether the technology primacy can be transformed in prosperity and sustainable wealth. To be independent in sciences and technologies will not automatically increase Chinese

---

[1] See T.C.R. van Someren, 1995

innovation competences. Under the economic necessity as well as historical and cultural embedded reasons, China needs to broaden its thoughts about innovation. When the Chinese can combine technical excellence with their strategic insights, the big leap forward to become a real economic power can be true.

Fourth, current thinking about corporate strategy and innovation does not fit to upcoming new world order and new growth curve accompanies by the rise of China and other non-Western countries. New conditions, assumptions, and conceptual models are necessary like what the SIT tries to do—to cope with the challenges of the twenty-first century.

The Western economy is increasingly developing the competence to create new business models. But as soon as China becomes innovative as well, the game is completely different. Then the outcomes are dependent on the organizational and institutional solutions to integrate Western with Chinese businesses. When innovation is institutionalized with good leadership and governance as foundation for business development, a competitive advantage from innovations is possible. Because of this way, again and again new fields of competition will be created. There comes room for both incumbents as well as innovative market entrants. What is the use of being technical innovative when the Chinese can copy everything within years or even weeks? If we only finance the R&D costs but pay no attention to make business out of innovation, the one who can will get the profit.

Only firms that are able to align the strategic innovation arenas in which a win–win situation can be created for both Westerners and Chinese will survive in China. For Western firms it is necessary to know how the current Chinese innovation system is and what the future opportunities are to share the Chinese innovation cake. There are opportunities because the Chinese innovation framework has to be developed almost from scratch. This is the best situation for creative entrepreneurs to get involved and to play a substantial role.

There is a big chance that the Chinese can succeed in strategic innovations but also a big chance that it will fail. As soon as Chinese firms enter the global market, either backed up by the Go Global Strategy of the Chinese central government or forced by overcapacity, Chinese firms have to reinvent their business model. Attracting Western customers with low-cost products is only an infant step. The cost levels of labor, resources, and capital are rising in China. The pressure increases to go into higher added value segments. Innovations are increasingly critical for the survival of Chinese companies. At the same time, the Chinese leadership realizes the pressure and is generating innovation policy to become more independent. A large bunch of Chinese entrepreneurs will back this policy due to their proudness of building a new nation. This effect may not be underestimated; it is like in the 1960s when President Kennedy announced to put a man on the moon. Not only NASA knew what to work on but the whole nation felt as entering into a new era.

On first sight, the race between China, the USA, and the EU is about technologies. But if the technologies are more or less the same or can be copied easily and fast, what is the battle of innovation then really about? In our opinion, not the content of technology but the creation of the context and the ability to mobilize

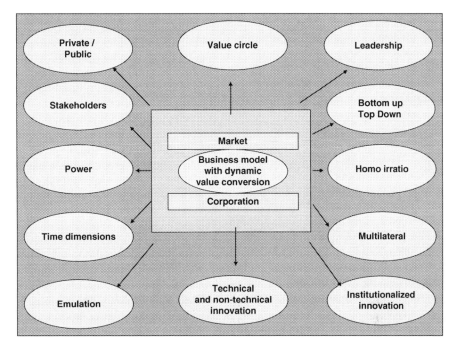

Fig. 6.2 Strategic innovation blurs the current borders of corporation

innovative entrepreneurship and knowledge will decide the winner. Therefore, the most crucial innovation battle is not only in the laboratory fought by technicians or high-tech teams. Instead, one of the decisive battles will be fought by the leaders about who can create and sustain the right context and can institutionalize innovation. Creative individuals and teams can leave firms and countries, but an institutionalized innovation process cannot. It is part of a firm or a network of firms. Therefore, in order to win the innovation battle, you need to know how to deal with leadership, behavior, negotiation, and organization, too. These are especially important in a Chinese business environment.

Strategic innovations as the future battlefield goes beyond creating new business models. Creating new business models may win the battle of yesterday within the context of Western market economy and in a safe world without China. The Chinese way of innovation blurs the current borders of corporations. Strategic innovation can help us to blow the market rules and to go beyond the creation of both a new business model and technology (see Fig. 6.2).

The main reasons are the new ways of business behavior, new market rules, and the new global issues like sustainability which accompany with the rise of China and the others. These issues change the traditional roles of government, the idea about corporate strategy and industrial development, the time dimensions, the different rational and irrational forms of behavior and decision making, the control of the value chain, the replacement of value chain by the value circle, the role of stakeholders in society and informal networks, and the cultural differences leading to a multilateral opportunities and challenges. A new world economy is being created based upon new rules, market structures, and behavior. We have to strategically renew our business to survive in this New World.

6.4   From Corporate Governance to Strategic Governance

The Chinese have not won the strategic innovation battle yet. The blurring of existing boundaries and extension of issues to deal with are not all in favor of Chinese parties. In fact, all main contenders, the EU, the USA, and China, have to deal with not only issues which they are comfortable with but also issues which are far out of their comfort zone. For example, the USA has to deal with long-term planning with regard to infrastructure for new mobility concepts and energy infrastructure. The EU has to create an integrated home market with competitive global players. China has to deal with bottom-up initiatives for realizing the desired indigenous innovative society.

The nature and behavior of the acting market participants will change as Fig. 6.3 demonstrates.

Both Anglo-Saxon Western enterprises focused on short-term profits and the primary role for shareholders and managers, and Rhineland-based stakeholder-oriented companies will have to compete and cope with Chinese firms based on government-supported or even government-owned world players. Chinese players go beyond the Western-involved stakeholders of suppliers, clients, and NGOs and additionally involve governments and public organizations. Moreover, the informal Chinese networks, depending on the situation, have an extended influence than the Western networks. On top of that, the ambiguous behavior of short-term and long-term behavior backed by governmental planning will prove to be a big challenge for Western enterprises. With regard to bottom-line behavior, in the Chinese perspective, it is not about replacing profit for Triple P but creating new economic dragons. Current approaches of either strategy focused on the corporation and markets or innovation focused on technology, as discussed in Chap. 4, cannot cope with the new frontier and need to be adapted and renewed. Strategic governance is the beginning of this renewed process.

6.5   The Future Battles Between the West and China

As Chap. 4 has demonstrated, the creation and emergence of a new growth curve will be accompanied by a complete new inner (market) dynamics. These new dynamics shape a new world order. In Table 6.1 the ten strategic innovation fields which can decide the winner are summed up. Of course, one need to keep in mind that one battlefield can disappear and new ones can emerge due to the ever-changing circumstances.

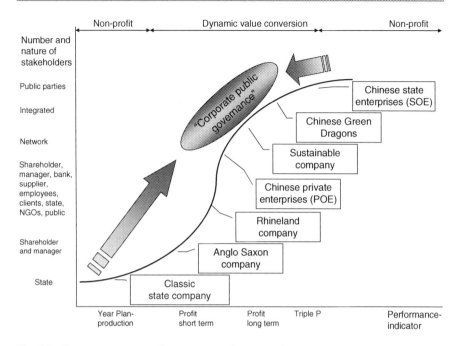

Fig. 6.3 Corporate governance becomes strategic governance

Table 6.1   The ten battlefields of strategic innovation between China, the USA, and the EU

	Battle fields	Main feature
1	World order	From free market to China market rules
		From Knowledge Economy to Entrepreneurial Economy
2	Government	From dichotomy public private to symbiosis
		From policy maker to activistic partner
3	Market governance	From shareholders or stakeholders to strongholders
		From defending IP to creating industrial standards
4	Resources assurance	From free market to ecolization
		From dependency to self supporting
5	Mode of value creation	From value chains to value circles
		From Triple P to Dynamic Value Conversion
6	Mode of innovation	From ad hoc innovation to institutionalized innovation
		From technology to strategic innovation
7	Strategy	From market strategy to industrial power
		From me too hypes to tailor made
8	Cross cultural	From mono to cross cultural leadership and management
		From separation city rural to metropolitan (cross nation) areas
9	Time perspectives	From Western time to Eastern time views
		From linear to circular time
10	Leadership	From content to context creating leadership
		From moral leadership to people's power
11	???	???

The new world order with the rise of non-Western countries will make the way of doing business completely different. Especially China, with its history of assimilating other cultures, introduces new rules sometimes completely different than Western rules while the Chinese economy is gaining importance in the world. For example, reproducing the knowledge of the master is an honor; the Chinese are very good at copying and improving the master's work. It is even praised in a Chinese phrase: "Green comes from Blue, but it is better than Blue." But only imitation will harm future prospects of innovation. When not only Western firms have a knowledge monopoly but China contributes to the knowledge too, the Chinese will not be happy if other people get rich with their knowledge. Rules to protect the knowledge but at the same time allowing (Chinese) business to benefit from it will be created. Only those who can cope with these new rules will be able to earn money from innovation in China.

Chinese government has a different and sometimes opposite role and power than Western governments. The general opinion in the USA and by some parties in the EU is "the smaller the government the better." Chinese governments are not only law and policy maker; they are active participants and stimulators in the economic process. The number one criteria to judge a Chinese governmental leader is the economic performance under his governance. Many governmental leaders are themselves former business leaders mostly in state-owned companies. Besides many prestige projects, this can also really generate very good business climate. The symbiosis between private and public organizations is easier to reach in China than in the West. The result is a different market structure and behavior leading to different outcomes than in Western situations. Becoming an activistic government has different scopes partly depending on culture and history. Activistic does not only mean developing government-owned enterprises in strategic sectors but also mean setting the right conditions for development. The latter is very difficult because it requires an even better knowledge of the market situation and market process in time than the individual market participant. It is very dangerous for Western governmental leaders to try to stimulate economy while either themselves or their civil servants lack of business knowledge and/or experiences. The Strategic Innovation Cycle has proven to be useful in the process to overcome this common problem in Europe.

With the rise of China, the industrial market governance will become more important than the Western focus on corporate governance. Whereas the West has to deal between the power between shareholders and other stakeholders including management, the Chinese governance focuses more on the whole industry together with preferred and selected industry leaders. American and European institutions like anti-cartel organizations to protect consumers from dominant market players play the opposite role. Moreover, the fight about IP rights might be overshadowed by the relevance of upcoming Chinese industry standards.

The free market principle is advocated by Western countries even for natural resources market except oil and gas. But for new materials the Western countries rely on market parties to secure resource supplies. The Chinese approach is almost the opposite. Instead of development aid, China secures resources worldwide by building up friendship relationships, investing in foreign countries, buying resources, and earning the money back by involving Chinese firms to carry out projects. This is "ecolization" as a phrase for economic colonization of foreign countries. At the same time, discovering own sources or developing new resources is heavily supported in China.

The conquest of the traditional value chain will be followed by the creation of a value circle indicating the emergence of a sustainable society. Furthermore, regarding sustainability as an economic issue, the Triple P will be replaced by the dynamic value conversion. It stresses the combination of short-term and long-term value creation with the exploitation of economies of scale, scope, and time. Applying the dynamic value conversion leads to different strategic decision making than traditional measures of profit and Triple P (Van Someren, 1992, 1995, 2005).

For the organizations which need innovation, the institutionalization of the innovation function will become pivotal for future progress and prosperity. The focus on R&D and technology needs to be replaced by the angle of strategic innovation to stress the relevance of non-technological innovations and to broaden the issue of innovation beyond product, process, and business model innovation. Organizational innovations like a combined top−down and bottom−up approach require both freedom and rules.

Corporate strategies based on current Western approaches are not sufficient anymore. Integration of existing concepts does not take into account the emerging new world order requiring fundamental new approaches. The instrument of power on the level of the industry instead of the corporation needs the involvement of governments. For those doing business in China or fighting Chinese competitors at home, the role of the government and how to get governmental support should become an important part of the strategy too.

Cross-cultural aspects make or break the innovation process and its output. Ignoring cultural aspects of innovation lowers the success rate of innovation or the implementation of national and corporate innovation systems. Moreover, diversity is a source of creativity and entrepreneurial activity keeping a society robust and alive.

The seven time dimensions are probably for most top managers and policy makers the most invisible and hard to grasp, but they can be more decisive than any other aspect of strategic innovation. The right timing together with an institutionalized accumulation of knowledge, capital, and experiences over time is a powerful instrument of dynamic wealth creation.

All the above aspects of strategic innovation together definitely change the requirements for leadership in private and public organizations. In the future battle, it is important to be able to create a context for institutional innovation, to integrate cross-cultural differences, to understand Western and Chinese requirements, and to lead industries. This is something else and much more difficult but at the end more rewarding than increasing short-term shareholder value by cost-cutting programs, carrying out mergers and acquisition, and reshuffling business portfolios.

Conditions	Creativity
• From free market to SINO-Western market rules • From dichotomy public private to new forms of symbiosis between private and public sector • From policy maker to activistic partner • From resource dependency to self supporting	• From ad hoc innovation to institutionalized innovation • From knowledge economy to entrepreneurial economy • From me too hypes to tailor made
Content	**Context**
• From value chains to value circles • From technology to strategic innovation • From market strategy to absolute industrial power • From free market to ecolization of natural resources • From economic to sustainable development • From Triple P to Dynamic Value Conversion	• From content to context creating leadership • From moral leadership to people's power • From shareholders or stakeholders to strongholders • From defending IP to creating industrial standards • From mono to cross cultural leadership and management • From differences to exploiting diversity • From linear to circular time • From Western time to Eastern time views

Fig. 6.4 The strategic innovation battle within the 4C framework

In short, the innovation battle can be the battle of leadership. The one who can manage the 4C framework (see Fig. 6.4) of the strategic innovation theory will have a bigger chance to win.

Figure 6.4 gives insight in the action areas of strategic innovation beyond the business model. Taking these actions will enable the leaders find the right balance between business model innovation, leadership, institutional innovation, business development, and governance.

In this battle, every player has different heritage, different starting positions, different accumulated assets, different abilities and competences, and different behaviors. Figure 6.5 shows the different challenges and opportunities which Triple E on a macroscale can bring to the USA, the EU, and China.

The Triple E potential leading to growth and prosperity in the USA, the EU, and China is still immense. However, the Triple E potential on the level of individual firms is even more relevant. Imagine what could happen when China is able to organize the bottom-up innovation process. The sheer number of eager employees and entrepreneurs would outperform any other country or region. The bottom-up innovation process would increase the economies of scope exponentially at the price of less central control—in Western eyes a Walhalla and in the eyes of Chinese a box of Pandora. This example shows the ice berg of measures and consequences behind each dimension of the Triple E.

United States

Economies of scale
- Exploiting scale of economy for industrial instead of military power

Economies of scope
- From unilateral to multilateral approach world economy
- Market based innovation broadened by federal governmental support for emerging industries
- Decreasing scope of states with regard to nation wide issues like sustainability
- Global sourcing strategy for resources instead of search for independency
- Increase relationship with America's and EU as countervailing power against Asia

Economies of time
- Adopting circular time for sustainable development
- Focus on long term relation with China instead of short term defense of status quo

European Union

Economies of scale
- One Europe: European integration or harmonization
- Creation of pan-European champions
- From low end social security support systems to investment in education, research, start ups and growth SMEs

Economies of scope
- Decreasing member state and increasing EU
- Meso level innovation system
- Quadruple Helix
- Applying and exploiting EU's variety and diversity
- Global sourcing
- Revive Atlantic relationship with US

Economies of time
- Increasing innovation intensity and time to market
- Faster decision making and implementation
- Circular time culture instead of linear
- Faster growth of SME

China

Economies of scale
- Creating home market for industry
- Chinese industry standards
- World class Chinese champions

Economies of scope
- From large scale single product manufacturing to multiproduct
- Control of global value circle
- Micro level innovation system
- Bottom up innovation
- Large market diversity Chinese home market

Economies of time
- Increasing innovation intensity
- Fast learning competence using for innovation and time to market
- Using circular time notion for dynamic value creation

Source: based on van Someren, 1991, 2005

Fig. 6.5 Illustrations of Triple E on a macroscale for the USA, the EU, and China

6.6 Global Strategic Innovation Index

To win the strategic innovation battle, one has to know the strength and position of oneself and of the counter partner. Knowing the strategic innovation position should be as important as knowing the GDP. The Strategic Innovation Index is meant to start strategic innovation benchmarking as presented in Table 6.2. The scores may be subjective, but they give an idea about what are the important factors to measure strategic innovation.

When compared to other benchmarks like the European Scoreboard or the Global Innovation Index, the Global Strategic Innovation Index score and ranking of China are on average much higher. The background is that the European Scoreboard and the Global Innovation Index measure from a Western perspective. The Western bias includes aspects like R&D and open innovation but leaves aside aspects like the seven time dimensions, the market governance, global sourcing, institutionalized innovation, and cross-cultural aspects. These aspects of strategic innovation are of utmost importance for the future innovation battle.

In conformity with the previous chapters, Table 6.2 demonstrates the high scores of China in global resource sourcing but their relatively low score for innovation within individual organizations. The USA scores high in market-based innovation but at the same time scores low for innovation in new industries like renewables due

Table 6.2 Global strategic innovation index

	Battle fields	China	USA	EU
1	World order	6	6	3
2	Government	8	4	3
3	Market governance	8	8	6
4	Resources assurance	8	6	2
5	Mode of value creation	5	6	5
6	Mode of innovation	2	7	4
7	Strategy	6	6	4
8	Cross cultural	2	5	5
9	Time perspectives	4	2	4
10	Leadership	2	4	4
	Total (max. 100)	51	54	41

to lack of governmental long-term planning. The strong market-based innovation performance of the USA gives them the lead. But China is catching up. The EU is lagging behind due to failing integration, absence of coherent and consistent policies, and too less innovative firms. The few countries and firms which perform well cannot compensate the rest of Europe.

The big question arises whether China should copy the West and the West should copy the central plan approach of China. The answer is no and yes. In Chap. 4 we concluded that the policies in China, the USA, and the EU are indeed converging. But the competences and results differ. The trend in China is towards including policies on the micro level such as innovation in the individual firm. The USA is formulating Blueprints for Innovation whereas the EU is trying to formulate Pan-European big plans such as the Innovation Union. But both China and the West will have their difficulty to copy each other because the institutional settings belonging to successful implementation are missing. The top–down central planning of China does not fit into the current institutional settings of the EU and the USA. At the same time in several cases such as nation grid for renewable energy requires a macro approach. The same holds for China. For China it will be very difficult to switch towards bottom-up innovation processes.

The only right conclusion is that tailor-made solutions have to be found which are dependent on context, industry, time, and place. China needs, for example, a bottom-up innovation process if it wants to achieve its aims of indigenous innovation, but it will be different from the European or American bottom-up process. Strategic innovation requires an approach which addresses some necessary building blocks and simultaneously allows for cultural differences. For this reason the Strategic Innovation Cycle© offers the approach to take into account the tailor-made requirement.

6.7   The Winning Weapon: Strategic Innovation Cycle©

The total strategic innovation potential is only exploited for about 50 % as the current Global Strategic Innovation Indexes show. China, the USA, and the EU have all huge opportunities to substantially increase their score. All have the chance

Table 6.3 Strategic innovation take-aways

Take aways Strategic Innovation Cycle (SIC)
• The SIC turns the black box of innovation into a white box making you understand what to do and how
• The SIC enables you to create a unique 'Corporation of the Future'
• The SIC makes Western firms ready for a new world order with China as a strong new contender
• The SIC makes Chinese enterprises ready for conquering the West
• The SIC necessarily moves beyond creating new business models due to issues like rise of China and sustainability
• The SIC moves beyond market position, competitor analysis, product innovation and hype driven single issue innovation like eco or social innovation
• The SIC includes a new value proposition 'Dynamic Value Conversion' enabling you to deal with Chinese rivals and markets
• The SIC offers the opportunity to integrate micro, meso and macro levels including the role of government in order to create favorable conditions for a new growth curve
• The SIC acknowledges the world wide emulation process and gives time dimensions such as timing, accumulation and speed a prominent place
• The SIC combines bottom-up and top-down innovation processes
• The SIC makes implementation easy and starts at day 1 of renewing your business
• The SIC enables you to involve all stakeholders to maximize the innovation output and to reduce risk of implementation failure
• The SIC is both aspirational and inspirational ('realizing your dreams') instead of mission statement and budget driven

to win when creating the right strategic innovation fitting to their own situation and what the world needs. For this purpose the strategic innovation cycle can be applied to increase the winning chance.

The Strategic Innovation Cycle (SIC) presented in Chap. 4 provides the practical framework for creating unique solutions to the opportunities lying ahead. The conditions, context, content, and creativity inherent to the SIC are different for China, the USA, and the EU.

The SIC enables to create tailor-made and unique solutions. This is important with regard to the future of strategic innovation in China, the USA, and the EU. We have demonstrated that innovation policies are now converging. China copies and adapts some Western policies on the meso and micro level, whereas the West imitates the Blueprint and macro views such as Innovation Union approaches. The macro-based top-down plans from the EU were not very successful and in the USA; the Blueprints have to show their effects. China is struggling with innovation policies on the micro level of individual organizations and individuals. Therefore, what is successful in one region does not necessarily have to work in the other. Strategic central plan making is a relative strength of the Chinese and not of the Europeans or Americans. The Europeans and Americans might be better off with focusing on their strength of bottom-up innovation which has a large potential for development. But sometimes central planning is necessary such as in case of renewables and future industrial standards. Therefore, only tailor-made and cross-cultural-dependent solutions will work. In Table 6.3 why Strategic Innovation Cycle can be the winning weapon is summed up.

In the next sections China, the USA, and the EU will be discussed showing the different approaches, opportunities, and challenges. In fact, every organization applying this approach will encounter the uniqueness of its own starting position and the unique own challenges and limitations. The cases in Chap. 5 have demonstrated some different ways on how to apply the main principles and steps of the Strategic Innovation Cycle. In a similar way both private and public organizations in China, the USA, and the EU have to apply the Strategic Innovation Cycle in order to be prepared for the future.

6.8   The Innovative Future of China?

6.8.1   China's Big Bang of Deng

China has a very long history of stable philosophical and cultural principles which are not innovation friendly as discussed in Chap. 2. In the tradition of these philosophies, the Chinese leaders paid a lot of attention to non-technological issues to organize China. The core issues were to create a stable governmental system with the necessary organizations and institutions. Technology did not matter too much. The opening of China by Deng was at the same time an attempt of revolutionary modernization of the house without taking away the load-bearing walls. The opening of China by Deng acted as a Big Bang and is a true strategic innovation. In Fig. 6.6 this inversion of thinking and priorities within the economic context is presented schematically.

The opening of China allowed for the creation and development of a Chinese mode of capitalism. In the early times of the opening, the phases of imitation and improvement were still based on the Confucian replication of knowledge. Moreover, the opening also allowed for radically changing the focus from nontechnical aspects of state organization to technology as the Holy Grail of future prosperity—a true inversion. Technology became the core notion of 5-year plans and policies on central and local governmental levels. This radical shift was in conformity with the increasing importance of the role of R&D and technology in Western scientific economic literature in the 1980s and thereafter. But again due to the Confucian doctrine of learning, the Western approaches and ways of thinking were adopted and technology became pivotal for future success. In the later phase of the imitation-improving scheme and in conformity with Sun Tzu, the desire to emulate by the adagio "learn in the West and surpass in the East" gained power. Home-grown technology independent of the West is the future aim of China.

The extreme inversion from changing state organization forms to technology demonstrates the current unbalanced or disharmonious innovation policies. China should reconsider their tradition of non-technological issues and revalue their contribution to the growth and development of China. But some renewal is necessary as well. The nontechnical issues should not be limited to the macro (state organization) and meso level (industries) but the micro level (individual companies and individual citizens) as well.

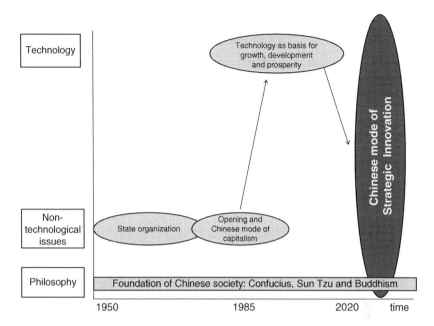

Fig. 6.6 Inversion of Chinese leading economic system

The most challenging Chinese paradox of the twenty-first century consists of the two opposites—technical and nontechnical issues. A synthesis in Chinese tradition is necessary to restore a balance and mutual reinforcement of the technical and non-technical issues. Strategic innovation is the solution. Chinese leaders from government and enterprises have to create a Chinese Mode of Strategic Innovation. The Chinese Mode of Strategic Innovation should integrate the cultural–philosophical heritage of Confucius, Sun Tzu, and Buddhism. Only then the desired harmonious society can be achieved.

But how should the Chinese Mode of Strategic Innovation be realized? The previous chapters have shown the dreams, ambitions, eagerness, will to win entrepreneurialism, and hunger for success of the Chinese government and business people. With this attitude to become prosperous, the Chinese were able to become at least a respected rival and a future challenger. As Fig. 6.7 demonstrates, China was able to create a breakthrough of the slow growth curve by the Chinese Manufacturing System.

For many centuries the agricultural sector and other industrial activities dominated the Chinese economic landscape. During the takeover of Western countries of the world economy, the Chinese economic development collapsed. Only very recently, the Chinese Manufacturing System gave way to a very steep growth curve of GDP and growth and development of various industries. But there is a flip side as has been demonstrated in previous chapters. The foundations of the growth curve are short-term based. The success of the Chinese spectacular growth is primarily based on comparative (labor) cost advantages coupled and imitation

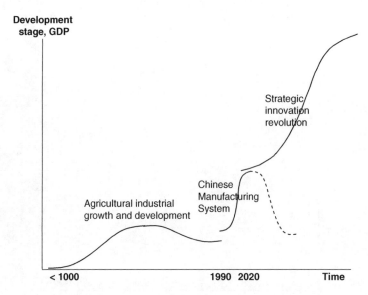

Fig. 6.7 Strategic innovation as the twenty-first-century core challenge

and improvement strategies resulting in dynamic value conversion based on economies of scale time. The mirror side of the growth curve based on Chinese Manufacturing System is the rapidly disappearing (labor) cost advantages and the risk of withdrawal of knowledge-rich non-Chinese enterprises to other promising markets. The steep growth can easily turn in a steep downturn.

For China, Strategic Innovation Revolution is the only way out of a potential economic disaster and consequently an unequaled world crisis. But strategic innovations require revolutionary changes in the way enterprises do business and how government supports the nontechnical part of the strategic innovations. Till now even in China, the innovation policies were rather ineffective. The success of the imitation–improvement phase disguises failing innovation bottom-line results. The top-down innovation policies are not as effective as top-down infrastructure construction programs. The most difficult and time-consuming changes are linked to bottom-up behavior, organized creativity, new educational programs, a national innovation system, formulating and implementing innovation culture, creating institutionalized innovation, creating strategic innovations, and many more. Strategic innovations will decide about the future of China and its people.

China has a long way to go; they have only started. To sum up, GDP is rising steadily, but the GDP per capita is far below Western levels; the size of the middle class is estimated to be around 200 million people, so more than a billion to go; despite rising wealth, the social inequality is rising; export levels belong to the highest of the world, but Chinese added value is still relatively low; although R&D output is rising, institutionalized innovation is in its infancy; Chinese firms enter Fortune 500 list, but world brands and global MNEs are scarce; and so on. Therefore, the proof of the Chinese pudding is the coming stage of strategic innovation. But the hunger for success and world dominance will make the Chinese in the short term insatiable.

With regard to conditions, the central planning and strong position of local governments determine the initial starting position. Furthermore, the top-down and hierarchical forms of Chinese leadership combined with the guanxi network influence the way stakeholders are defined and how they are involved in the Strategic Innovation Cycle.

The trends of the increasing urbanization undermine old tradition of social system of younger family members taking care for elderly people, social inequality and environmental problems leading to health problems undermine legitimacy and stability of Chinese societal system, rising labor costs force to develop higher added value activities, the jump from imitation–improvement to innovation and internationalization is a huge challenge, and institutional innovation requires new social behavior and systems far beyond existing practices and deep-held beliefs based on hierarchical order and deep-rooted culture of top-down decision making.

In the strategic sectors, free competition is replaced by regulated competition, and industry policies determine the future path of more than individual corporate strategies.

The economic engine is the search for higher added value activities along the value chain or even value circle. The development of higher added value capabilities like branding, marketing, and innovation competences is the logical consequence.

In the Chinese 4I developments scheme from imitation to improvement to innovation and internationalization, strategic innovation is indeed the next hurdle to take. In the recently developed Total Innovation Management approach, discussed in Chap. 5, it does focus on important areas of innovation (see Fig. 6.8).

In this respect the Total Innovation Management (TIM) as discussed in Chap. 4 and 5 is insufficient for the aim of indigenous innovation. The bottom line of TIM is the improvement of innovation output, whereas dynamic value creation tries to focus on creating new wealth. The six functional areas of TIM fit into the existing top-down culture innovation process. Moreover, the TIM is an attempt to address the internal organization of innovation, thereby focusing on the micro level of the individual firm. Paradoxically, these characteristics of TIM prevent indigenous innovation. The reason is that indigenous innovation requires, for example, bottom-up initiatives.

As soon as Chinese powerhouses replace Western organizations with the aim to become independent of Western technology, the institutionalization of innovation becomes relevant. The corporate governance of mobilization and organization of creativity, entrepreneurship, and knowledge within and between enterprises will be the greatest challenge. For China, the corporate governance of bottom-up innovation process is a greater issue than improving the industrial governance of public–private symbiosis. The mobilization and organization of creativity, entrepreneurship, and knowledge within and between enterprises are interwoven with bottom-up process. Furthermore, the allowance of failures and rewards of

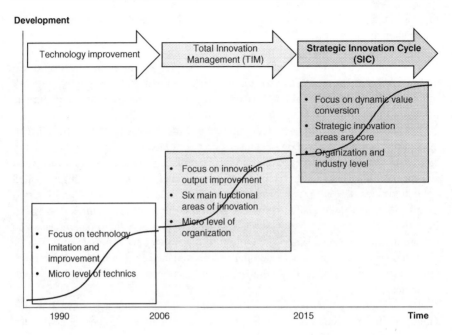

Fig. 6.8 Strategic innovation as the next step

individuals instead of groups is an extra dimension which does not fit to current Chinese practices and history.

Moreover, the strategic innovation areas replace the six functional areas of innovation. Apart from individual organizations, the network or guanxi of involved parties in the whole industry becomes relevant.

Managing the power of the people will be the biggest challenge for the People's Republic of China. As soon as Chinese powerhouses enter the global economy, the focus on dynamic value conversion requires an active involvement of stakeholders. The challenge is to organize a bottom-up innovation process. For Chinese, it is an inversion of their cultural mindset and to allow subordinates to have an equal contribution to innovative solutions.

The future power of the people is based not on the scale but on the scope and time effects of their exploitation and self-development. The number of annually graduated Chinese technicians is impressive, but it is more important how these academic knowledge and qualifications are used and implemented within enterprises and knowledge institutes. It fits to the Chinese desire to be your own boss.

The top-down leadership and command control behavior fitted to the imitation–improvement era. But the coming innovation–internationalization era requires additionally bottom-up and context-creating leadership—a huge challenge for Chinese.

Therefore, the Strategic Innovation Cycle (SIC) is a necessary next step towards becoming an Innovative nation and emulating the West. The Strategic Innovation Cycle is the instrument to realize these aims and dreams.

6.8.2 The Chinese Game

The future innovation battle will be characterized by some typical behavioral aspects based on their long history as explained in Chap. 2. Chinese strategic behavior for expansion is for Westerns much more difficult to interpret because here we have to read between the lines of official statements. The West has to know the Chinese future strategic behavior to win the Chinese game:

From underdog back to the center of the world. China acknowledges the leading role of the USA and some countries and firms in the EU in technology. They often play the underdog to stimulate the technology transfer. However, as soon as technologies are imitated and emulated, they will be proud to be the center of the world of innovation.

China is a developing country and rich countries are obliged to help. The modesty of China can be used strategically too. On the one hand, being aliens with other developing countries makes China a very powerful negotiator in international community; on the other hand, emphasizing the shortcoming enables China to leap forward without being challenged.

China pledges for harmony, but it should be an organized harmony. By pleading for harmony, China refers to its painful history when chaos and wars only brought economic disasters. But the Chinese harmony will always be a hierarchical harmony. There will be a number one and the rest should follow. It is natural that the Chinese wants to be number one too as it once was in world's history. To realize this dream, China has to create a society in which every Chinese can participate and share in the wealth and prosperity. For this aim the cooperation with the West is sometimes necessary. But China will act like number one when it turns to be the real number one.

Talk about market economy and walk state capitalism. China makes use of freedom of negotiation of individual countries, governments, and firms and tries to adept to the rules of the Western market economy. But the collectiveness and the hierarchical structure will enable China to conquer the world market. China has the potential to combine the advantages of both the market and the government. An ultra-state capitalism can be the case for China in the future.

Avoid conflict and compete to death. To avoid losing faces for both sides, conflicts will always be avoided on the surface. But it does not mean that the Chinese do not want to win the competition. In fact, the competition underneath has the killing effect.

Start small and end big. The Chinese can be very good at long marches. All global activities of China on macro and micro scale start with a small step. A minor cooperation and a small acquisition of a single company can be used to build up key points in a Chinese network. Once the points are connected, the oil drop effect will show. It is like playing GO chess; one can win big if all the surrounding grounds are taken.

Imitation leads to innovation. Trying to stand on the shoulders of a giant is the first step of Chinese innovation. Imitation is not an end goal; it is an intermediate step towards indigenous innovation.

Knowledge should be as fruit on a tree. The fruit belongs to the one who can pick it. Getting as much relevant knowledge as one can and to do something with it to generate benefit is very often the Chinese enterprise innovation strategy. This is a good ground for non-technological innovations.

Corporate responsibility does not only come from the corporate enterprises. In the Chinese case, the government will always play a role in business. The government will not only try to help Chinese cooperate to perform better through macro and meso instruments; it will also play the role of the referee when the corporate does not take its responsibility.

Learn in the West and surpass in the East. Many Chinese students study on Western universities. Chinese firms set up R&D center and carry out mergers and acquisitions in foreign countries. Western knowledge and innovation can flow to China with the talents and firms. It can be worse if the Chinese are able to emulate the innovation to a better market alternative and to bring it back to world market.

Chinese and Western win–win are not the same. Western win–win is to have a fair share in profits. Chinese win–win is to become as strong as possible and try to win the whole battle. If not, the share will be divided according to the hierarchy. This means that the weaker should have more willingness to share.

The Chinese business game is quite different from the Western one. Not knowing the rules of the game is the source of Western frustrations even conflicts such as the IP rights discussion reveals. But to play the Chinese game well needs balance between paradoxes. An even more difficult situation emerges as soon as overreaction comes into play as the next section shows.

6.8.3   The Chinese Strength and Weakness

Paradoxically, the Chinese strength is also their weakness. When the Chinese lose sight of the balance, a behavior of overreacting due to a perceived strong position, overenthusiasm, or hidden anger can be their worst enemy. Many Chinese are not defeated by their enemies but by themselves. In the situations of overdoses, the starting position can transform in counterproductive extreme situations. The

Table 6.4 Examples of counterproductive innovation overdoses

Fostering	Counter productive overdoses
Strong clear leadership	Dictator/weak leader
Clear hierarchical structure	Spider web/chaotic matrix structure
Mission driven future aim	Hindering bottom-up, flexibility and new ideas
Formal channel for feedback	Informal loose network
Institutionalized innovation	Rigid innovation with no freedom
Competition between groups	Cutthroat competition
Cooperation within groups	Absence of initiatives
Trust (space and time for mistake)	Arrogance and privileges
Long term	Wrong investments
Risk taking	Gambling
Big picture	Failures on details destroys big picture
Pragmatic and second movers	Pig cycle and hindering indigenous innovation (homegrown basic and radical innovation)
. . .	. . .

bottom-line result often ends in the opposite of the original aim. For example, the cutthroat competition in industries like toys, shoes, and solar panels comes from me-too behavior. The success of export for years blinded the eyes of some entrepreneurs. Overcapacity is the result. The big ones which were fighting a very dangerous price war were the first to be hit by a broken capital chain. In Fig. 6.7 some illustrations of counterproductive innovation overdoses are presented. These give some examples of the strength and weakness of the Chinese (Table 6.4).

The innovation overdoses is a form of irrational behavior. In China strong leadership is admired and asked for. Innovation in China can profit from strong leadership when applied in the right time and the right place. But when it is pushed too far, it ends in dictatorship or even worse a weak leadership trying to cover up the weakness with excessive decisions.

How can the Chinese strength be turned into weakness? A good example is the desire of Chinese managers for a clear hierarchical structure which indicates who is responsible for what. But a too-strict organization is neither efficient nor innovative. Especially when the official hierarchy does not fit the informal power fields, the structured organization works very inefficient. Many cases of our clients who complained about bad communication can be traced back to the inefficient organization. The Chinese will not risk taking the responsibility of someone else's function. If you ask the wrong Chinese, you will just get no feedback. On the other hand, in some cases of innovation cooperation between Western and Chinese partners, organizational forms like matrix management are used. The Chinese may turn the matrix into a spider web. There is only the choice between a web without spider or with a too-dominant spider ending with disappointing innovation output.

For the Chinese a matrix structure is a chaotic horror (and for many Westerns as well). Even the well-known notion of trust can end in a disastrous behavior resulting in a detrimental effect on innovation output. When trust or the space and time for mistakes are pushed too far, a counterproductive behavior of arrogance accompanied by privileges destroys a context for effective innovation.

The same holds for the praised long-term attitude of Chinese. A myopic behavior based on long term can lead to holding on to the wrong investments. A pragmatic attitude of, for example, copying instead inventing the wheel again hinders a culture and behavior necessary to foster homegrown indigenous innovation.

These behavioral attitudes represent pitfalls for the future Chinese innovation. China can overcome its own trap by strategically renewing itself in these aspects. The West can win by knowing and using these aspects as directions for strategic innovations.

6.8.4 Golden Tips for Chinese Government

National innovation system. The instruments of 5-year plans and other central plans have proven to work in China. However, to realize the ambitions of becoming an innovative nation, an integrated national innovation system suits the Chinese way better. The national innovation system generates the necessary knowledge and provides the necessary organizations to realize indigenous innovation. In fact, the Quadruple Helix of private and state-owned firms, knowledge institutes, and central and local government as regulator and capital provider form together the organizational structure of the innovation system. The key for the Chinese is integration. This can only be realized when the following points are taken into account too.

The heritage of nontechnical innovation should be exploited. A radical change in current innovation vision with its focus on technical innovation is necessary. Nontechnical innovations instead of new technology should get the most attention of Chinese leaders. Nontechnical innovations are the real source of long-term uniqueness. The Chinese have proven to be able to renew the soft part. The Strategic Innovation Index reveals that the soft side of innovation such as the bottom-up innovation process will determine the success or failure of Chinese innovation aspirations.

Strategic innovation. The Chinese embrace strategic thinking and keeping balance. Strategic innovation comprises the harmonious balance between technology and nontechnical innovation. The Chinese Mode of Strategic Innovation will be to find a Chinese way of dealing with leadership, institutionalized innovation, business development, and governance. In this respect, the 4I scheme of development fitted well to the consecutive plan-making phases in the past but should be replaced by eternal emulation of which strategic innovation is the driving force.

Organized creativity. In order to support the national innovation system and strategic innovation, it is unavoidable to organize creativity within the cultural and institutional boundaries and conditions of China. It starts in education and later on in private and public organizations to implement the contribution of creativity to a harmonious society. A link between the governmental plans and aims and the contribution of creative solutions requires attention to exploiting creativity and its organizational setting.

Public innovation. As soon as enterprises are able to create strategic innovations from the inside, a new growth and development dynamism will change China from bottom-up. Public organizations and policies need to renew themselves in order to establish a new symbiotic relation.

Industry strategy. In the current growth curve of imitation and improvement, a parallel strategy of state-owned enterprises (SOE) and allowing private-owned enterprises (POE) is not contradictory. But the jump to the growth cycle based on innovation and internationalization characterized by bottom-up innovation may make the POEs bigger and even become rivals of the preselected preferred SOEs. A new industry strategy is necessary to cope with this issue.

Worst-case scenario. The increase of control of the whole value chain beyond manufacturing together with the protection of Chinese enterprises may lead to a withdrawal of Western firms. The rise of other emerging countries, lack of Chinese market share, and rising costs in China may drive Western firms to other regions. With less Western firms, the speed of development generated by new innovation and internationalization will slow down. Potential rivals such as India may present themselves as a better option and take advantage of the Chinese losing ground, attracting both short-term thinking Western business leaders and world game-playing political leaders. The mentality and behavior linked with IP rights, copycats, squeezing Western partners in alliances, and using market power to exclude non-Chinese parties will harm China in the long run. A worst-case scenario is necessary preparing for a "China Only" innovation path.

SMEs as backbone of harmonious society. The current governmental focus is on both strategic sectors and a selection of preferred leading companies and private companies. The other side is the unknown innovative SMEs. Most of them have to survive without governmental and/or bank support. This forces them to be very innovative in especially nontechnical aspects of the business. With the decreasing job opportunities and the increasing education level, more and more Chinese will find their way to setting up their own companies. The future innovative strength of China will have to be based on the midsized firms using their scale and scope to contribute to innovation. These midsized companies will have to grow to the backbone of the Chinese economy due to their innovative power and ability to serve the whole Chinese home market. The increasing urbanization together with the rise and growth of middle income groups together with new megacity challenges opens the opportunity for innovative SMEs to contribute to new solutions and inland market development. For a sustainable and stable future China, the SMEs are the linking pin between innovative economic growth and social harmonious society. They should be treated as the future backbone of the Chinese economy with sound governance for them.

Innovation culture. In China the national innovation culture is connected with individual culture within organizations. Institutional aspects such as norms and values during childhood, education, philosophy, and expected behavior can hamper innovation in China. Chinese creativity output depends on changing these institutional structures over a long time. The success of Chinese in Silicon Valley depends more on the institutional context and culture than on the level of individual creativity.

6.8.5   Golden Tips for Chinese Enterprises

Strategic Innovation. Use the Chinese strength in strategic thinking for innovation. Besides improving and developing new technology, nontechnical strategic innovations may generate more growth of the enterprise. Especially for those enterprises which enter global markets or want to become independent of Western technology, the strategic innovation approach will be a priority number one.

Implementation of Institutionalized Innovation. The approach of Strategic Innovation Cycle (SIC) should be adopted as successor of the Total Innovation Management (TIM). SIC supports to focus on future demand and customer needs requiring new technology and nontechnical innovations instead of increasing innovation output. The cycle makes innovation a continuous process which generates better and better innovations.

Creativity Organization. The conditions for becoming a creative enterprise required to change some Chinese behavior. The top-down management style needs to be accomplished with an organization in which people's creativity and knowledge will be mobilized and exploited.

Internationalization and Cross-Culture Management. In the emulation process of Western firms, internationalization and cross-culture management will become crucial in satisfying non-Chinese customers. Together with the expansion in the value chain, the nontechnical aspects of doing business will become relevant for future success.

Stakeholder Involvement Beyond Guanxi. In non-Chinese markets, stakeholder involvement goes beyond managing the own guanxi. The ranking of the stakeholders is very different than in China. In Chinese eyes "powerless" NGOs or SMEs can turn out to be crucial for a business in Europe.

6.9   The Innovative Future of the West?

6.9.1   New US Stars or Losing Magnitude?

US enterprises swiped away many competitors as did textbooks on management in the educational world. Some were breakthrough magnitudes; others were hypes. Can the Americans be as successful as last century? Despite issues like (federal) debts, unsustainable development, loss of manufacturing capabilities, deteriorating infrastructure, and education system, which are gasping for renewals, the USA is still an entrepreneurial and innovative society. Figure 6.9 shows the steady growth and development based on burst of innovative entrepreneurship from individuals, enterprises, and sometimes alliances between government, knowledge institutions, and private industries.

The American Manufacturing System created a mass market based on standardization respectively modularization of parts and economies of scale followed by economies of scope. The increasing role and contribution of science, R&D, and technology together with managerial innovations created the second wave of market-based innovation. In this world the USA became the new superpower and in the last decades the unilateral economic and military superpower. With the rise of China, the supremacy of the USA will change and a multilateral world will emerge. At least the economic power and share of world GDP will shift to other regions in the world including China. More importantly, among others the norms and values will change, business behavior will change, power relations will change, and industrial business development will change. The American way of doing business has to adapt to these new circumstances by means of strategic innovation too.

The ability to create innovations and new industries based on mobilization of entrepreneurship, creativity, and knowledge of the USA has more superpower than the military power. This ability of the USA is their biggest asset. The higher innovation output in USA is based on nontechnical aspects like freedom to think and act as precondition for indigenous innovation. This is the most powerful weapon the USA possesses which is also very difficult to be copied. But this weapon needs to be aimed at future innovation targets. The US government has to declare not a war against terror but an economic war on sustainability, deep sea resources, or space.

One of the main assumptions is that American technical ingenuity will overcome all current weaknesses and problems. These apparently sudden bursts of waves or pinpoint innovation waves can be compared to pulsars. Regularly innovative entrepreneurs working in the USA are able to astonish the world by new inventions

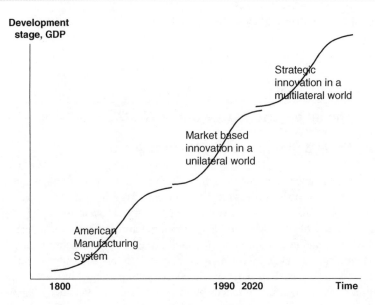

Fig. 6.9 Strategic innovation as the next pulse in US economy

and innovations. This attitude leads to an extension of the existing growth curve instead of creating a new future for the USA. The shale gas revolution illustrates the American fossil fuel Pavlov reaction. Another core assumption is the deep belief in market-based innovation in which government has to play only a minor role. All these assumptions will be challenged by newcomers like Innovative China.

The great challenge of the USA is to combine their market-based innovation with the core challenges of the world like sustainability, global R&D facilities, and the rise of China. Involvement of government is necessary which should go beyond accusing China to keep their RMB exchange rate low, breaking IP rights, and not providing equal playing fields for US firms in China. However, it is not a pledge for more or bigger government but to support and pave the wave for the new growth curve by replacing regulations hindering enterprises and setting new boundaries for the new growth curve.

The economic relevance of, e.g., deep sea and space will increase in the future and will require large investments to explore and exploit. National laws and environmental state agencies but also space agency NASA can be combined to a new powerful government creating the necessary conditions for a market-based sustainability innovation program. Therefore, the biggest challenge for the USA is strategic innovation with regard to sustainability and coping with new powers like China.

The role of government in strategic innovation has to be redefined. Market-based innovation in the field of sustainability requires governmental action for creating the necessary infrastructure or institutional settings. For example, creating a smart

Table 6.5 US innovation pitfalls

Fostering	Counter productive overdoses
Individual entrepreneurship	Dependency on heroic and worshipped entrepreneurs and forgetting global economic power play like sourcing and resources assurance
Strong CEO	Top-down innovation
Technology	Creative and cheap non-technical solutions get out of sight
Market based innovation	Lack of long term, context creating and public innovation with high societal return
Competition	Cutthroat competition
Triple Helix	Time consuming business development
US world order	Sustainability and Chinese (non-Western) values change the rules of game
Short term	Focus on improvements and loosing grip on basic innovation and denying dynamic value conversion effects
Education	Watch your 'Lawyers to engineer ratio' and traditional education system
Single issue/aspects of innovation	Hype driven and loosing sight on strategic innovation (big picture)
First movers	Copycat behavior of others take away value creating potential
. . .	. . .

grid structure throughout the whole USA requires large investments and central planning. US market innovations have to fight against Chinese market innovation plus Chinese governmental support.

6.9.2 US Pitfall of Not Renewing

The great innovation successes from the past can lead to arrogance hindering the renewal of the American innovation system. Table 6.5 shows some illustrations.

The rise of Innovative China is not only introducing new market rules; they also change the game. Sticking to past success formulas such as protecting your knowledge by lawyers or short-term based innovations needs to be supplemented. Some issues like sustainability or global resources sourcing require the involvement of the US government. The market-based innovation has been and will maintain great, but societal-based innovations offer great opportunities as well. The single-issue approach of innovation has the drawback of not seeing the big picture anymore.

6.9.3 Europe's Archipelago of Bright and Dark Stars

In the past centuries the economic zone of Europe is characterized by rise and decline of several countries. Simultaneously, some Pan-European developments such as the acknowledgement of science and the private-based entrepreneurship

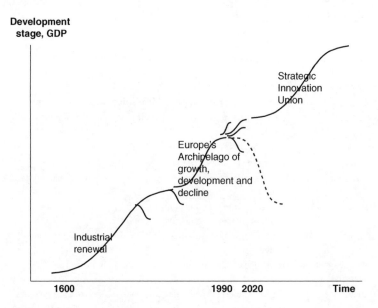

Fig. 6.10   Europe's archipelago of countries' growth and development

and creation of new industries. Taken together the group of nations showed a growth and increased prosperity as shown in Fig. 6.10.

From a Eurocentric point of view, several European countries successively took over the economic powerful position of China as of 1500. Several industrial renewal processes in agro-food, transport, finance, and manufacturing contributed to the rise of Europe as a whole. But Europe has never been united and can be described as an archipelago of independent countries. In different times different countries emulated each other. When the USA took over as dominating economic power in particular as the innovation leader, Europe as a whole was slowly falling back despite growth. Europe's main project of integration was largely limited to political–institutional measures and structures such as European industrial regulations, the Euro, and European Court.

With regard to innovation, the strategic integration failed and the contribution of the different islands of innovation within Europe is dominant. Empty phrases and top-down policies such as the Knowledge Economy and Innovative Union are not followed by measures and implementation. As the previous chapters have shown, European member state innovation policies are relatively ineffective. The EU is dependent on several private firms creating and introducing to market strategic innovations. Also in the private sector, the archipelago as a metaphor can be applied. The consequence is that the potential of Europe from the perspective of home market and innovation is not exploited. China is playing the different countries against each other. Moreover, the EU has no plan or strategy on how to cope with the rise of China. With the rise of China and the power of the USA, a next wave towards an integrated form is necessary to create a countervailing power of old and new economic superpowers.

The features of today's EU boil down to social security instead of entrepreneurial economy, knowledge for invention instead of innovation, demographic aging problem, absence of Pan-European policies and enterprises, lack of integration not compensated by exploitation of diversity, lack of earning power except Germany and Switzerland, too much regulation by member states, slow decision making, and lack of policy implementation leading to an elite without any understanding of the real entrepreneurial world.

Bureautechnocratic Europe overshadows Entrepreneurial Europe. Nevertheless, on the micro level, there are some very innovative and successful enterprises. But measured to the size of the EU, there are too less of these companies. The EU looks like a small galaxy full of bright stars and brown stars fighting with their death.

At first sight, the future of the EU looks grim, but there is a spark of hope. European dreams exist on paper and in the heads of the political elite but not in reality. The European Commission governs a disintegrated area full of rules, civil servants issuing new rules but the European people are far away from the Brussel mandarins. The political–bureaucratic–law-based approach towards European integration denies basic economic laws. The missing economic competence in political and governmental levels leaves an open space for Chinese rivals. The world view of the EU is indeed one of an ancient man.

The European society is based on social security, aid programs, redistributing wealth from money earners to societal free riders, moral superiority, and the idea that the EU is a leading region even in the future. The Euro crisis is a self-made crisis due to ignoring the law of dynamic value creation. Debts being made to finance the social welfare state and growth plans based on infrastructure projects financed by redistributed money from member states will not lead to growth and development. The EU needs a clear vision on the New World shaped and shaked by the USA, China, and some other countries. The EU needs to invest in the top of the society and not in the bottom being the welfare state. It requires favorable conditions for wealth creators and not for wealth redistributors.

Furthermore, the fight between member states to dominate the European Union weakens the EU. China creates government-supported private-owned and state-owned global powerhouses. The USA admires innovative entrepreneurs and their social system is based on the freedom of these breed of people. In the EU, the focus is on the weak in the society and in the world that need help. Governmental programs supporting an innovative economy often fail target because the two worlds of private and governments are separated. The members of these two worlds do not speak each other's language; they do not share the same dreams and do not understand each other's world. On the European level, these notions are not shared at all and the member states follow their own aims. European powerhouses do exist but they have a private history and not a history due to European policy. European economic policy is based on comitology and not building a sound strong new economy. European member states are played against each other in attracting Chinese investments. Therefore, also the EU needs strategic innovation on all levels.

The discussions about the European integration projects hide the insufficient performance of the private sector in creating strategic innovations. On average, European firms lag behind on innovation compared to US firms measured as R&D investments. Moreover, innovation output also depends on non-R&D expenditures and nontechnical innovations and on effectiveness of R&D investments. Despite all these amendments, it is crystal clear that the innovation potential of the EU is largely underexploited. There are huge opportunities for Triple Helix development and Pan-European innovation, using the diversity within the Union and export for internal European and world markets.

In particular, the inbound and outbound relation with China needs a fundamental change of course. The Europeans have no strategic answer on both the long-term development of the Chinese market and the direct investments by Chinese in the EU. With regard to upcoming Chinese brands, Chinese trademarks, Chinese R&D, Chinese innovations, and Chinese powerhouses, a China strategy is necessary.

The key issue is not to create a Knowledge Economy but a Strategic Innovation Union in which both creative entrepreneurialism and intrapreneuralism foster strategic innovations. If the EU wants to maintain its extremely expensive social security system, it is obliged to create the worldwide highest dynamic value conversion. Otherwise, the USA and China will emulate the EU. The core of the future EU is not its political unification and all its institutional structures and organization but a Pan-European increase of its earning capacity by means of strategic innovation on all levels and at public and private organizations.

It can be concluded that strategic innovation will become the future battlefield of old involved players especially the USA, the EU, and China.

6.9.4   EU Pitfall of Arrogance and Slow Moving

Like the Chinese, the Europeans are proud on their culture and historical achievements. The clock time is, for the EU, the same as for China and the USA. But the other time dimensions such as speed, accumulation, flexibility, and future orientation are changing rapidly. Connected with the time dimensions are some issues which can lead to European arrogance and slowness as demonstrated in Fig. 6.11.

The strength of the EU is in the bottom-up processes and leadership based on empowerment of subordinates based on the idea of societal equality, cooperation, knowledge sharing, openness, and network organization. However, we forget about the flip sides of these assumptions and starting points like slow decision making, competition on knowledge, being the best, emulating others, and industrial power.

Fostering	Counter productive overdoses
European integration	Additional European taxes, bureaucracy
Supporting leadership and empowerment	Absence of decision making
Entrepreneurship	Taxing entrepreneurship and risk takers
Bottom-up	Time consuming democratic processes without leadership
Top-down	Right context for acceptance, commitment, competence and implementation is missing
Network based innovation	Meetings without bottom line results
Societal equality	Brilliance not respected and rewarded
Social security	Low or even absence entrepreneurial activity
Governmental support	Waiting on government attitude
Cooperation	Forgetting essential flip side of competition and emulation
Tailor made member state innovation system	Lack of cross border innovation and loss of European scale
Separation between market and government	Lack of industrial power
Single issue / aspects / hypes of innovation	Losing sight on strategic innovation
...	...

Fig. 6.11 EU innovation pitfalls

6.10 Golden Tips for the West Creating the Twenty-First-Century Growth Wave

The eternal innovation symbol ∞ also means that the West will be able to rise together with China if they comprehend strategic innovation, the Chinese culture of dealing with paradoxes and creating a Western form of private–public symbiosis.

6.10.1 Strategic Innovation Is Core

The previous chapters clearly demonstrated the emergence of a new world order and the emergence of a new growth curve. Figure 6.12 demonstrates the consequences of the entrance of China in the world economy.

The new growth curve will not develop autonomously but will be shaped by all actors. The jump to the new growth curve will be accompanied by several strategic innovations in the four areas of leadership, institutional innovation, business development, and governance. Both enterprises and public organizations in China, the USA, and the EU have to reinvent themselves and prepare themselves for the twenty-first century.

Development

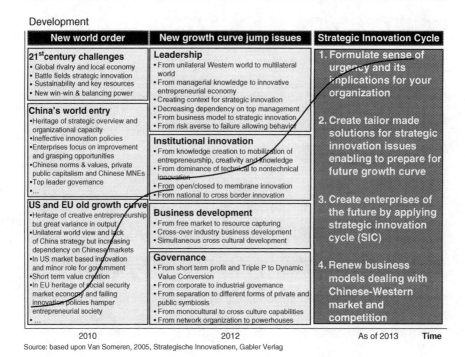

New world order	New growth curve jump issues	Strategic Innovation Cycle
21ˢᵗcentury challenges • Global rivalry and local economy • Battle fields strategic innovation • Sustainability and key resources • New win-win & balancing power	**Leadership** • From unilateral Western world to multilateral world • From managerial knowledge to innovative entrepreneurial economy • Creating context for strategic innovation • Decreasing dependency on top management • From business model to strategic innovation • From risk averse to failure allowing behaviour	**1. Formulate sense of urgency and its implications for your organization**
China's world entry •Heritage of strategic overview and organizational capacity •Ineffective innovation policies •Enterprises focus on improvement and grasping opportunities •Chinese norms & values, private public capitalism and Chinese MNEs •Top leader governance •...	**Institutional innovation** • From knowledge creation to mobilization of entrepreneurship, creativity and knowledge • From dominance of technical to nontechnical innovation • From open/closed to membrane innovation • From national to cross border innovation	**2. Create tailor made solutions for strategic innovation issues enabling to prepare for future growth curve**
US and EU old growth curve •Heritage of creative entrepreneurship but great variance in output •Unilateral world view and lack of China strategy but increasing dependency on Chinese markets •In US market based innovation and minor role for government •Short term value creation •In EU heritage of social security market economy and failing innovation policies hamper entrepreneurial society •...	**Business development** • From free market to resource capturing • Cross-over industry business development • Simultaneous cross cultural development **Governance** • From short term profit and Triple P to Dynamic Value Conversion • From corporate to industrial governance • From separation to different forms of private and public symbiosis • From monocultural to cross culture capabilities • From network organization to powerhouses	**3. Create enterprises of the future by applying strategic innovation cycle (SIC)** **4. Renew business models dealing with Chinese-Western market and competition**

| 2010 | 2012 | As of 2013 **Time** |

Source: based upon Van Someren, 2005, Strategische Innovationen, Gabler Verlag

Fig. 6.12 Strategic innovation is a core challenge for the twenty-first century

6.10.2 Becoming Successful with Chinese: Synthesizing Paradoxes

Synthesizing paradoxes is one of the keys for being successful in Chinese business. Westerners have to get insight and knowledge of this powerful tool to cope with apparent contra dictionary and unsolvable situations van Someren, T. C. R., & Someren-Wang, S. (2012).

Synthesizing paradoxes is also a way to generate strategic innovation (van Someren, 2005). How to do it depends on specific situation and here only the general principle on how to create your solution is presented. In Fig. 6.13 the paradox of Chinese business development versus Western business development is presented as an example. For simplicity reasons the characteristics of each starting position is kept simple.

The predominant starting position for China is characterized by top-down and long-term development, and the Western position is by bottom-up and short term. When using the methodology of paradox synthesis, a possible outcome could be the development of alternative business development options by a group and combining low-hanging fruit results with mid- and long-term results. The underlying principle for this specific paradox synthesis is to develop mutual increasing interests.

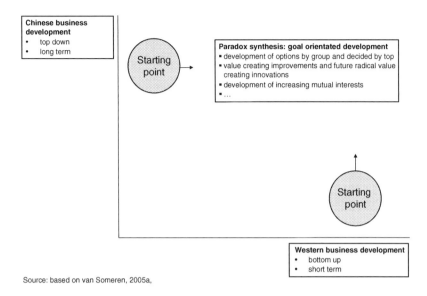

Source: based on van Someren, 2005a,

Fig. 6.13 Paradox synthesis

6.10.3 Becoming Successful with the Chinese: Symbiosis Between Private Business and Government

The close relationship between Chinese enterprises and government has played an important role for the rise of Chinese strategic industries. Western businesses entering Chinese markets are mostly not used to these forms of cooperation. For those who rely on the growing market in China, symbiosis between public and private sector can be a direction for their strategic innovation. Western governments and enterprises cannot and should not copy the Chinese behavior but should find a way to fit into both Chinese and Western practices. Figure 6.14 shows the difference between the old approach fitting to the old growth curve and the new approach fitting to the new growth curve.

In Table 6.5 the old approach of a separation between private and public organizations and government is shown in the upper part. The butterfly-shaped graph fits to the free market ideology that governments are no good entrepreneurs and should only be involved in support of embassies, consulates, and investment agencies delivering market information, organizing matchmaking events, and opening doors. Because governments are not better entrepreneurs than the market, in the Western world the involvement in the right part of the butterfly is minimal. It is indeed true that in general the market participants take better entrepreneurial decisions than governments or civil servants. But when dealing with China there is a flip side due to the great stake of government in business.

Western enterprises experience the greatest difficulties in the right-hand part of the butterfly-shaped graph. The main reason is failing strategic innovations to adjust

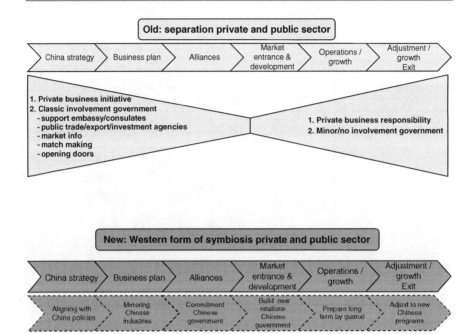

Fig. 6.14 Old and new forms of private and public sector

to Chinese circumstances. By the way, the same holds for Chinese enterprises entering Western markets.

In our experience, the role of Western government involvement is beyond giving market information and opening doors. Table 6.5 shows that the key of success is that the government should play a role in every phase of the market development by Western enterprises. However, we stress that our suggestion here is not to copy Chinese practices but to create a Western form of symbiosis respecting the core role of entrepreneurs for market development and not governments.

Figure 6.15 shows how the methodology of the Strategic Innovation Cycle has been used to formulate a systematic approach for a Western form of symbiosis.

The SIC makes it possible that the Western enterprises stay in the lead, but the government is actively involved in all phases of the Chinese market activities when necessary. This can only be achieved through a SIC process in which the communication between all parties from top-down to bottom-up and from macro through meso to micro is stimulated (van Someren, 2005). Even important is the continuity of the process to renew what did not work. That is why a kind of central coordination between the Western private and public parties as well as between the Western and Chinese counterparts is necessary. The root of failing innovation policies and governmental economic initiatives can very often be traced back to lack of SIC processes. By the way, the same principle is also valid if the Chinese really want to continue to explore the possibilities of government and private symbiosis.

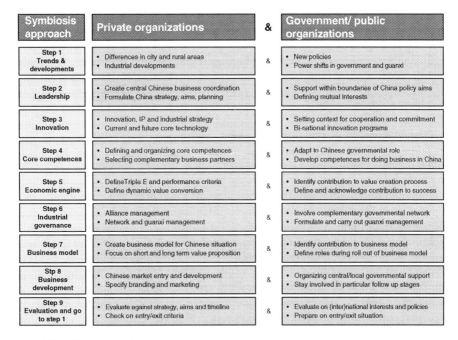

Symbiosis approach	Private organizations	&	Government/ public organizations
Step 1 Trends & developments	• Differences in city and rural areas • Industrial developments	&	• New policies • Power shifts in government and guanxi
Step 2 Leadership	• Create central Chinese business coordination • Formulate China strategy, aims, planning	&	• Support within boundaries of China policy aims • Defining mutual interests
Step 3 Innovation	• Innovation, IP and industrial strategy • Current and future core technology	&	• Setting context for cooperation and commitment • Bi-national innovation programs
Step 4 Core competences	• Defining and organizing core competences • Selecting complementary business partners	&	• Adapt to Chinese governmental role • Develop competences for doing business in China
Step 5 Economic engine	• Define Triple E and performance criteria • Define dynamic value conversion	&	• Identify contribution to value creation process • Define and acknowledge contribution to success
Step 6 Industrial governance	• Alliance management • Network and guanxi management	&	• Involve complementary governmental network • Formulate and carry out guanxi management
Step 7 Business model	• Create business model for Chinese situation • Focus on short and long term value proposition	&	• Identify contribution to business model • Define roles during roll out of business model
Stp 8 Business development	• Chinese market entry and development • Specify branding and marketing	&	• Organizing central/local governmental support • Stay involved in particular follow up stages
Step 9 Evaluation and go to step 1	• Evaluate against strategy, aims and timeline • Check on entry/exit criteria	&	• Evaluate on (inter)national interests and policies • Prepare on entry/exit situation

Fig. 6.15 Western symbiosis approach for private enterprises and government

6.11   Future Stars of the Economic Universe

It has become clear that the current Chinese resurrection based on unsustainable imitate–improve growth and development has to be replaced by a sustainable innovate–internationalize growth model. Both strategic innovation and greening of the society have become a necessity. China also realizes that it will become an integral and probably leading part of the world society. On the short term, an interdependency between China, the US, the EU, and other countries and regions will be the result. In the long run we are not all dead but some nations will better survive than others.

Our message is simple, but it needs courage and effort. Due to the different histories, contexts, and future visions, it is useless to copycat each other's policies. A good China strategy is not to imitate big plan making but to reinforce the strong points in the framework of leadership, institutional innovation, business development, and governance but taking into account the changes China will introduce. The same holds for China; the successful top-down leadership style should not be replaced by bottom-up approach but be complemented by an organized bottom-up system reinforcing each other. But for all same mantra holds: in the coming growth cycle, only strategic innovations starting within the single enterprises support any aim on the national level.

For managers, the easiest way is to throw money at R&D, technology development, and sexy IT and to put pressure on the technicians for breakthrough results. The smarter way is to rethink your organization in a new future and how to contribute to a New World changed by the rise of China. For governments, the easiest way is to throw money at innovation hypes and regularly formulate new policies and be silent about its bottom-line results and implementation. The smarter way is to realize that the earning power of a society is dependent on new-growth-curve-ready public organizations. For both managers and governmental leaders, strategic innovation is the only road to be on the edge of the new growth curve. Luckily the uniform SIC methodology can deliver necessary tailor-made multiple answers.

Creating and building strategic innovations will decide about the future prosperity in China, the USA, and the EU. The innovation–internationalization phase in China requires inversions in the core of the existing practices, instruments, and vehicles to create welfare. Nontechnical innovations complementary to technical innovations, bottom-up innovation complementary to top-down policies, creative SMEs complementary to government-governed MNEs, organized bottom-up creativity complementary to leader innovation preferences, and increasing power of individuals due to increasing wealth will be part of the society to realize the aims of the desired innovation state being independent of the West.

The crises force the EU to renew integration, but China forces the EU to strategically innovate. In the EU the current and past constellation of rivaling self-centered nation states fighting for leadership role in the EU will have to be inverted too. The EU has been used by member states to avoid war and tame each other but not to become a world power. Forced by the rise of China, the member states are now forced to invert the aim of the EU from a self-defense against each other to a firewall against China and platform to launch European-based innovations. Strategic innovations in private and public organizations are necessary to stay competitive in the next growth curve. Corporate leaders need to discover the value of strategic innovation. It is better to stimulate bottom-up entrepreneurial initiatives instead of a transformation towards a bureaucratic European headquarters trying to issue top-down policies.

The greatest asset of the USA, bottom-up innovative entrepreneurial activity, and its freedom of creativity and self-development should be kept for the new growth wave. But the USA has to transform from a unilateral to a multilateral world perspective and to take account of non-American norms and values, long strategic term behavior, and industrial corporate governance into private and public organizations.

The future development of the current mutual power relations and strength between the regions will be dependent on the ability to renew itself and generate future-earning capacity by means of strategic innovation in a new world order with new rules. Therefore, becoming number one is not the ultimate aim for Chinese leaders but the result and side effect of creating and implementing strategic